AF541997

India and the Bangladesh Liberation War

India and Bangladesh achieved a historic victory in the 1971 war. Yet fifty years later, important questions remain about India's aims and policy in the war. Did India have a plan to break up Pakistan? When and why did it involve itself with the Bangladesh freedom struggle? When did India decide to prepare for military action? Why was no other country prepared to support the cause of an independent Bangladesh? How was India able to counter the US–China–Pakistan axis that emerged dramatically midway through the liberation struggle? How did India persuade the Soviet Union to shed its initial reluctance to support the liberation war? Did India 'win the war but lose the peace' by signing the Simla Agreement?

Drawing on previously unexplored Indian records, eminent diplomat and historian Chandrashekhar Dasgupta dispels many myths as he sheds fascinating new light on these and other questions. Deeply researched over eighteen years, this authoritative, lucid and compellingly narrated book also reveals why and how India fashioned an overarching grand strategy, employing every instrument of national power – political, diplomatic, economic and military – to help the Bangladesh freedom fighters speedily liberate their country.

India and the Bangladesh Liberation War

[illegible] Bangladesh [illegible] history [illegible] the 1971 [illegible] the most important [illegible] policy in the war. Did India want a war to break up Pakistan? When and why did it [illegible] the Bangladesh [illegible] struggle? When did India decide to prepare for military action? [illegible] country [illegible] support [illegible] an independent Bangladesh? [illegible] course [illegible] Pakistan [illegible] changed dramatically [illegible] the liberation struggle? [illegible] support of the liberation war? [illegible] India [illegible] the war [illegible] signing the Simla Agreement?

Drawing on [illegible] India's eminent diplomat [illegible] new light on these and other questions. Deeply researched [illegible] this [illegible] compellingly [illegible] book [illegible] how India [illegible] an extraordinary [illegible] power – political, diplomatic, economic and military – to help the Bangladeshi freedom fighters [illegible] their country.

Praise for the book

'Deeply researched and lucidly and fluently narrated, this unusual book answers all the remaining questions and conundrums relating to India's most successful diplomatic and military achievement: aiding in the Liberation of Bangladesh in 1971. An invaluable contribution to the extant literature, which puts an end to numerous conspiracy theories that have hitherto clouded and distorted the true story of a milestone in South Asian history.' **Mani Shankar Aiyar**

'Illuminating and instructive' ***Daily Star***

'This is the definitive account of Indian diplomacy during the Bangladesh crisis of 1971. Using hitherto untapped sources, Chandrasekhar Dasgupta has, with great lucidity, brought out the complexities of decision-making in those fateful ten months. The book will alter existing perceptions of the period.' **Swapan Dasgupta**

'Grippingly told, this account gives us more than the story of Bangladesh's birth. It tells us how political freedom can be lost in the name of religion and culture, and spectacularly retrieved in the cause of human dignity.' **Gopal Gandhi**

'Drawing on a host of documentary material . . . anyone curious about how India midwifed the emergence of Bangladesh could do no better than reading this.' ***India Today***

'This book is a tour de force of contemporary history. Dasgupta examines in one succinct and readable volume how domestic politics in Pakistan, Indian grand strategy, diplomacy, broader geopolitical shifts and military strategy led to the birth of Bangladesh. That it was done within fifty years of the events it describes makes it an even more remarkable achievement. Judicious and sober in its judgements, this is how history should be written, driven by evidence, logic and facts. Dasgupta's own experience and knowledge illuminate this brilliant book that will be indispensable for scholars, diplomats, political scientists and anyone interested in the formation of the modern Indian subcontinent.' **Shivshankar Menon**

'Ambassador Dasgupta is amongst the most scholarly of Indian diplomats with a passion for archival research. Here is another masterpiece of his in which he debunks a couple of powerful myths that surround the historic events of 1971. He unravels India's "grand strategy" in the political and diplomatic spheres that guided military actions that year and that remade subcontinental geography.'
Jairam Ramesh

'This is one of the finest political histories of recent times, and confirms Ambassador Dasgupta's reputation as a scholar whose meticulous research and rigorous analysis are unparalleled. It provides us with an insider's view of the complex and rapidly evolving geopolitical backdrop against which the dramatic saga of the birth of a nation took place. Above all, its value lies in demonstrating the importance of an overall national strategy to deal with the extraordinary challenge, where objectives were achieved, inspired – as the author says – by "a common clearly defined overarching national aim".' **Shyam Saran**

'There are very few diplomats who research the subjects they write on with such diligence and analytical skill as Chandrashekhar Dasgupta. This book, like his earlier book *War and Diplomacy in Kashmir, 1947–48*, is truly eye-opening, revealing aspects of the subject that were unknown. It not only tells an untold story but will lead to new interpretations and conclusions that will change the way we view the history of that period.' **Karan Thapar**

'In *India and the Bangladesh Liberation War*, Chandrashekhar Dasgupta focuses a sharp eye on India's role in the era-defining conflict that led to the creation of Bangladesh. Rich in detail and primary research, this insightful book weaves a compelling narrative. Highly recommended – not just for military buffs, but for anyone seeking to understand India's role on the world stage in that tumultuous period of history.' **Shashi Tharoor**

'Brilliantly researched' ***The Hindu***

India and the Bangladesh Liberation War

India and the Bangladesh Liberation War

Chandrashekhar Dasgupta

juggernaut

JUGGERNAUT BOOKS
C-I-128, First Floor, Sangam Vihar, Near Holi Chowk,
New Delhi 110080, India

First published in hardback by Juggernaut Books 2021
Published in paperback by Juggernaut Books 2024

10 9 8 7 6 5 4 3 2 1

P-ISBN: 9789353458621
E-ISBN: 9789391165581

The international boundaries shown in the map are representational only and not to scale.

Typeset in Adobe Caslon Pro by R. Ajith Kumar, Noida

Printed at Replika Press Pvt. Ltd.

In memory of my parents
Sachindra Nath and Renu Das Gupta

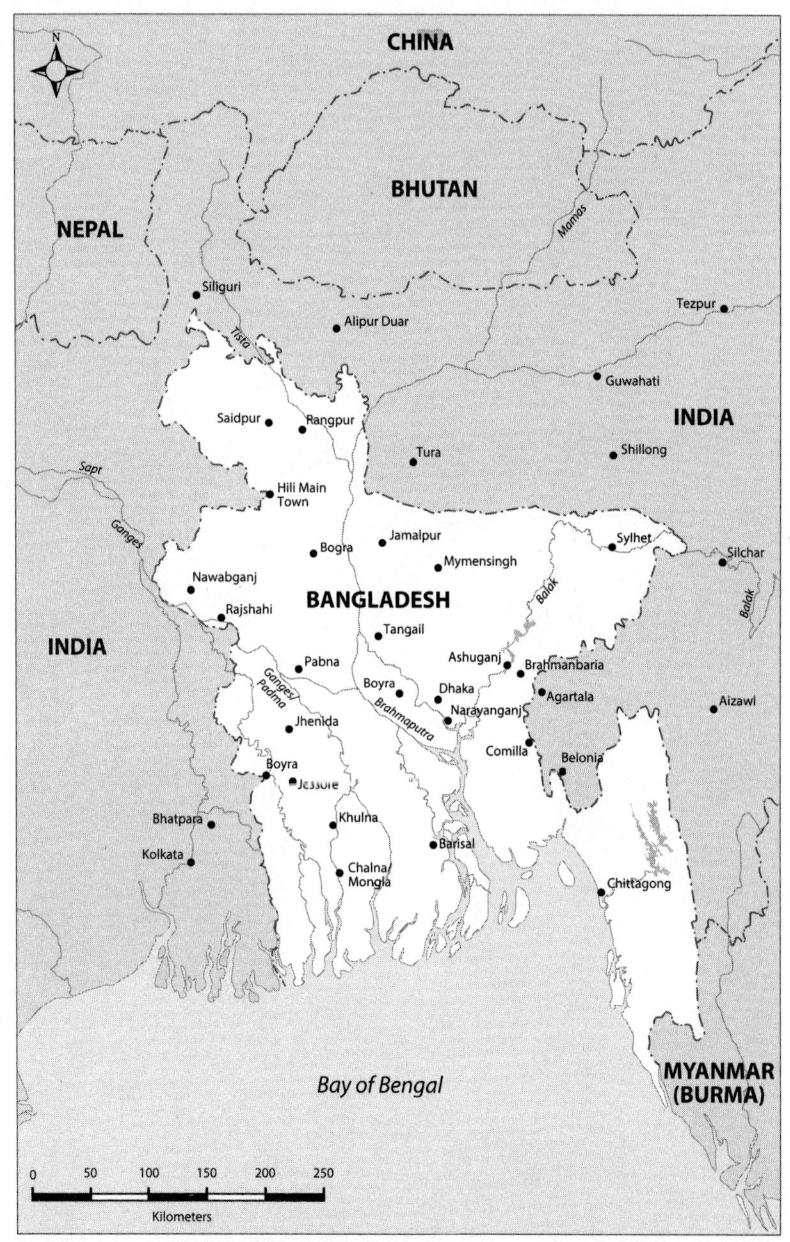

The international boundaries shown in the map are representational only and not to scale.

Contents

Introduction

The Bangladesh Liberation War came to a triumphal conclusion on 16 December 1971, when the Pakistani forces in the Eastern Theatre surrendered unconditionally to the India–Bangladesh Joint Command. This was the finale of a spectacular feat of arms, one without parallel in the recent history of South Asia. In January 1972, India opened an embassy in Dhaka, becoming the first country to establish diplomatic ties with the People's Republic of Bangladesh. The embassy was redesignated as a high commission later in the year, when Bangladesh became a member of the Commonwealth.

I had the privilege of serving in this mission in the early years of independent Bangladesh, from March 1972 to mid-1974. Officers selected for the new embassy were instructed to rush to Dhaka as soon as possible, leaving their families behind in India. We were informed that we would be unable to find any time for them. Bangladesh was just beginning to recover from the devastation it had suffered during the liberation war. We assisted the Bangladesh authorities in rehabilitating ports and railways, repairing roads and bridges, assuring them supplies of basic food items, medicines and other essential commodities. We also helped them resettle the millions of refugees who had taken shelter in India during the Pakistani crackdown in Bangladesh. We worked from morning to night, seven days a week. It was only after the first six months that we were allowed to take the afternoon off on Sundays.

These were exciting and eventful times. Within days of my arrival in Dhaka, I witnessed two historic events. On 12 March 1972, the Indian army staged a spectacular, impeccably choreographed farewell parade at the Dhaka stadium. The stadium was packed to capacity long before the event, and a vast overflow surged outside the gates. We had to fight our way through the crowd to reach our seats. Taking the salute at the farewell parade, Bangabandhu Sheikh Mujibur Rahman paid homage to the valiant officers and jawans of the Indian army who had sacrificed their lives in the liberation war. Five days after the farewell parade, Indira Gandhi arrived in Dhaka to an unforgettable welcome. Tens of thousands had poured into the capital from the outlying districts to catch a glimpse of the Indian prime minister and hear her speak at the Suhrawardy Udyan. The streets of the city were festooned with posters bearing her portrait alongside effusive expressions of gratitude and admiration.

To enable the embassy to meet the unprecedented challenges it faced, exceptional powers were delegated to it, dispensing with time-consuming bureaucratic procedures. It was assumed that formal financial sanction would follow automatically in all cases of expenditure approved by Ambassador Subimal Dutt. I recall, for example, that we received an appeal for assistance from the Bangladesh government to deal with a major cholera epidemic. A massive inoculation campaign was urgently required to deal with this public health emergency, but the proportionately massive requirements of vaccine were not available in war-devastated Bangladesh. Under Dutt's instructions, I rang up the concerned desk officer in the ministry of external affairs (MEA) and informed him that the ambassador had asked for the requisite quantity of cholera vaccine to be airlifted to Dhaka within forty-eight hours. The task involved coordination between the ministries of external affairs, health, defence and finance, as well as between these civilian agencies and the air force. In normal times this would have taken weeks, if not months, with each organization raising its own issues at every step. In the event, in April 1972, two Indian Air Force planes delivered the urgently needed vaccines in Dhaka in thirty-six hours! This is only a small example of the way the Government of India functioned during and after the 1971 war. The contrast with the stately pace at which the government normally moved could not have been more startling. It was possible to execute tasks so speedily only because everyone involved was inspired by a common, clearly defined, overarching national aim.

This period of frenetic activity drew to a close as normalcy was restored and an increasing number of countries, including the principal western aid donors, accorded diplomatic recognition to Bangladesh. This enabled Bangladesh to diversify its sources of assistance, relieving India in the process of a massive economic burden that it could not have borne beyond a few months. The embassy gradually settled down to more normal working hours and, at long last, our families were allowed to join us in Dhaka.

During these eventful years in Dhaka, I had no detailed knowledge of the historical background of our association with the Bangladesh freedom struggle. We received only a cursory briefing before we took up our posts in Dhaka. This was intended to prepare us for addressing the urgent tasks in hand, not for historical inquiry. Some of my colleagues in the Dhaka mission provided fascinating accounts of our links with the Bangladesh freedom fighters. I learned a great deal about our 1971 operations from a dear friend and foreign service colleague, Arundhati ('Chuku') Ghose, who had been posted in Kolkata in our liaison office with the Bangladesh government-in-exile. Our military attaché, Maj. Gen. (later Lt Gen.) B.N. Sarkar, was the principal link between the Indian army and the Mukti Bahini before the war. He was the source of many valuable insights concerning our military operations. Another guide to these operations was the naval attaché, Cdr M.N. Samant, who had helped establish the naval branch of the Mukti Bahini and had led many daring covert operations. Samant was awarded the Maha Vir Chakra for conspicuous gallantry in the 1971 war. Quite a few of our Bangladeshi friends told us about their clandestine contacts with our authorities before the war. All of these were fascinating anecdotes, but they did not add up to a complete picture. Many basic questions remained unanswered. When and why did India decide to involve itself in the Bangladesh freedom struggle? Did India have a plan to break up Pakistan? What was the impact of the massive influx of refugees fleeing from Pakistani oppression? What conclusions did India draw from the dramatic geopolitical transformation signalled by Kissinger's secret trip to China midway through the Bangladesh liberation struggle? Above all, did India react in a piecemeal manner to challenges as they arose, or did it have a comprehensive grand strategy early in the day?

Three decades later, after my retirement from the foreign service, I sought answers to these questions in the archival records.

The archives throw new light on many perplexing questions. They show that far from planning to break up Pakistan, Indian policymakers hoped, right up to 25 March 1971, for a peaceful transition to democracy in Pakistan and the installation of an Awami League-led government in Islamabad. New Delhi believed that this held out the only hope for a breakthrough in Indo-Pakistan relations. These hopes were belied when President Yahya Khan decided to crush the aspirations of the eastern province through a murderous terror campaign, thereby triggering off an armed independence struggle. Only then did India decide to actively assist the Bangladesh freedom fighters in order to bring their struggle to an early conclusion. This decision was based on New Delhi's concerns about the spillover effects of an extended guerrilla war across India's porous eastern borders; it also reflected deep public sympathy in India for the people of Bangladesh. The records conclusively disprove the story popularized by Field Marshal Manekshaw that he had dissuaded Prime Minister Indira Gandhi in April from sending an unprepared Indian army into East Pakistan. They reveal that the prime minister and her principal advisers had already decided against premature intervention on political and diplomatic grounds, fearing this would result in loss of international support for the Bangladesh cause. Most importantly, the archives indicate that as early as in April–May 1971 India had formulated a comprehensive outline plan or grand strategy encompassing military, diplomatic and domestic initiatives, with the aim of bringing the liberation war to a successful conclusion before the year end. They throw new light on how these decisions were made and executed amidst dramatic changes in the international environment. They throw new light on the close coordination of military and diplomatic moves by India during the December war, and on how Indian diplomacy thwarted US and Chinese moves in the UN Security Council to abort the freedom struggle by imposing on India a premature ceasefire. Finally, they dispel the widespread belief that India 'won the war but lost the peace' in the Simla summit by giving up its intention of converting the Line of Control into an international boundary. The records prove that at every stage in the Simla conference India specifically reserved a final settlement of the Kashmir issue for future meetings. India did, indeed, push for an *eventual* settlement on the basis of the Line of Control, but Indira Gandhi feared that an *immediate* agreement on these lines would expose her to the charge that she had 'surrendered' Pakistan-occupied Kashmir.

This is not a book about the military operations in December 1971; that task has been undertaken by several distinguished military historians. Nor is it a global history of the war – the subject of an illuminating work by the eminent historian Srinath Raghavan. This book is about India's grand strategy in 1971. The term 'grand strategy' has been defined in more ways than one. I use it to mean a comprehensive and coordinated plan for employing all the resources available to a state – diplomatic, military and economic – to achieve a defined political objective. This book seeks to explain why India intervened in the Bangladesh liberation struggle; the diplomatic and military challenges it faced; and how its defence, foreign and domestic policies were shaped and integrated so that they played mutually supporting roles in achieving an overarching political aim.

1

Prelude: The Alienation of East Bengal

Pakistan is a unique country having two wings which are separated by a distance of more than a thousand miles. These two wings differ in all matters, excepting two things, namely, that they have a common religion, barring a section of the people in East Pakistan, and that we achieved our independence by a common struggle ... With the exception of these two things, all other factors, viz., the language, the tradition, the culture, the costume, the custom, the dietary, the calendar, the standard time, practically everything is different. There is, in fact, nothing common in the two wings, particularly in respect to those [things] which are the sine qua non to form a nation.

– Abul Mansur Ahmed (Awami League), speech in the Pakistan Constituent Assembly, 16 January 1956[1]

The Pakistan that came into existence in 1947 was a geographical and political anomaly. The geographical gap of over 1,000 miles between its western and eastern wings was matched by a corresponding gulf in their language, culture and socio-economic conditions. These, in turn, gave rise to divergent political aspirations. The failure of the Pakistani state to accommodate the aspirations of the Bengalis of East Bengal and to reconcile the divergent interests of the political elites of its two wings resulted in the increasing alienation of East Bengal and the ultimate emergence of an independent Bangladesh.

The divide between the two wings first manifested itself over the question of the state language. Pakistan's central government, with strong support in the western wing, decreed that Urdu – the lingua franca of West Pakistan – would be the national language. East Bengal demanded that Bengali, too, should be recognized as a national language, alongside Urdu. This was rejected by the central government as inconsistent with the requirements of national unity. Central leaders charged that advocates of Bengali were Indian agents and enemies of Pakistan. The ensuing language movement in East Bengal pitted the two wings of Pakistan against each other.

There was also a radical difference in the socio-economic structure of the two wings. Feudal landlords and tribal chieftains dominated society in West Pakistan. By contrast, East Pakistan was largely free of landlord domination. In the pre-Independence period, the vast majority of the big landlords or *zamindars* in the province were Hindus. Land reforms were speeded up with the departure of most of the Hindu landlords to India during and after Partition. The Estate Acquisition and Tenancy Act passed by the East Bengal legislature in 1950 set a ceiling of 33 acres on landholdings and protected the rights of the tiller. The political elite in the eastern wing were drawn largely from an emerging middle class – lawyers, teachers and journalists – not landlords and tribal chieftains. The few industrial entrepreneurs in Pakistan were based almost exclusively in the provinces of Punjab and Sind in the western wing. They had close ties to the West Pakistani political elite, which favoured a policy of promoting economic development by providing incentives and other support to the emerging entrepreneurial class. By contrast, political leaders in the eastern wing called for an expanded role for the state in economic development, including nationalization of the jute trade and government support for East Bengal's cottage industries. Jute exports from the eastern wing were the major source of Pakistan's foreign exchange earnings. The central government channelled this foreign exchange to industries in Sind and

Punjab. East Bengal demanded that the foreign exchange earnings from its jute and tea exports should be utilized for its own development in order to reduce the wide gap in per capita income between the two wings. Rejection of this demand provided grounds for the charge that the western wing was treating East Pakistan as a colonial possession.

Unlike the western wing, East Bengal had a sizeable, though shrinking, Hindu minority. This raised the question of the role of religious minorities in the new state of Pakistan. Though attacks on the minorities were distressingly common, most political leaders of the eastern wing advocated a secular, or non-communal, approach. In 1953, the Awami Muslim League redesignated itself as the Awami League, reflecting its essentially secular political programme. The other party with mass support in the province – Fazlul Huq's Krishak Sramik Party (Peasants and Workers Party) – similarly pursued a non-communal agenda. By contrast, there was little support for secular politics in West Pakistan. Political leaders in West Pakistan were committed to separate electorates for religious minorities, while their counterparts in the eastern wing demanded a joint electorate.

The political demands of the two wings differed even in the sphere of foreign and defence policy. For the central government and the western wing, Kashmir was the core problem of the country's foreign and defence policy – to be resolved, if necessary, through recourse to arms. In sharp contrast, the Kashmir issue generated no heat in the eastern wing, where the public favoured a peaceful resolution of differences and normalization of ties with India. With strong support from West Pakistan, the central government entered into an alliance with the United States, with a view to building up its military capabilities vis-à-vis India. Perceiving no threat from India, political opinion in the eastern wing favoured a non-aligned foreign policy.

The armed forces and civil services, which soon took on a central role in Pakistani politics, were led almost exclusively by West Pakistanis, principally Punjabis and *mohajirs*. Some measures were, indeed, taken to remedy the imbalance in the civil services through the introduction of a quota system. Even so, in the mid-1950s, there was not a single Bengali officer at the topmost civil service level of secretary, and only three Bengali officers figured among the forty-one joint secretaries.[2] The absence of Bengali representation was even more glaring in the armed forces. In 1955, there was only one Bengali brigadier, one colonel and two lieutenant colonels in the Pakistani army.[3] Field Marshal Ayub Khan ascribed the deficiency to a 'lack of qualities of leadership' among the Bengalis.[4]

It might have been possible to reconcile these differences, deep as they were, through the give and take of a political democracy, and by the devolution of powers from the central government to the provinces. Pakistan's failure to evolve such a system foreclosed the possibility of a mutually acceptable solution. This rejection of a democratic option by the West Pakistani political, military and civil service leadership led to mounting discontent, protests and mass movements in the eastern wing, to which the central authorities responded with brute repression. The central theme in the history of East Pakistan from 1947 to 1970 is its progressive alienation from West Pakistan.

Early years: The language movement and the demand for autonomy

The alienation of the Bengalis began within months of the birth of Pakistan, and in the lifetime of its founder, Muhammad Ali Jinnah. In the opening session of the Pakistan Constituent Assembly in February 1948, a Congress party member from East Bengal, Dhirendra Nath Dutta, proposed that Bengali, along with Urdu, should be recognized as a national language of Pakistan. Rejecting the proposal outright, Prime Minister Liaquat Ali Khan alleged that it was inspired by the intention to divide the Muslims of Pakistan. Dutta's proposal was, however, widely acclaimed in East Bengal, even within the ruling Muslim League. The student wing of the party, the Chhatra League, formed an all-party Rashtrabhasa Sangram Parishad (National Language Struggle Committee) to press the demand for Bengali as a national language.

Disturbed by the rising swell of public opinion, Jinnah decided to pay his one and only visit to East Bengal after the founding of Pakistan. Not one to mince his words, he delivered a tough message in a public address in Dhaka on 21 March 1948, alleging that the demand for making Bengali a state language was inspired by communists and foreign agents who wanted to destroy Pakistan and reunite its eastern wing with India. A heated exchange broke out when he met later with members of the student-led State Language Working Committee. Among the members of the committee were two individuals who were destined to play a central role in the events of 1971 – Tajuddin Ahmed and Syed Nazrul Islam.[5]

Protests from students and other political groups continued to gather strength. When the government re-emphasized its national language policy in January 1952, massive student-led protests broke out in Dhaka. On 21 February that year, police opened fire on the protesters, killing five. This brutal act converted five unknown youngsters into immortal martyrs for the Bengali cause. Tributes are paid to them on 21 February every year at a solemn public ceremony at the Martyrs' Memorial in Dhaka. The significance of the language movement in the history of the eastern province can hardly be overestimated. In the words of the Bangladeshi political scientist Talukder Maniruzzaman, '[The] state language movement secularized the political atmosphere of East Bengal. The success of the movement showed that the politically relevant section of Bengalis, and particularly students, could no longer be diverted from substantive political issues through slogans of Islam, anti-Indianism and anti-Hinduism.'[6]

The language movement gave a great boost to the demand for autonomy in East Pakistan. Prominent Bengali Muslims pointed out the Lahore resolution adopted by the Muslim League in 1940 had called for constitution of 'independent states' in the Muslim-majority areas in the North, Western and Eastern zones of the subcontinent. Ignoring the position of the central leadership, in 1950 the East Bengal Muslim League Working Committee on the Constitution called for 'maximum autonomy' for the eastern wing. The government's rejection of the demand for recognition of Bengali as a state language and the brutal suppression of protests brought the autonomy question to the forefront.

Reflecting the mounting discontent with the central leadership, a major section of the ruling party in the eastern wing broke away in 1949 to form the East Pakistan Awami [People's] Muslim League. In 1953, the new party dropped the word 'Muslim' from its name, restyling itself as the Awami League and signalling its secular approach in politics.

In 1953, the main opposition parties in the eastern wing – the Awami League, the Krishak Sramik Party of Fazlul Huq and the Nizam-e-Islam – came together to form the United Front. The common twenty-one-point programme of the United Front included recognition of Bengali as a national language, full autonomy for East Bengal, the raising of an East Bengal armed militia, shifting of the naval headquarters from Karachi to Chittagong, release of all prisoners detained without trial, open trials of persons accused of treason, nationalization of the jute trade, subsidies for cottage industries, and labour rights.

The United Front swept the polls in the first election to the provincial assembly, held in 1954. It won 223 of the 237 Muslim seats, routing the Muslim League, which won only nine seats. In April, a United Front government took office in East Bengal under the veteran leader Fazlul Huq.

Interregnum (1951–57)

Meanwhile, a major transformation had occurred in the political structure at the Centre. Jinnah's Muslim League lacked a grassroots organization, drawing all its strength from its charismatic leader. It suffered a severe blow when Jinnah died in September 1948, barely a year after the birth of Pakistan. His principal lieutenant, Liaquat Ali Khan, who took over the reins of power, was assassinated in 1951. After these two stalwarts of the Pakistani movement had passed from the scene, the ruling Muslim League was left rudderless. Power passed progressively from the hands of political leaders to the civil-military bureaucracy. A former civil servant, Ghulam Muhammad, took over as governor general in 1951, with the backing of the army.

The rise of the civil-military bureaucracy was closely linked to a shift in Pakistan's defence and foreign policy. Led by Army Commander-in-Chief Ayub Khan, senior generals and civil servants sought a US alliance, ignoring public opinion in East Bengal as well as widespread misgivings in West Pakistan among supporters of the Palestine cause. Contemptuous of politicians and public opinion, Ayub assured the US embassy that the army would 'take no nonsense from the politicians', nor allow the public to 'ruin the country'.[7]

In April 1953, Pakistan experienced its first 'constitutional coup'. With the active connivance of General Ayub Khan and senior civil servants, the governor general dismissed Prime Minister Nazimuddin, replacing him with a political lightweight, Mohammed Ali Bogra.[8] For the next five years, the country was ruled by a governor general supported by the army and the civil service. Domestic and foreign policy was formulated by the governor general, acting in tandem with the army and civil bureaucracy. Governments were appointed or dismissed by the governor general, depending on their willingness to follow his policies.

In October 1954, Governor General Ghulam Muhammad dismissed the Constituent Assembly, which had the temerity to call for certain legal restraints on his powers. A new 'cabinet of talents' was installed, in which Iskandar Mirza occupied the post of interior minister while the army chief, General Ayub Khan, doubled as defence minister. Over the next four years, supreme authority was to pass successively from Ghulam Muhammad to Iskandar Mirza and, finally, to Ayub Khan. In October 1955, with the support of the army, Mirza seized power from the ailing Ghulam Muhammad. The façade of civilian rule was finally discarded in 1958, when Ayub compelled Mirza to resign and go into permanent exile in England.

The first target of the military-civil service clique which assumed power in 1953 was the democratically elected United Front government in East Bengal. The twenty-one-point programme, Chief Minister Fazlul Huq's friendly sentiments towards India and the United Front's espousal of a non-aligned foreign policy were anathema to the central government. The East Bengal chief minister was charged with treason, dismissed from office, and placed under house arrest. The democratically elected government of East Bengal had a brief life of two months. Governor's rule was imposed on the province, bringing it under the direct control of the Centre.

For the Bengalis, the transfer of power to the hands of a military-civil service clique had a twofold implication. Since they were basically unrepresented at the highest echelons of the armed forces and civil services, the Bengalis were effectively marginalized in the formulation of state policies. Second, the armed forces and the civil services were in the main hostile to Bengali aspirations, partly because of their provincial origins but mainly because Bengali demands for provincial autonomy, normalization of relations with India and a non-aligned foreign policy were inimical to the institutional interests of the military. The military and civil service leaders favoured a centralized state and were strongly opposed to the demand for 'full regional autonomy'. However, Bengali politicians were not excluded from high office if they were prepared to toe the line. In the words of the historian Ayesha Jalal, the 'only acceptable Bengali in office in Karachi was a captive Bengali'.[9] Despite this severe handicap, ministerial office and membership of the legislature made it possible for Bengali politicians to squeeze occasional concessions from the ruling clique.

The career of the Awami League leader Huseyn Shaheed Suhrawardy provides the best illustration of the limitations of and possibilities for a Bengali politician in the central government. Suhrawardy was dedicated equally to promoting the rights of the people of East Bengal and to preserving the unity of Pakistan. Appointed law minister in the central cabinet in 1953, he made a bold effort to frame a set of compromise proposals that could serve as the basis of a constitution. In order to allay fears of Bengali numerical domination, Suhrawardy conceded the Punjabi demand for consolidation of the West Pakistan provinces into a single unit ('One Unit'), with parity in parliamentary seats for West and East Pakistan. In exchange, the parity principle would apply also to representation in the civil and military services, in order to rectify the imbalance between the two wings. East Pakistan would get 'full autonomy', a joint electorate, and recognition of Bengali as a state language alongside Urdu. The proposals were summarily rejected by Governor General Iskandar Mirza. Suhrawardy was obliged to resign from his post, and the Awami League joined the ranks of the Opposition.[10]

The constitution that was finally adopted in 1956 offered a single concession to the eastern wing. Bengali was accepted as a national language. This was due in no small measure to the persistent advocacy by Suhrawardy and the Bengali prime minister, Mohammed Ali Bogra. The constitution, however, ignored the demand for 'full autonomy', renamed East Bengal as East Pakistan, despite strong protests from the province, and conceded parity in parliamentary seats to West Pakistan, notwithstanding East Pakistan's larger population. The Awami League walked out from parliament in protest before the constitution was adopted. A few months later, however, in this game of political musical chairs, Suhrawardy was sworn in as prime minister in a coalition government, after he had accepted three conditions laid down by President Mirza. These reflected the foreign and defence policy priorities of the military-civil service clique; adherence to a pro-western foreign policy; non-interference in military matters; and keeping under control Maulana Bhashani, the leader of the left wing of the Awami League and a strong advocate of an independent, non-aligned policy.[11]

Suhrawardy had little choice but to work within the system. He became an ardent advocate of 'One Unit' and Pakistan's pro-west foreign policy. His defence of Pakistan's military pacts led to a split in the Awami League. Its founder president, Maulana Bhashani, resigned from the party and subsequently formed the National Awami Party. Yet, working within the system, Suhrawardy and his minister for commerce and industry, Abul Mansur Ahmed, were able to achieve a modicum of success in advancing the economic interests of East Pakistan. Industrial development was transferred to the list of provincial subjects, enabling the East Pakistan government to take its own initiatives in this field. The powerful Import–Export Controller opened an office in Chittagong to facilitate issue of import licences to provincial businessmen. Issue of licences to newcomers in the commercial field was made easier. A trade agreement was concluded with India. Steps were taken to ensure for East Pakistan a fairer allocation of foreign aid received from the United States.

These modest measures to redress the economic imbalance between the two wings proved to be the undoing of the Suhrawardy ministry. They drew strong protest from vested business interests in the western wing. Some of Suhrawardy's allies withdrew their support and the governor general demanded Suhrawardy's resignation. The Awami League–led coalition had lasted barely a year.

A new cabinet was appointed, but the days of the recently adopted constitution were now numbered. It suffered from a fatal flaw: it required periodic elections, the uncertainties of which were unappealing to the governor general. Moreover, the concept of division of powers between the Centre and the provinces was suspect in the eyes of the commander-in-chief, General Ayub Khan. 'The constitution, by distributing power between the President, the Prime Minister and his Cabinet, and the provinces, destroyed the focal point of power and left no one in a position of control,' he was to write later.[12] President Mirza, on his part, was apprehensive about the outcome of the general elections required under the constitution. With the army chief and the president on the same page, the constitution was doomed. On 30 September 1958, President Iskandar Mirza imposed martial law, abrogating the constitution, dismissing the central and provincial governments, dissolving the central and provincial assemblies and banning all political parties.

Mirza failed to recognize in good time that by handing over power to the army, he had made himself superfluous. The army was no longer restricted to a behind-the-scenes role. The generals forced Mirza to resign on 27 October and sent him into permanent exile in London. Pakistan's transition to military rule is often ascribed to the failure of democracy in the country. In reality, the army seized power in order to pre-empt the emergence of democracy in Pakistan.

The Ayub Decade (1958–68) and the Six-Point Demand

General (later Field Marshal) Mohammad Ayub Khan did not come unprepared to shoulder his new responsibilities. He was convinced that in politics, as in the military, there should be a single 'focus of power'. As early as in 1954, the commander-in-chief had set down his political ideas with military clarity in a 'short appreciation of present and future problems of Pakistan'. In his opinion, the Pakistani people could easily be led astray by communists and unscrupulous politicians. 'Unfettered democracy' was, therefore, a danger to be avoided. Pakistan needed a 'controlled form of democracy' in which the president, as Head of State, would have powers to dismiss the cabinet. Provincial governors, appointed by the president and answerable to him, should have similar powers in their respective jurisdictions. The president should have 'over-riding powers to assume control should things go wrong in the provinces or the centre'. Ayub deplored the introduction of universal franchise, but was resigned to the fact that it was too late to reverse the position. His answer was to introduce checks to prevent 'irresponsible' behaviour on the part of the electorate. This could be achieved through a system of indirect elections, in which universal franchise would be restricted to the election of local electoral colleges, which would then elect members of the provincial and central assemblies, as well as the president. Ayub had an unflattering opinion about the Bengalis. Not only were they lacking in soldierly 'leadership qualities' but they also had 'all the inhibitions of down-trodden races and have not yet found it possible to adjust psychologically to the requirements of the new-born freedom'. They suffered from 'complexes, exclusiveness, suspicion and a sort of defensive aggressiveness'.[13]

Ayub lost no time in putting his plan into action. Large numbers of the detested class of politicians were imprisoned or debarred from future political activity on charges of corruption or treason. At the same time, energetic measures were instituted to speed up administrative procedures and bring to account corrupt politicians and civil servants. Development activity was speeded up, and the Ayub years witnessed impressive GDP growth rates in both wings of Pakistan. Within weeks of proclamation of martial law in the country, the army returned to the barracks, leaving the civil services to resume their normal role.

On the constitutional front, Ayub took the first step towards 'controlled' democracy by issuing the Basic Democracies Order in October 1959, providing for the election of 80,000 Basic Democrats – 40,000 from each wing of Pakistan. In February 1960, the newly elected college of 80,000 Basic Democrats lived up to Ayub's expectations by expressing their confidence in his leadership by a majority vote of 95.6 per cent – an impressive achievement even for a despotic regime. On this basis, Ayub – who had meanwhile elevated himself to the rank of field marshal – claimed to be the first 'elected' president of Pakistan.

In March 1962, a new constitution was introduced. This provided for a president empowered to act as the single 'focal point' of power. Provision was made for a national assembly as well as for provincial assemblies for each of the two wings of the country. Rejecting the Bengali demand for representation in proportion to population, Ayub's constitution provided for parity between the two wings in the National Assembly. Legislation enacted by the National Assembly could pass into law only if it received the president's approval. The president was empowered to appoint and dismiss central ministers and the two provincial governors without reference to the National Assembly. The provincial governors had similar powers to appoint and dismiss cabinets in their respective jurisdictions, without reference to the provincial assemblies. They were answerable to the president alone and held office at his pleasure. Ayub detested political parties, and his constitution initially had no provision for them. However, legislation was later enacted to permit their functioning, partly because of public pressure and partly because it dawned on Ayub that parties were not totally devoid of merit – they could be used to 'organize members on the basis of party rule and discipline' and to 'explain government policies to the people'.[14] He saw no role for political parties in the decision-making process.

Ayub's announcement was greeted with outraged protests from politicians, intellectuals and the general public in both wings. Demands were raised for abrogation of the new constitution and restoration of fundamental rights. In Dhaka, university students went on strike, burnt copies of the constitution and demanded the release of Suhrawardy and other political leaders who had been incarcerated on grounds of national security. The National Democratic Front launched by Suhrawardy brought together political parties from both wings on a common platform for democratic rights. 'The country started behaving like a wild horse that had been captured but not yet tamed,' Ayub complained in his memoirs. 'Every time you try to stroke it affectionately or feed it, it bites you and kicks you.'[15]

In the presidential elections held in 1964, Ayub defeated his rival, Fatima Jinnah, sister of the revered founding father of Pakistan. The outcome was a foregone conclusion, given the dependence of the Basic Democrats on official patronage.

The centralization of power in the hands of the president, Field Marshal Ayub Khan, deprived the Bengalis of even the modest degree of political influence they were able to exercise earlier through directly elected legislators. Through their representatives in the legislature, the Bengalis had been able to exercise a modicum of influence in national affairs, even though the power balance was heavily tilted against the eastern wing. By giving himself a virtual monopoly of state power and by reducing the role of the legislature to insignificance, Ayub deprived the

Bengalis of the only toehold they had in the policymaking process and unwittingly contributed to a sharpening of regional Bengali demands. In the words of the political scientist Rounaq Jahan, '... political movements in East Pakistan changed from competitive participation in the national system to radical provincial autonomy movements'.[16]

Furthermore, by virtually extinguishing hopes of redressal of Bengali grievances through the political process, the martial law regime created ripe conditions for clandestine revolutionary activities. In 1961, a group of student leaders formed a secret organization, the Swadhin Bangla Biplobi Parishad (Revolutionary Council for Independent Bengal). Separately, a few Bengali military and civilian officials set up an outfit called Bengal Liberation Force under Lt Cmdr Moazzem Hossain. The patron of these secret cells was the rising star of the Awami League, Sheikh Mujibur Rahman.[17] A follower of Suhrawardy since his student days in pre-Independence India, Sheikh Mujib was deeply involved in the language movement in the early years of Pakistan. He became the general secretary of the East Bengal Awami League in 1953, at the age of thirty-three. A charismatic orator, he soon emerged as Suhrawardy's right-hand man and political successor.

After the imposition of the martial law regime, Mujib would follow a dual strategy in his struggle for the rights of East Bengal. He called with increasing insistence for full autonomy for East Bengal in his public speeches, while at the same time taking the tentative first steps in planning for the contingency of being prevented from achieving his goal through constitutional means. Suhrawardy sensed the change in the ranks of his followers. Shortly before his death in 1963, he wrote: '[Mujibur Rahman] is prepared to accept the objective of democracy for Pakistan as the sole issue ... But he has doubts that national unity and national integration will solve the problems of East Pakistan.' Looking at the future, he reflected that 'one contingency which we were probably approaching was the mass upheaval in East Pakistan against West Pakistan'.[18]

The 1965 War

The 1965 war between Pakistan and India was the turning point in Ayub's political fortunes. From a narrowly military viewpoint, the war ended in a stalemate, but its political and economic consequences undermined the Ayub regime. A UN Security Council resolution finally brought hostilities to an end. Peace – and the ceasefire line – were restored in 1966 at a summit conference in Tashkent, where the Soviet premier, Aleksei Nikolayevich Kosygin, played the role of conciliator between Ayub and Prime Minister Lal Bahadur Shastri of India.

These events aroused powerful but contrasting emotions in the two wings of Pakistan. In the western wing, the war to seize Kashmir was hugely popular and its termination was condemned as a 'sell-out'. Fed on incessant official propaganda, public opinion expected the war to end in a glorious victory in Kashmir. Acceptance of the UN ceasefire resolution and the Tashkent agreement were seen as acts of betrayal by the government. The ambitious and unscrupulous foreign minister, Zulfikar Ali Bhutto, who was largely responsible for persuading Ayub to embark on the misadventure, now chose to distance himself from the president by joining the critics of the Tashkent accord. Seizing the political opportunity, Bhutto founded the Pakistan People's Party (PPP) in November 1967, and launched a popular campaign against Ayub with the slogan of 'democracy, an independent foreign policy and a socialist pattern of economy'.

Public reactions to the war in East Pakistan were very different, though they also led to mounting opposition to the Ayub regime. The war brought into sharp focus the fact that the Pakistani military doctrine had no credible provision for the defence of East Pakistan. Only a single army division was located in a province that accounted for the major share of the country's population. The war exposed the hollowness of the doctrine that the defence of the eastern wing lay in the west – that the Pakistani army had the capability of marching on New Delhi to enforce an Indian withdrawal from the eastern wing. The fact that India showed no intention of attacking East Pakistan offered little consolation to the Bengalis, who had long demanded that they should have the capacity to defend their province.

The Bengalis did not share the West Pakistani obsession with Kashmir. As the political scientist Rounaq Jahan points out, they '. . . resented the fact that they were exposed to the danger of Indian occupation for the sake of Kashmir'. Thus the 1965 war precipitated an intensified and more radical demand for full regional autonomy in East Pakistan. 'The [1965] war may truly be called a watershed in East Pakistan's relationship with the centre,' Jahan observes.[19]

The Six-Point Demand

Capturing the popular mood, Sheikh Mujibur Rahman, now the Awami League president, proclaimed the historic Six-Point Demand in 1966. This called for restricting the powers of the central government only to defence and foreign affairs, all other powers being vested in the regional governments. Powers of taxation would vest exclusively in the regional governments; the central government would have no right to raise taxes but would receive a share of the taxes raised by the regions. East Pakistan would have its own fiscal and monetary policy. Notwithstanding the role of the Centre in foreign affairs, the regional governments would have powers to conduct trade relations, enter into commercial agreements and establish trade offices in foreign countries. East Pakistan would have its own militia or paramilitary force. Mujib later added another demand to these six points: that representation in parliament should be proportional to the population of each wing.

The Six-Point programme was more radical than previous Bengali demands for 'full regional autonomy'. East Pakistan had previously called for autonomy within a loose federation; in contrast, the Six-Point programme verged on a demand for a confederal state. Mujib hoped to secure acceptance of the Six-Point programme by political means, avoiding the horrific sacrifices that are an inescapable feature of an armed struggle. However, as Suhrawardy had surmised, he doubted whether the repressive military regime, with its West Pakistani power base, would ever accept the Bengali demands. Sheikh Mujib's followers included champions of constitutional reform as well as a growing number of youthful advocates of armed action. The Six Points catered to both sections.

In 1965, Mujib confided to the Indian deputy high commissioner in Dhaka, Asoke Ray, that his ultimate goal was independence for East Pakistan. Shortly after launching the Six-Point movement in 1966, Mujib informed Ray that he visualized the Six Points as a bridge to independence.[20]

The Six-Point movement aroused tremendous enthusiasm throughout the eastern wing. Students once again took the lead in mobilizing public support and they were soon joined by industrial workers in the major cities. Once again, the central role of language and culture in forging a new sense of national identity was on display. The Awami League's student wing, the East Pakistan Student League, led a drive to replace all English and Urdu signboards with Bengali versions, achieving almost total success in a matter of days. 'A West Pakistani feels like a foreigner in Dacca,' Ayub complained bitterly in his diary.[21]

The Six-Point programme was anathema to Ayub. It directly contradicted his conviction that Pakistan could survive only as a strongly centralized state under the guardianship of the army. Ayub's response to the Six-Point programme was to extend the state of emergency declared after the 1965 war, imprison the top Awami League leaders and shut down *Ittefaq*, the major pro-Awami League newspaper.

The Agartala Conspiracy Case

In December 1967, a number of Bengali politicians, civil servants and military personnel were imprisoned on charges of conspiring with India to secede from Pakistan. Sheikh Mujib was soon added to the list of alleged conspirators, in what came to be known as the Agartala

Conspiracy Case. Though many of the charges were fabricated, some contained more than a grain of truth. One of the principal accused, Captain Shawkat Ali, revealed in 2010 in the Bangladesh Parliament (he was at the time the deputy speaker) that '. . . as a matter of fact, several military officers and civil servants were involved in the case as we wanted to liberate the country from Pakistan through an armed revolution under the leadership of Bangabandhu Sheikh Mujibur Rahman'. Shawkat Ali confirmed that a navy steward, Mujibur Rahman (not to be confused with Sheikh Mujibur Rahman) and an educationist, Mohammad Ali Reza, went to Agartala to seek Indian assistance.[22] They did not, however, succeed in securing an Indian commitment.

The central government had a long record of imprisoning Bengali political leaders on trumped-up charges of sedition and other offences. Hence, public opinion in the eastern wing reacted with disbelief and outrage to the Agartala Conspiracy charges. But this case against Mujib had the unexpected result of investing him with the halo of a hero. Massive and unabated protests, demonstrations, strikes and public protests brought about a virtual collapse of administration in the eastern wing, finally forcing the government to drop the conspiracy case and release Mujib and his fellow prisoners.

Mujib's popularity rose to even greater heights. He was hailed as the *Bangabandhu* – the champion of the Bengali cause. In November 1969, the Bangabandhu declared that 'East Pakistan' would henceforth be known as Bangladesh.[23]

End of the Ayub regime

By March 1969, with mounting disturbances in both wings of Pakistan, it became evident that the Ayub regime could not be further sustained. The 1962 constitution provided that in the event of the president's resignation he would be succeeded by the speaker of the National Assembly. In this case, the speaker, Abdul Jabbar Khan, happened to be a Bengali. The unthinkable prospect of placing a Bengali civilian at the centre of power was averted by abrogating the constitution and declaring martial law. On 24 March, Ayub announced his resignation and handed over power to the army chief, General Agha Mohammad Yahya Khan, who assumed office as president and chief martial law administrator. In his farewell address to the nation, Ayub declared: 'I have always told you that the secret of the continued existence of Pakistan is in a strong centre . . . But now it is being proposed that the country be divided into two parts, the centre be made weak and helpless, the defence forces be paralysed completely and West Pakistan's political position be ended. I cannot preside over the destruction of my country.'[24] This parting shot was aimed at the Awami League's Six-Point Demand, which was diametrically opposite to his basic conviction that Pakistan could survive only as a highly centralized state, with an army that had unquestioned authority to decide its budgetary allocation, and a political system dominated by West Pakistan, the army's recruitment ground.

In a cable to the US State Department in April, the American Ambassador to Pakistan, Benjamin Oehlert, Jr, explained that '[the] major objectives [of imposition of martial law] probably were to maintain intact [a] strong government, to protect [the] existing power structure in West Pakistan and to prevent East Pakistan from obtaining national political power proportionate to [its] population'.[25]

Fragile unity

By 1969, the fragility of the Pakistani state was apparent to close observers. In February, the director of intelligence and research in the US State Department prepared an analysis entitled 'Pakistan on the Brink'. It concluded that 'in East Pakistan opposition to Ayub has taken on strong overtones of anti-West Pakistani sentiment to the point that secession can no longer be ruled out as a possible consequence of political convulsion'.[26]

India's external intelligence agency, the Research and Analysis Wing (RAW), offered a prescient assessment in April 1969. Highlighting the massive popular support for the Six Points and reactions to the Agartala Conspiracy Case in East Bengal, RAW anticipated:

'The [Pakistan] authorities would have to resort to large-scale use of the Army and other paramilitary forces in East Pakistan to curb a movement which has already gained considerable strength. The use of force is likely, in turn, to lead to a situation where the people of East Pakistan, supported by elements of the East Pakistan Rifles (who are known to be sympathetic towards the secessionist movement as evidenced from the recent East Pakistan Conspiracy Case), may rise in revolt against the Central Authority and even declare their independence.'[27]

2

Birth of a Nation

On assuming office as president and chief martial law administrator, Yahya announced his intention of holding free and fair elections to pave the way for a new constitution. He conceded the Bengali demand for parliamentary representation in proportion to population. (This gave East Pakistan a majority of 162 seats in the 302-member National Assembly.) The assembly thus elected was to draw up a new constitution within sixty days – a formidable task, considering that it took Pakistan almost twenty years to produce its first constitution. To ensure that the new constitution protected the interests of the army, Yahya decreed that his 'authentication' was required for it to come into effect.

Pakistan held its first general elections in December 1970, almost a quarter of a century after gaining independence. In the eastern wing, the Awami League, under Mujib's leadership, succeeded in converting the election campaign into a virtual referendum on the Six Points. Right-wing parties calling for a strong Centre found no support from the public. Left-wing parties championed the regional cause, but questioned whether the rights of East Bengal could be achieved through constitutional means. The veteran peasant leader Maulana Bhashani called for independence and declared that his party, the National Awami Party (B), would boycott the elections.

In the event, the Awami League won 160 of the 162 East Pakistani seats for the national legislature, thereby gaining an absolute majority in the house of 300. In West Pakistan, Bhutto's PPP won 81 of the 140 seats. Significantly, the PPP did not contest a single seat in the eastern wing, while the Awami League fielded only seven candidates in West Pakistan, all of whom were defeated. The Pakistani general elections saw two separate campaigns – in East and West Pakistan, respectively – featuring different parties and contrasting issues.

The results took Yahya by surprise. Military intelligence estimates had predicted that the Awami League would win no more than 46–70 of the 162 East Pakistani seats.[1] Yahya had expected an outcome that gave no party an absolute majority in the National Assembly, leaving him free to play on party and personality differences in the time-honoured manner. Yet, the Pakistani army was not altogether unprepared to deal with a recalcitrant Mujib. Even before the polling, the army had begun to draw up contingency plans for a military crackdown in the event of Mujib proving to be uncooperative. On 11 December, within four days of the declaration of electoral results, Lt Gen. Yaqub Khan, chief martial law administrator for East Pakistan, issued a contingency plan, named 'Operation Blitz', to be implemented in certain emergency situations, such as open defiance of the martial law, a mass movement jeopardizing the integrity of Pakistan, or a declaration of independence. The general, a student of Napoleonic strategy, believed at the time that a 'whiff of the grapeshot' would suffice if Mujib and his followers refused to 'behave'.[2] The army was determined to preserve its prerogatives.

Bhutto fired the first salvo of West Pakistani intransigence. In a public speech on 20 December, he declared that 'a majority alone does not count in national politics',[3] emphasizing that real power at the Centre rested in Punjab and Sind. He declared that a constitution could not be framed either, without the cooperation of his party, nor a government formed at the Centre unless it included the party. Bhutto clearly believed that in the final analysis he could turn to the army to coerce the Bengalis into accepting the traditional dominance of West Pakistan.[4] A familiar pattern was repeating itself. As the Awami Leaguer

Kamal Hossain points out, '. . . a minority, unable to contain a majority within a democratically constituted representative institution had always fallen back on military force'.[5]

Mujib's sweeping electoral victory and the unbounded Bengali enthusiasm for full autonomy made Mujib a willing prisoner of the Six-Point Demand. He risked a strong reaction from his followers if he were to water down the programme. On 3 January 1971, he led the newly elected Awami League legislators in solemnly swearing their commitment to full realization of the Six-Point programme. Addressing a massive public rally, he declared that the Awami League would never compromise on the Six Points. He called for friendly relations with neighbouring countries and peaceful settlement of all disputes.[6] These included Kashmir – an issue that aroused little emotion in East Pakistan – as well as the Farakka Barrage issue and the equitable utilization of the flows of the Ganges River between India and East Pakistan.

In this tense situation, the Awami League leaders feared that the Pakistani army might precipitate hostilities with India in order to divert attention from the internal crisis and whip up nationalist sentiment to thwart their demand for autonomy. It alerted its contacts in Indian intelligence to this possibility and appealed to India to refrain from responding to Pakistani border provocations.

Indian reactions – January 1971

On receiving the Awami League's message, Ramji Kao, head of India's external intelligence agency RAW, sent a lengthy report to the prime minister's influential secretary, Parmeshwar Narain Haksar. Haksar and Indira Gandhi knew each other well since their student days in England in the late 1930s. In the words of his biographer Jairam Ramesh, 'Haksar contributed heavily to the making of Indira Gandhi, especially in the first six or seven years of her prime ministership . . . They formed an awesome duo: she with her charismatic appeal, he with his intellectual gravitas. Ultimately, she took all the decisions, no doubt, but she was influenced heavily by him at every turn.'[7] Haksar would play a central role in the crisis of 1971.

In his report to Haksar, Kao offered the assessment that in the event of a constitutional impasse in Pakistan, the martial law authorities would seek to divert public attention from the internal crisis by initiating a military confrontation with India or an infiltration campaign in Kashmir. In this context, Kao drew attention to the considerable increase in Pakistan's military capabilities since the 1965 India–Pakistan war.

The possibility of another Pakistani military adventure in Kashmir was never far from Indian minds. Only five years had passed since the latest Pakistani attempt to seize Kashmir by force. Kao's report only confirmed Haksar's own apprehensions. He alerted the prime minister: '. . . with the overwhelming victory of East Pakistan Wing, the solution of internal problems of Pakistan have become infinitely more difficult. Consequently, the temptation to seek a solution of these problems by external adventures has become very great.'[8] Though the prime minister (and Haksar himself) were preoccupied at the time with a bitterly contested general election, they found time for a series of meetings with the service chiefs to discuss the problem and identify deficiencies in India's defence equipment. A list of requirements was handed over to the Soviet ambassador. Moscow's response was prompt and positive.[9] Thus, at the beginning of the year, India was preparing to meet a Pakistani threat to Kashmir on the lines of the last war.

Senior Indian diplomats and intelligence officers met at the MEA on 6 January to consider the broader implications of developments in East Pakistan. Kao brought up the question of the Awami League's appeal for forbearance in the event of Pakistani border provocations. Though there was great sympathy for the Awami League, it was decided that border incursions by Pakistan could not go unchallenged. Kao was asked to inform the Awami League that India would strictly refrain from initiating any incident, but it would be compelled to retaliate if Pakistan were to violate the border.

The discussion centred on the prospects of a constitutional accord in Pakistan, the possibility of a secessionist movement in East Pakistan, and the implications of these developments for India. It was generally accepted that formidable difficulties stood in the way of agreement on the constitution and that there was a very real possibility of a secessionist movement if the Awami League's demand for autonomy were to be rejected. Officials were, however, divided on the question as to whether a secessionist movement was inevitable – or desirable – from an Indian viewpoint. The senior MEA officials, Secretary (East) S.K. Banerji and High Commissioner in Pakistan B.K. Acharya, argued that secession could not be treated as a foregone conclusion. Acharya argued that Bhutto might well accept the Six-Point programme for autonomy, with each wing of Pakistan going its own way, if he himself could be all-powerful in West Pakistan. The differences between the Awami League and the army were more problematical. The Pakistani army would never accept a constitution under which it would have to depend for its finances on subventions from the federating units. However, argued Acharya, it could not be altogether ruled out that the Awami League might agree to a compromise on the financial implications of the Six Points.

Acharya and Banerji adhered to the conventional line that secession was not in India's interest. Even before the announcement of the Pakistan electoral results, Acharya had spelled out this view in a dispatch to New Delhi. While recognizing the real possibility of a secessionist movement, he argued that the only hope of a breakthrough in Indo-Pakistan relations lay in a transition to democracy in Pakistan, with the Awami League forming a government at the Centre. India's efforts to improve relations had so far been met with 'unrelenting hostility from the central Pakistani Government dominated by West Pakistanis'. He wrote:

> Majority control of the Central Pakistan Government by East Pakistanis seems to be our only hope for achieving our policy objectives towards Pakistan and overcoming this stone-wall resistance of West Pakistan.

> *In order that this hope may become a reality, however, it is essential that Pakistan (with its East Pakistan majority) should remain one,* so that we may pursue our policy objectives through the leaders of East Pakistan [emphasis in original].[10]

Acharya also pointed out that a prolonged armed struggle in East Pakistan was likely to pass under the control of pro-China Naxalite elements. (In 1971, West Bengal was still in the final stages of suppressing a prolonged and destructive Naxal insurgency.) Finally, the high commissioner noted that a secessionist movement in Pakistan's eastern wing might also give rise to demands for a 'Greater Bengal', threatening India's own territorial integrity. This may seem far-fetched today, but for people of Acharya's and Banerji's generation, the 1947 proposal for an independent undivided Bengal launched jointly by Suhrawardy, Sarat Bose and other prominent provincial politicians was more than just a historical footnote.

There was general agreement in the meeting about the danger of a drawn-out guerrilla war passing into the hands of the extreme left, with the attendant dangers to India's security. However, Kao disagreed with Acharya and Banerji on the prospects of a constitutional compromise. He insisted that the West Pakistan establishment would never accept a dominant role for the eastern wing. The RAW assessment was that the Pakistani army would reject any fundamental shift in the existing power structure. Kao also emphasized that Mujib's own hands were tied and that he could not afford to accept a compromise. If he deviated from the Six-Point programme, he would be swept aside by popular sentiment. Kao added that he had received information that Mujib himself viewed secession as a distinct possibility and was preparing for such an eventuality. He argued (as he had done earlier, in 1969) that India should have the capacity to offer the assistance that the Awami League might require if it launched an independence movement. An independence struggle would have to progress on a multi-directional front, encompassing a political movement to maintain continuing popular support, and the raising of a volunteer army to reinforce the Bengali regulars declaring for independence. Among the MEA officials present, only the head of the Pakistan division, Asoke Ray, agreed with Kao. (Ray, it will be recalled, had direct contacts with Mujibur Rahman in 1965–66.)

Thus, the divergence between the MEA and RAW perspectives, visible even in 1969, remained unresolved. The MEA view remained dominant in official circles. As we shall see further, it was shared by the Prime Minister's Office (PMO) at its highest level, right up to 25 March 1971.

In retrospect, it is clear that the RAW anticipated events correctly, but as of early January, none of the major protagonists – Mujib, Yahya and Bhutto – had ruled out the possibility of reaching an agreement on the constitution, even though each of them was also preparing for a breakdown in the talks. (Indeed, as we shall see below, both Mujib and Bhutto were to explore the possibility of a constitutional accord on the lines anticipated by Acharya in early January.) Neither was it inevitable that the Pakistani army would pursue its institutional interests at the cost of national unity. The seniormost officers in East Pakistan, Admiral Ahsan and Lt Gen. Yaqub Khan, would warn Yahya in early March about the folly of a crackdown.

Initial explorations: Mujib, Yahya and Bhutto in January 1971

Yahya visited Dhaka in mid-January for talks with Mujib and the Awami League high command. As Acharya had anticipated, Mujib took the opportunity to explain that the Six-Point programme would accommodate the institutional interests of the army. The size of the army would not be reduced. Adequate finances for the army and the central government could be ensured by incorporating a suitable provision in the constitution. Mujib offered Yahya the post of president, catering also to the general's personal interests. Mujib urged Yahya to convene the National Assembly by 15 February. When he requested Yahya to spell out any objection he might have to the Six-Point programme, the president said that he himself had no objection, but Mujib would have to carry the West Pakistani leaders with him. He thus obliquely brought up a question of importance for the army – the composition of the new central government and inclusion in it of a reliable counterpoise to the Awami League.

The Awami League's thinking on the constitution was explained in greater detail when its legal expert, Kamal Hossain, met with Lt Gen. Peerzada, Yahya's principal staff officer (PSO). Kamal Hossain explained that constitutional provisions would ensure that a certain portion of the revenues and foreign exchange earnings would be automatically appropriated by the central government. Regarding control over foreign trade and aid, Hossain said that the regional governments could resolve any differences through negotiations held within the framework of the country's foreign policy. Finally, Hossain dismissed the possibility of a conflict between the Centre and East Pakistan, pointing out that both governments would be led by the Awami League.[11]

Before his departure from Dhaka, Yahya made a statement describing Mujib as the future prime minister of Pakistan. The positive tone of the statement was soon to be belied by events. After Dhaka, Yahya proceeded to Larkana in Sind, where he was Bhutto's guest at a shikar (shooting party) on his extensive estates. Bhutto reportedly criticized Yahya for naming Mujib as the future prime minister even before the National Assembly had met. Bhutto said that Mujib was a 'clever bastard' who wanted the National Assembly to meet at an early date so that he could 'bulldoze' an Awami League constitution through the assembly. He argued that a consensus on the constitution must be reached *before* convention of the assembly. Time would be needed to protect the interests of West Pakistan and the army. If Mujib were a 'true' or 'loyal' Pakistani, he would not object to this delay.[12]

The events that followed show that Bhutto's arguments had made an impression on Yahya. After Larkana, the president did not again refer to Mujib as the future prime minister. More importantly, the National Assembly was not convened in the time frame requested by Mujib.

At the end of January, Mujib and Bhutto met in Dhaka. Mujib focused on constitutional issues and the need for convening the National Assembly at an early date. Bhutto dwelt on power-sharing arrangements, demanding the post of deputy prime minister and foreign minister or, as an alternative, the presidential post. He showed scant interest in constitutional details, apart from rejecting provincial control of foreign trade. Mujib was angered by Bhutto's arrogance – at his demand for sharing power as a matter of right and at his hints that the army would never agree to hand over power to a Bengali party unless he, Bhutto, were given a prominent role in the government.[13]

The Awami League suspected, not without reason, that Bhutto and the army leadership were hatching a plot against the Bengalis. (Bhutto's close confidant, Rafi Raza, has produced convincing circumstantial evidence of collusion between his leader and Yahya prior to each important development from mid-January to 25 March.[14]) On 29 January, Yahya confided to US ambassador Farland his apprehensions about the future of the country, declaring that he had no intention of accepting a constitution that could lead to a split-up of Pakistan.[15]

Suspecting collusion between Bhutto and the army leadership, the Awami League began to plan for a mass movement. On 21 January, RAW reported that Awami League leaders were not optimistic about an accord on the constitution and were thinking of launching a mass movement. In early February, RAW confirmed that Mujib was planning to build up the party's capacity to launch a mass movement.[16] In early February, dismayed by the delay in the announcement of dates for the convention of the National Assembly, the Awami League leaders had held a secret meeting to consider the option of declaration of independence. Sheikh Mujib and the Awami League general secretary, Tajuddin Ahmed, had carefully examined the measures needed to implement a unilateral decision. Kamal Hossain and Tajuddin were tasked to draw up a formal proclamation of independence.[17]

The contrasting positions of Bhutto and Mujib concerning India were highlighted when two Kashmiris hijacked an Indian passenger plane to Lahore at the end of January 1971. The hijackers were given sanctuary in Pakistan and the plane was blown up at the airport. Bhutto rushed to the airport to hail the hijackers as heroes and announced that his party would assist the terrorist group in whatever manner they wanted. Mujib deplored the failure of the authorities to prevent the destruction of the aircraft, called for an official inquiry and alerted the public against attempts by 'vested interests' to 'create abnormal conditions with the ulterior purpose of sabotaging the peaceful transfer of power to the people'.[18]

There was a brief parting of the clouds on 13 February, when Yahya announced that the National Assembly would meet in Dhaka on 3 March. The Awami League welcomed the announcement, but its hopes were soon to be dashed. Bhutto declared that he would boycott the meeting. Yahya made no serious attempt to dissuade him, despite the fact that other parties from the western wing were ready to participate in the National Assembly. Rather, Yahya decided on 20 February that Mujib must be made to 'see sense'.[19] On 22 February, Bhutto's PPP declared that a grave national crisis had arisen on account of the constitutional deadlock, implying that it rejected the Six-Point formula. On the same day, Yahya met with his provincial governors and martial law administrators to inform them of his decision to indefinitely postpone the National Assembly session. The governor of East Pakistan, Admiral Ahsan, argued strongly against the decision. He was supported by the Sind governor, General Rahman Gul, but the warnings of the two provincial governors were summarily rejected by Yahya. Ahsan was instructed to inform Mujib of the decision on 28 February, on the eve of the presidential announcement to be made on 1 March.[20]

Preparations went ahead for applying a 'whiff of the grapeshot' to the Bengalis. On 27 February, Maj. Gen. Khadim Hussain Raja, General Officer Commanding (GOC), 14 Div. and deputy martial law administrator, issued orders to the army to prepare to put 'Operation Blitz' into action any time after midday on 1 March. Troops fanned out to the district towns to deal with disturbances that might arise following the announcement the next day of the indefinite postponement of the National Assembly meeting.

On the evening of 28 February, Governor Ahsan informed Mujib and Tajuddin of the president's decision to postpone the National Assembly session indefinitely. Having carried out his distasteful duty, the governor sent in his resignation, warning the president that a 'point of no return' had been reached.[21]

Non-cooperation

Shortly after 1 p.m. on 1 March, Radio Pakistan announced Yahya's decision to postpone the National Assembly session to an unspecified 'later date' in view of the failure of political leaders to reach a consensus on the main features of the constitution, and the risk of a confrontation between the political leaders of the two wings. As Kamal Hossain points out, this meant in effect that the '... ruling minority would have a veto on constitution-making and, indeed, unless there was a prior understanding with them, the Assembly would not be convened'.[22]

The US Consulate General in Dhaka was situated at a central location on the topmost floors of one of the city's few multistoreyed buildings. The consul general, Archer Blood, surveyed the scene in the streets below after the radio announcement. Sensing the mood of the crowds below, the consul general reported to Washington that he had just witnessed the 'beginning of the break-up of Pakistan'.[23]

A powerful undercurrent of nationalism was visible everywhere. Student groups were in the forefront, raising the slogans '*Joi Bangla*' [Victory to Bengal] and '*Bir Bangali, ostro dhoro, Bangladesh swadhin koro* [Brave Bengalis, take up arms, liberate Bangladesh]'. Militant processions converged on the Purbani Hotel, where the Awami League leaders were holding a meeting. The crowd carried sticks and staves, and raised the cry of 'independence'.

The mass movement that began on 1 March was planned by Mujib, but it was also the spontaneous reaction of a people who had been denied their democratic rights once too often. Mujib harnessed the protests to launch a comprehensive non-cooperation movement. This began with his call for a peaceful, countrywide hartal (strike), including closure of government offices and the courts. Certain specified services, such as the post office, public utilities, railways and other public transportation, factories and markets, were exempted from the strike. The call met with total compliance. The army was unable to obtain provisions from the market as shopkeepers refused to transact business with the military. Curfews declared by the army were systematically defied by the populace.

The resultant situation has been described by the deputy martial law administrator, Maj. Gen. Khadim Hussain Raja.

> The Martial Law Administrator, at this stage, was left with no one to answer his commands except his troops. Even in the matter of troops, it became clear to us that the Bengali troops would not shoot at the Bengali crowds. In fact, it seemed obvious that on a clarion call from Sheikh Mujib, they would even take up arms in his support.[24]

Raja consulted other senior officers in Dhaka about the feasibility of conducting Operation Blitz in the prevailing situation. He records, 'Each one of them was of the opinion that it would be sheer "lunacy" to conduct the operation at that time as the whole basis, and all the prerequisites for attempting it had been knocked out with one blow.'[25]

The futility of military repression in the face of massive public resistance was clear also to the author of Operation Blitz, Lt Gen. Yaqub Khan. An intelligent and perceptive analyst, Yaqub Khan followed Ahsan in cabling his resignation to Yahya. He explained:

> Only solution to present crisis is a purely political one . . . I am convinced there is no military solution which can make sense in present situation. I am consequently unable to accept the responsibility for implementing a mission, namely military solution, which would mean civil war and large-scale killings of unarmed civilians and achieve no sane aim.[26]

Undeterred by the warnings of his two seniormost colleagues in the eastern wing, Yahya decided to replace them with an officer with a reputation for carrying out operations against civilians with unquestioning brutality. Lt Gen. Tikka Khan, famed as the 'Butcher of Baluchistan', was appointed governor and martial law administrator of East Pakistan, in succession to Lt Gen. Yaqub.

Lt Gen. Tikka Khan soon discovered the ground realities in Dhaka. Arriving at the governor's house, he found that all the Bengali staff had disappeared! The governor was obliged to move to the cantonment as Maj. Gen. Raja's guest.[27] A little later, he was to discover that none of the judges of the Dhaka High Court was prepared to swear him in as governor of the province. Non-cooperation extended to the judiciary too.

Developments in the eastern wing rapidly gained momentum. Student and youth groups, in particular, were pressing Mujib to make a formal declaration of independence in his scheduled speech on 7 March. Kamal Hossain recalls that by 7 March, 'anything less [than independence] would not be acceptable to the students, the younger elements, and indeed large sections of politically conscious people'.[28] However, Mujib had also to contend with the fact that an immediate declaration of independence would precipitate a massive military onslaught on the people. In the early hours of 7 May, Maj. Gen. Raja sent a message to Mujib, warning him that if he were to proclaim independence, the army would be sent in to wreck the planned public rally and 'raze Dhaka to the ground if required'.[29]

On 7 March, Mujib addressed a massive public rally in Dhaka's Race Course grounds (now Suhrawardy Udayan). In a masterpiece of oratory, he gave a rousing call to the people to be prepared to fight for freedom, stopping just short of an outright declaration of independence. He listed as his immediate demands: (1) withdrawal of martial law; (2) sending the troops back to their barracks; (3) an inquiry into the killing of civilians; and (4) transfer of power to the elected representatives of the people.[30]

The non-cooperation movement rapidly developed into an effective governing system. The initial call for a hartal was progressively modified to ensure that the public were not subjected to avoidable inconvenience and that economic activities could be sustained in a manner consistent with the Six-Point Demand. This was achieved through a series of directives issued by Tajuddin Ahmed, operating from a room in Mujib's home, and by the Bangabandhu himself. Thus, banks were allowed to conduct domestic transactions, while ensuring that no remittances were effected outside 'Bangladesh'. Postal and telegraph services were to operate within but not outside 'Bangladesh', except for press cables. Essential services were to be maintained.

On 14 March, a new set of directives replaced previous regulations. The hartal directive was relaxed to allow the administration to maintain law and order, as well as development activities, in cooperation with the local Awami League Sangram Parishads (Struggle Committees). Port authorities were to carry out their normal functions, but would refuse the use of their facilities for transportation of troops or military materials. Customs duties were not to be credited to the central government account; they were required to be deposited in special accounts to be operated in accordance with Awami League instructions. Railways were to resume their normal functions, but were to refuse facilities for transporting troops or materials. All provincial taxes were to be credited to the account of the 'Government of Bangla Desh'. Direct central government taxes were not to be collected till further notice. Customs duties and all other indirect central taxes were to be deposited in special accounts to be operated in accordance with directives issued by the Awami League authorities. Thus, by mid-March, the government offices, law courts, banks and other public services in 'Bangla Desh' were effectively operating under Awami League directions. The administrative and judicial authorities functioned under Awami League control; only the military forces remained under effective central control.

Taking note of the cascading developments in the eastern wing, Bhutto threw out a feeler on 14 March. He suggested, in a deliberately ambiguous public speech, that the Awami League might form a government in East Pakistan and the PPP in West Pakistan. A leading

Urdu newspaper reported the speech under the headlines '*Udhar Tum, Idhar Hum*' (You There, We Here).[31] (Acharya was not wide of the mark!) Bhutto dropped the proposal when it drew negative reactions in West Pakistan.

Mujib's appeal for India's assistance

While launching the mass movement at the beginning of March, Mujib recognized the danger of a military crackdown and the need to be prepared for this contingency. On 2 March, RAW chief Kao informed Indira Gandhi that an appeal had been received from the Awami League for arms and ammunition, communications and signal equipment, a radio transmitter, a small passenger aircraft for speedy movement on the Indian side of the border, as well as medicines and food supplies. It was apparent that Mujib contemplated the possibility of waging a resistance war, with sanctuaries along the Indian border. This was the first time that a comprehensive and specific list of requests had been received from the Awami League. It was also evident that the list was drawn up in haste, without careful calculation; thus, the requirement for food supplies was fixed at the incredible level of 3 million tons!

The request raised complex issues for Indian officials. Was the break-up of Pakistan in India's interests? How would Pakistan react if India were to get involved? Would it retaliate across the Kashmir ceasefire line? Should Indian assistance be preceded by recognition of Bangladesh as an independent state? How would the international community react to Indian intervention in a Pakistani civil war? Would China come to Pakistan's assistance? Under the prime minister's instructions, a committee headed by the cabinet secretary was formed to examine these questions. The committee included Secretary to the Prime Minister P.N. Haksar, Foreign Secretary T.N. Kaul, Home Secretary Govind Narain, and RAW chief R.N. Kao.

Kao, who had long anticipated the separation of Bangladesh, emphatically pressed for a positive response:

> ... the longer the liberation struggle takes to achieve success, the greater are the chances of its control passing into the hands of extremists and pro-China communists ... Therefore, it would be in our own interest to give aid, adequate and quick enough to ensure the early success of the liberation of Bangladesh.[32]

Tajuddin Ahmed followed up the request in a meeting with Deputy High Commissioner K.C. Sen Gupta in the first week of March. The Awami League general secretary inquired whether India would offer political asylum and other support in the event of a Pakistani crackdown.[33]

While Indian officials grappled with the complex questions raised by these requests, Mujib was impatient for an immediate response. A few days after Tajuddin's meeting with Sen Gupta, Mujib sent another emissary, Capt. Sujat Ali, to convey to the deputy high commissioner his dissatisfaction over India's failure to make a definite response to his appeal. To goad India into prompt action, Mujib's emissary spun a yarn about an American offer to assist the liberation movement in exchange for a naval base facility in the Bay of Bengal! Capt. Sujat Ali also communicated Mujib's concern over the withdrawal of some Indian troops from the West Pakistan border. (These troops had been sent to the border in the wake of the hijacking incident in January.) Mujib felt that the withdrawal had made it easier for Pakistan to transfer troops to the eastern wing. He, therefore, appealed to India to intercept Pakistani troops, ships and aircraft on the pretext of border violations.[34]

From his vantage point in Dhaka, Sen Gupta was convinced that Mujib had no alternative but to fight for independence and, furthermore, that an independent Bangladesh would prove to be a friendly neighbour. Since Sen Gupta's urgent cables proposing full support to the Bangladesh cause elicited no clear response from New Delhi, the deputy high commissioner decided to present his case in person to the Indian authorities. To throw Pakistani intelligence off the scent, he concocted a story about a wedding in his family that required his presence in India. Just before emplaning, however, he received instructions to remain at his post and to stay in touch with the rapidly changing situation. Sen Gupta ignored the message and flew to Kolkata so that he could at least explain his case to New Delhi over a secure telephone line.

On his return to Dhaka, Sen Gupta met Tajuddin on 17 March. According to a generally reliable Bangladeshi account, he told Tajuddin that the Indian high commissioner in Islamabad was not yet convinced that a military onslaught was imminent. However, if such a contingency were indeed to arise, India would offer all possible cooperation to the victims.[35] This guarded response avoided specific commitments. It was agreed that the two would meet again on 24 March, by which date Tajuddin hoped to obtain Mujib's authorization to discuss the specifics of the required assistance. The planned meeting did not, however, materialize, partly because of other pressing demands on Tajuddin and partly because he received no further instructions from Mujib.[36]

Mujib and the United States

Mujib was determined to achieve his goal by peaceful means, if possible, or by a liberation war, if necessary. He hoped to preserve the first option by persuading the United States to use its influence in favour of a peaceful solution, while he turned to India to prepare for the latter contingency.

As we saw in the previous chapter, Washington, like New Delhi, had foreseen the possibility of a break-up of Pakistan as early as in 1969. The assessments in the two capitals continued to show striking similarity right up to 25 March 1971, a similarity all the more remarkable in the context of their divergent policies during the Bangladesh liberation war.

Washington commenced contingency planning in February 1971 for a possible declaration of independence by Sheikh Mujib. As in the case of the parallel Indian exercise initiated in January, no conclusive decision emerged, and the outcome was a wait-and-see approach. On 16 February, Henry Kissinger, President Nixon's national security adviser, called for a contingency study on US options in the event of an East Pakistan secessionist movement. Meanwhile, he advised President Nixon:

> The U.S. position has been that we support the unity of Pakistan . . . [H] owever, we could before long be faced with a declaration of East Pakistani independence . . . That raises the issue of whether or not we should be adopting a more neutral stand toward Rahman, who is basically friendly toward the U.S., as a hedge against the day when we might have to deal with an independent East Pakistan. A realistic assessment would seem to recognize that there is very little material left in the fabric of the unity of Pakistan. This would argue for adjusting our posture, but against that is the fact that the division of Pakistan would not serve U.S. interests.[37]

Nixon's first reaction was not wholly negative. He underlined the words 'more neutral stance towards Rahman', commenting, 'not yet – correct – but not any position which encourages secession'.[38]

The sense of an impending crisis was strengthened when American ambassador Farland met President Yahya and Mujib in the last week of February. The ambassador reported that Yahya 'spoke in a tone of despair of the "blood and chaos" which might ensue if the Bhutto–Mujib impasse was not resolved. He dropped a broad hint that he might have to defer the National Assembly session'.[39] Mujib told Farland that the political impasse was not caused solely by Bhutto's machinations; Bhutto's position would have been untenable but for the support of certain military leaders. Bhutto's foreign policy was abhorrent, Mujib said, citing Bhutto's intransigence against India and his love for communist China. It was essential to establish good relations with India and reopen traditional trade routes. Mujib said that he did not want separation, but rather a form of confederation. Mujib sounded out the ambassador regarding Washington's policy at this critical juncture. Pointing to the leverage provided by US economic aid it extended Pakistan, he appealed to the United States to exert its influence with the Pakistani army in order to ensure a peaceful resolution of the crisis. Following instructions, Farland '. . . in no way conveyed a sense of concern regarding Pakistan's future in such a manner as to suggest an unalterable U.S. opposition to Bangla aspirations'.[40]

On 1 March, the massive and spontaneous Bengali reaction against Yahya's decision to postpone the National Assembly session created a powerful impression in Washington. Archer Blood's assessment that it signalled the 'beginning of the end of a united Pakistan' was broadly accepted in the capital. Kissinger's staff alerted him: '*Events in Pakistan today took a major step toward a possible early move by East Pakistan for independence.*' They raised two questions. Should the US hedge its bets with East Pakistan against its possible secession? Should the US try to avoid bloodshed in the event of secession?[41]

On Kissinger's instructions, the National Security Council (NSC) staff prepared a contingency study in early March on the East Pakistan situation. Its cautious recommendation was: 'Unless and until separation is certain, any shift in our position would be against our continuing interest in seeing Pakistan remain unified.' The stance bore a certain similarity to that adopted by the external affairs ministry in New Delhi. As in New Delhi, the US intelligence agency, the CIA, advocated a more proactive role. The CIA pointed out that a split would bring the pro-Chinese Bhutto into power in West Pakistan. A loose confederation would be preferable, since it would check Bhutto's pro-Chinese and anti-India policies. The CIA therefore argued that Washington should urge Yahya to reach an accommodation with Mujib, but 'if separation becomes imminent, but before it is announced, we should . . . let East Pakistani leaders know privately that, should East Pakistan become independent, we would recognize the new state'.[42]

Kissinger chaired a meeting of senior officials on 6 March to review the East Pakistan situation. Deputy Secretary of State Alexis Johnson summed up the prevailing situation as follows:

> While we have maintained a posture of hoping the country can be brought together and its unity preserved, the chances of doing so now are extremely slight. It is only a question of time and circumstances as to how they will split, and to what degree the split is complete or may be papered over in some vague confederal scheme . . . [In the circumstances]

> if Mujib approaches us, we will have to walk a tightrope between making him think we are giving him the cold shoulder and not encouraging him to move toward a split if any hope remains for a compromise . . . [If Yahya were to use force against the Bengalis, the] judgment of all of us is that . . . the result would be a bloodbath with no hope of West Pakistan reestablishing control over East Pakistan.

Johnson emphasized that '. . . this is not an East–West, or a US–Soviet, or a US–Indian confrontation. The US, USSR and India all have an interest in the continued unity of Pakistan and have nothing to gain from a break-up.'

His assessment was that India would probably not intervene in the short run in the event of a Pakistani crackdown, but if the turmoil continued it might feel impelled to do so.

When Johnson referred to the option of discouraging Yahya from using force in East Pakistan, Kissinger cautioned the Senior Review Group to bear in mind Nixon's 'special relationship' with Yahya. The president would be reluctant to press Yahya to exercise restraint and, in any case, the Pakistanis 'wouldn't give a damn'. Following this intervention, the officials concluded that a policy of 'massive inaction' would be appropriate in the circumstances. It was decided to instruct Consul General Blood to simply refer the matter to Washington if Mujib were to sound him out over a declaration of independence.[43]

On 10 March, Mujib's emissary Alamgir Rahman met Blood to convey that the Awami League leader was anxious to arrive at a political settlement with Yahya. Mujib's question to Blood was: Does the United States want to see military confrontation with the prospect of eventual communist domination of Bengal, or would it prefer a political solution to the crisis? Mujib was obviously hoping that Washington would apply pressure on Yahya to desist from a military solution. Blood parried the question by replying blandly that the United States hoped for a peaceful political solution and believed that this was desired by both Mujib and Yahya![44]

In March 1971, there was nothing to indicate that the United States would see the break-up of Pakistan as a contest between the superpowers or as anything more than a South Asia issue. Kissinger had dropped a broad hint about the president's 'tilt' in favour of Pakistan, but its laboured geopolitical rationalization was yet to make an appearance.

To the brink and beyond

On 15 March, at a time when the ground realities were evolving at an incredible speed, Yahya arrived in Dhaka, ostensibly for negotiations with Mujib. Outside the limits of the military cantonments, the entire province was by now effectively controlled by the Awami League. The army was bringing in reinforcements to cope with the situation, but movement of military supplies was being systematically obstructed by the public, precipitating confrontations between the military and the civilian population. Except for some fringe elements, the entire Bengali population was united in its demand for immediate implementation of the Six Points, now being interpreted as independence by an ever-increasing number of people. The emotional ties between the two wings of Pakistan had been reduced to a mere thread by this time.

Yahya's actions cast doubts on his stated intention of finding a political solution. His first act on arriving in Dhaka was to convene a meeting of senior military officers to take stock of the security situation. On 17 March, after his initial talks with Mujib, Yahya ordered his generals to prepare plans for a massive crackdown. On 20 March, midway through the talks, Yahya approved the new plan, code-named 'Operation Searchlight'.[45]

When Mujib had called on Yahya on 16 March, he had pressed for acceptance of the demands he had made in his public speech on 7 March – immediate withdrawal of martial law, and transfer of power to the elected representatives of the people in the provinces as well as at the Centre.[46] Yahya raised no substantive objection, but said he had been advised that there were legal difficulties in withdrawing martial law before promulgation of a new constitution. This would lead to a 'legal vacuum' in the intervening period. The legal point was discussed between Lt Gen. Peerzada, PSO to the chief martial law administrator, and Kamal Hossain, the latter contending that a presidential Interim Arrangements Order (in effect, an interim constitution) would prevent a legal vacuum. Lengthy debates followed between the two legal teams.

On 17 March, discussions began on the procedures for framing new constitutions for the regions and the Centre. The Awami League proposed a presidential proclamation, under which the elected representatives of the two wings would meet separately to draw up constitutions for their respective wings. The constitution for the eastern wing would be based squarely on the Six Points. Thereafter, the elected representatives of both wings would meet together to draw up a constitution for the whole of Pakistan. Yahya's adviser, Justice Cornelius, took the position that this would require a prior resolution of the National Assembly. On the same day, while these legal confabulations were in progress, Yahya issued instructions for preparations for 'Operation Searchlight'.

On 19 March, after another futile round of discussions on the same legal issues, the presidential team decided to recommend a modified formula to Yahya. Under this proposal, national and provincial assemblies would be invested with the legislative powers available under the 1962 constitution; national and provincial cabinets would be formed; and the martial law administration in East Pakistan would be abolished, while keeping the post of chief martial law administrator intact. Instead of withdrawing martial law, as demanded by the Awami League, the proposal was only to suspend its operation in East Pakistan. Moreover, the Six Points could not be accommodated within the 1962 constitution without basic amendments in its provisions. The generals in Yahya's entourage raised strong objections even to the modest concession proposed by his legal team, but after some hesitation the president finally instructed the latter to prepare a draft martial law regulation on the proposed lines.

While the negotiations proceeded at a snail's pace, the situation at the ground level was becoming more tense by the hour. The army was bringing in reinforcements as speedily as possible and the Bengalis were doing everything in their power to oppose the build-up, knowing that it was to be used against them. The army had repeatedly opened fire on crowds opposing movement of troops and military equipment. During one such incident on 19 March, there was an exchange of fire between the army and civilian groups. It was one of the earliest instances of armed resistance by the Bengalis against military rule.

This incident touched off a heated exchange between Yahya and Mujib when they met on 20 March. An irate Yahya told Mujib that negotiations could not proceed unless such incidents were stopped. The Awami League leader angrily replied that if the army opened fire on the unarmed masses, the latter might indeed be compelled to take up arms. The army should remain in the barracks and desist from further provocation. After tempers had cooled down, Yahya and Mujib took up the threads from the previous session. The president said he had no objection in principle to Mujib's proposals, but he was advised that it would create a legal vacuum. Moreover, it was essential to consult political leaders from West Pakistan, in particular, Bhutto. Anticipating that Yahya and Bhutto would close ranks against him in trilateral negotiations, Mujib replied that the president was free to consult Bhutto but that he himself would not participate in discussions with Bhutto in a trilateral format.

Up to this point, the Awami League demand was for a transfer of power at both the Centre and the provinces. The mounting tide of Bengali nationalism, however, raised questions about this formula. On arriving at Mujib's residence on the morning of 21 March, Kamal Hossain found his leader engaged in deep discussion with Awami League secretary general Tajuddin Ahmed. Mujib informed his constitutional adviser that it would not be expedient, in view of the popular mood, for the Awami League to take over power at the Centre; it should only insist on an immediate transfer of power at the provincial level. This was a significant change in the party's position. The student leaders in particular were arguing forcefully that the Awami League might find itself compelled to accept compromises on the Six-Point Demand if it were to form a government at the Centre. To avoid this, the party should assume office only in the eastern wing. An Awami League provincial government, free of central entanglements, would also be able to build up the paramilitary East Pakistan Rifles (EPR) and the police force to prepare for the contingency of armed confrontation.

Thus, on the morning of 21 March, Mujib and his team held an unscheduled meeting with Yahya and presented their revised proposals. These called for: (i) immediate appointment of an East Pakistan governor selected by the Awami League; (ii) martial law to be lifted totally, as soon the governor assumed office; (iii) an interim constitution based on the 1962 constitution, with amendments incorporating the Six Points; and (iv) continuation of the president in office at the Centre. The Awami League hoped that the last provision would make the package palatable to Yahya.

The significance of the shift in Mujib's position was not lost on the president's advisers. It deepened Cornelius's fears that even a brief 'constitutional vacuum' might be exploited by the Bengalis to declare independence. But Yahya, who had already set in motion steps towards another 'solution', instructed Cornelius to proceed with the drafting exercise. As in the earlier talks in January, Yahya's tactics were to affect the posture of a neutral referee, counting on Bhutto to shoot down the Awami League proposals.

Bhutto arrived in Dhaka on 21 March, and on the following day Yahya had separate meetings with Mujib and Bhutto. Bhutto also had an informal conversation with Mujib outside the conference room. After the president had briefed Bhutto about the Awami League proposals, Bhutto predictably opposed them, warning that they would create two Pakistans. Neither he nor Yahya recognized that rejection of the Awami League proposals would inevitably destroy the last remaining links between the two wings of Pakistan. In the afternoon, a working draft of the presidential proclamation prepared by Yahya's legal team was handed over to Tajuddin and Bhutto. Bhutto promptly raised objections to the draft, demanding that the post of chief martial law administrator should remain in position; that there should be no erosion of the Centre's powers in the fields of defence and foreign policy; that safeguards be incorporated to guarantee adequate finances for the Centre's role in these and other areas; and that no legislation should be enacted unless approved by a majority of members of each wing in the National Assembly. In other words, he demanded a veto even for constitutional changes relating to the eastern wing.

The events that unfolded the next day vividly demonstrated the increasing depth of Bengali nationalism. Pakistan's National Day, 23 March, was observed in the eastern wing as 'Resistance Day'. The green-and-red flag of Bangladesh fluttered atop private and even official buildings all over Dhaka, with the exception only of the army cantonment. Motor cars flew the Bangladesh flag. Innumerable groups of students, youths and other activists paraded through the streets, carrying the flag of Bangladesh and raising pro-independence slogans. Mujib and his entourage arrived at the president's house flying the Bangladesh flag on their cars, arousing deep anger among the generals.

The Awami League delegation brought with itself a heavily revised version of the draft presented to them the previous evening by the president's team. Reflecting a fundamentally different approach, the revised draft incorporated extensive amendments to the 1962 constitution to fully incorporate the Six-Point programme. It envisaged an almost immediate revocation of Martial Law. It provided for elected representatives of each wing to meet separately to draw up constitutions for their respective wings; thereafter, they would meet in a joint session to draw up a constitution for 'whole of Pakistan'. Under the Awami League draft, all powers of taxation would vest in the provinces. For the military, this was an unacceptable limitation of its hitherto unchallenged authority to decide the size of the defence budget. In short, the Awami League draft envisaged a 'Confederation of Pakistan', in which the West Pakistani power elite, comprising the armed forces and political leaders, would no longer be in a position to impose its will on the 'State of Bangladesh'.

Even while the two delegations were engaged in formal debates on these proposals, Yahya Khan was in the cantonment, instructing his generals to speed up preparations for Operation Searchlight. Generals Khadim Raja and Farman Ali were airborne soon after to communicate the decision in the greatest secrecy to the brigade commanders in the field.

Negotiations continued on 24 March in a desultory fashion, but by then the Awami League leaders had begun to suspect that the negotiations were a smokescreen for an imminent military crackdown. Mujib sent his emissary Alamgir Rahman to Consul General Blood to request the US to use its influence with Yahya in favour of a political solution. Following his instructions, Blood offered no assurance.[47] The same day, Washington instructed Ambassador Farland to avoid playing an intermediary role. 'We do not believe we can play [a] useful role as middlemen or mediator in [an] essentially Pakistan[i] domestic concern,' the ambassador was advised.[48]

Operation Searchlight

On the fateful day of 25 March, in anticipation of a crackdown, Mujib instructed his senior colleagues to leave the city secretly and head for the countryside. He himself would stay on and face the consequences, hoping that this would reduce the ferocity of the army's assault on a defenceless population. Yahya flew out of Dhaka secretly, hours before the Pakistani army launched Operation Searchlight. By orders of the army, foreign journalists were confined to the Intercontinental Hotel, pending expulsion. The *New York Times* correspondent, Sydney Schanberg, provides a vivid account of the scenes he witnessed from the hotel.

> Huge fires could be seen in various parts of the city, including the university area and the barracks of the East Pakistan Rifles ... [Soldiers]

> set ablaze large areas in many parts of Dacca after first shooting into the buildings with automatic rifles, machine guns and recoilless rifles . . . [At the offices of the *People*, a pro-Mujib newspaper, they] fired a rocket into the building and followed this with small arms fire and machine-gun bursts. Then they set fire to the building and began smashing the press and other equipment . . . Moving further along, they set ablaze all the shops and shacks behind the bazaar and soon the flames were climbing high above the two-storey building . . . At 4:45 a.m., another big fire blazed, in the direction of the East Pakistan Rifles Headquarters.[49]

Sheikh Mujib was arrested by the army and incarcerated in prison in West Pakistan.

'Here in Dacca we are mute and horrified witnesses to a reign of terror by the Pak military,' reported Consul General Archer Blood to Washington on 28 March, in a telegram with the headline 'Selective Genocide'.

> Evidence continues to mount that the MLA authorities [Military Law Authorities] have a list of Awami League supporters whom they are systematically eliminating by seeking them out in their homes and shooting them down . . . Among those marked for extinction, in addition to A. L. [Awami League] hierarchy are student leaders and university faculty.

The streets, he reported, were flooded with people fleeing the city.[50]

The ruins of a united Pakistan lay buried under a mountain of corpses. The Pakistani army unleashed a reign of terror in Bangladesh, carrying out massacres, rape, loot and arson on a diabolic scale. Over the next eight months, no less than 10 million people would flee for their lives and honour to neighbouring India.

3

Towards a Grand Strategy

Reports of the slaughter of unarmed civilians in East Bengal aroused deep emotions among the Indian public. There was strong condemnation of Pakistan across the political spectrum and demands that the government extend full support to the Bangladesh cause. The population of the border areas displayed an extraordinary degree of solidarity in receiving and hosting the tidal wave of refugees fleeing into India. Powerful voices were raised in favour of formal recognition of an independent Bangladesh. On 31 March, the doyen of India's strategic thinkers, K. Subrahmanyam sounded a call for early military intervention by India to install an independent Bangladesh government in Dhaka, urging the Indian government to seize the historical opportunity. The highly respected and influential analyst found wide support.

Some accounts of the 1971 war depict India as seizing the golden opportunity offered by the Bangladesh uprising to pursue its plot of dividing Pakistan. The documentary evidence disproves this view. As we saw in the previous chapter, Indian policymakers were apprehensive about the consequences of a break-up of Pakistan. They had pinned their hopes on a transition to democracy in Pakistan and a transfer of power to a Bengali-led government at the Centre. Intervention was contemplated only in the event of a civil war, which, if prolonged, was likely to be taken over by pro-Chinese communist militants or

'Naxalites'. As we have seen, Washington correctly assessed the Indian position in March.

Indian policymakers reacted with horror and disbelief as news trickled in of the military crackdown. For the first few days they found it difficult to believe that the Pakistani army would pursue its institutional interests by conducting savage massacres that could only lead to a total collapse of national unity. New Delhi was still reluctant to shed all hopes of a negotiated political settlement between the army and the Awami League. A senior Indian official later recalled:

> First reports about the crackdown were alarming, yet we continued to believe that negotiations would be resumed after a brief show of military might . . . It was difficult to understand why the Pakistani rulers would go over the brink and start a full-scale civil war. For at stake were the territorial and ideological foundations of the state, matters too serious to be trifled with.[1]

Thus, on 27 March, Foreign Secretary T.N. Kaul suggested to the US ambassador in Delhi, Kenneth Keating, that even at this late hour it might still not be too late for Washington to convey to the Pakistan government that it hoped for a political solution to the crisis. Kaul said India was concerned that there could be a threat to its security. Refugees were arriving from across the border and the exodus might assume proportions that would exceed India's ability to cope with the problem. Keating replied that the US position was that the conflict was an internal matter that should be settled internally.[2]

An agitated Indian Parliament met on 27 March to hear a statement by the foreign minister on developments in Pakistan. Knowing the deep feelings aroused by the crackdown, Indira Gandhi met informally with opposition leaders before the session in order to take them into confidence about government policy on the matter. A brief prepared by her aide P.N. Haksar summed up the official thinking:

> While our sympathy for the people of Bangladesh is natural, India as a State has to walk warily. Pakistan is a State. It is a member of the U.N. and, therefore, outside interference in events internal to Pakistan will not earn us either understanding or goodwill from the majority of nation-States.

Haksar, who had earlier served as high commissioner (ambassador) in Lagos, drew attention to the case of the Nigerian civil war and the failure of the Biafra secessionist movement. '[W]here a state of civil war exists, international law and morality only accords legitimacy to a successful rebellion.' He emphasized that '[w]hatever the Government may or may not do, should not become a subject-matter of public debate, as such a debate would defeat the purpose of giving such comfort as we can to democratic forces in Pakistan as a whole'.

It is noteworthy that even at this late stage, Haksar spoke of 'assistance to democratic forces in Pakistan *as a whole*'. In the immediate aftermath of the military crackdown there were confusing and often contradictory reports emerging from East Pakistan; New Delhi still clung to hopes of a transition to democracy in Pakistan through a negotiated settlement between Yahya and Mujib.

Thus, on 27 March, Foreign Minister Swaran Singh made a bland statement in parliament registering India's 'grave concern' over the suppression of the people of 'East Pakistan'. He expressed the hope that 'even at this late stage it would be possible to resume democratic processes leading to the fulfilment of the aspirations of the vast majority of the people there'.

The statement failed to respond to the mood in parliament. The respected veteran Member of Parliament Hiren Mukherjee derided it as 'lifeless'. Other leading parliamentarians called upon the government to raise the issue at the UN, to extend formal recognition to 'Bangladesh', and even to blockade Chittagong port to prevent Pakistan from reinforcing its troops. Mrs Gandhi took the floor to calm down the agitated members. She said the latest developments had belied hopes of a 'new situation in our neighbouring country which would help us to get closer'. Assuring members that the government 'fully share the agony, the emotions of the House and their deep concern', she appealed to them to understand that 'we have to follow proper international norms', and that 'in a serious moment like this, the less we, as a Government say, I think the better it is at this moment'. Significantly, she spoke of 'East Bengal', in place of 'East Pakistan', indicating a neutral position on the question of its status in relation to Pakistan.[3]

On 29 March, parliament unanimously adopted a resolution moved by the prime minister, expressing its 'profound sympathy and solidarity with the people of East Bengal in their struggle for a democratic way of life'.[4]

Indira Gandhi's observation that India's hopes of closer ties with Pakistan had been belied by the latest developments and her references to East Pakistan as 'East Bengal', indicate that she was a step ahead of her advisers. She had quickly grasped the fact that the brutal military crackdown launched on 25 March had delivered the final death blow to Pakistan's unity. She shared the sense of outrage over the crackdown voiced by the members of parliament, but she would not be pushed into premature action. Official policy statements, such as the parliament resolution of 29 March, eschewed any reference to an independent Bangladesh, expressing support only for the democratic rights of the people of 'East Bengal'.

Critically important details of the actual situation remained unclear for several days after the crackdown. Wildly exaggerated and contradictory reports poured in from across the border. There was uncertainty about Mujib's fate and his whereabouts, and of the plans of other Awami League leaders. The fog of uncertainty shrouding the latest events in East Bengal began to clear at the end of March, as Awami League leaders and rebel military officers began to arrive at the border. On 30 March, the Awami League general secretary, Tajuddin Ahmed, who had earlier in the month approached Deputy High Commissioner Sen Gupta seeking India's cooperation for the freedom movement, crossed the border into

India. Taking Indian border officials by surprise, Tajuddin immediately demanded a meeting with Prime Minister Indira Gandhi. He met with the topmost Border Security Force (BSF) officials, Inspector General Golak Majumdar and Director General Rustomji, and persuaded them to fly him to New Delhi.

A historic meeting

In the first week of April, Tajuddin had two secret meetings with the Indian prime minister. Realizing that an appeal from an individual Bangladesh political figure would have little impact, Tajuddin concocted the story that a declaration of independence had been made immediately after the commencement of the crackdown and that Mujib had formed a government constituted of members of the Awami League Working Committee. This daring claim was made at a time when Tajuddin had yet to re-establish contact with other members of the Working Committee after the crackdown. Providentially, while these talks were in progress, Indian intelligence sources reported that rebel East Bengal military officers had met in Teliapara, near the Indian border, and had resolved to form a central command for conducting the war of liberation. The rebel officers also called upon political leaders to immediately form a government.

Tajuddin's total dedication to the cause of an independent Bangladesh made a deep impression on the Indian prime minister. She gave an assurance to Tajuddin that India would provide asylum to the freedom fighters and that they could operate without let or hindrance from Indian soil. She also offered a general assurance of broader assistance, but did not specify its nature or scale, and she made no reference to military support. However, Tajuddin surmised that her initial assurances would grow to encompass comprehensive political and military support if Pakistan refused to end the crackdown and if the liberation war was properly directed.[5] The Awami League leader had correctly read Mrs Gandhi's mind.

The historic importance of the talks between Tajuddin and Indira Gandhi can hardly be overestimated. By early April, the Indian government had shed all vestigial hopes of a transition to democracy in Pakistan. It was clear that the Pakistani military was determined to persist with its policy of brutal subjugation of the people of East Bengal and that the latter were resolved to take up arms to achieve an independent Bangladesh. It was of vital importance to India that the liberation war should achieve success in a short duration, before control of the armed struggle passed into the hands of extreme leftist groups linked to China or the Indian Naxalites. Tajuddin impressed his interlocutors with his unshakeable dedication to the Bangladesh cause, displaying also the leadership qualities required to guide the liberation struggle in the absence of the Bangabandhu.

As promised by Mrs Gandhi, Tajuddin was enabled to run his operations from 'Mujibnagar' (actually Kolkata). Premises for a secretariat were provided in No. 8, Theatre Road (now Shakespeare Sarani), together with the necessary financial and logistics support. A radio transmitter was provided for broadcasts from Swadhin Bangla Betar Kendra (Radio Free Bangladesh). RAW helped establish clandestine contacts between Mujibnagar and Bengali personnel in Pakistani diplomatic missions, generating an impressive flow of intelligence.

On 12 April, just days after Tajuddin's meetings with Indira Gandhi, New Delhi adopted a plan named 'Operation Jackpot'. Its broad objective was:

> To build up the strength of Bangla Desh Forces to keep West Pakistani forces tied down in a running struggle and to consolidate their hold on peripheral territories with a view to roll West Pak forces back and administer a crushing blow with such open assistances as may be needed eventually.[6]

In the next few weeks, India took a number of policy decisions, which in their totality constituted a grand strategy to assist the birth of an independent Bangladesh and secure speedy recognition of the new state by the international community. These decisions encompassed assistance to a government-in-exile, asylum for the torrent of refugees fleeing the place, mobilization of resources for their sustenance, a slew of diplomatic initiatives, training and equipping of freedom fighters, and military plans for Indian intervention at the final stage. All the resources of the state – military, political and economic – were mobilized to serve the national aim.

Nature of the challenge

Stung by public criticism of the government's 'inaction', some of Mrs Gandhi's cabinet colleagues were asking for immediate military intervention in April. To silence them, the prime minister asked the army chief, Gen. Sam Manekshaw, for his opinion, knowing full well that he would need time to prepare for a major unplanned contingency.[7] Failing to see through the prime minister's political ploy, Manekshaw, a gifted raconteur, circulated a colourful tale about how he had restrained Mrs Gandhi from ordering the Indian army to march into East Pakistan in April. The true reason for the government's decision have been spelled out by Maj. Gen. Sukhwant Singh, who served as deputy director of military operations in 1971. Sukhwant Singh recollects:

> . . . political compulsions clinched the issue [of timing] . . . if the creation of an independent Bangladesh was achieved by Indian military action, how was its domestic and external viability to be assured without its recognition by the international forum, the United Nations? If India intervened without clearly justifying the action in foreign eyes, the charge that it was engineering the break-up of Pakistan would be established and Bangladesh would be refused recognition by the majority of nations.[8]

As we noted earlier, within hours after news of the crackdown in East Bengal reached New Delhi, the prime minister's principal adviser,

P.N. Haksar, had cautioned her that most countries would view Indian intervention at that early stage as unwarranted interference in Pakistan's internal affairs. He had emphasized that the Awami League leaders would have to establish their legitimacy through a successful revolt, culminating in control of the territory of Bangladesh – or, at least, the greater part of the territory – before they could expect international recognition as an independent state. Haksar made sure that these factors were understood by ministers and influential members of parliament across the political spectrum. When the prime minister met opposition leaders in early May, he urged her to explain matters to them: 'We cannot, at the present stage, contemplate armed intervention at all . . . It would evoke hostile reactions from all over the world and all the sympathy and support which the Bangla Desh [sic] has been able to evoke in the world will be drowned in [an] Indo-Pak conflict.'[9]

A precipitate march into East Bengal would not have served the higher political aim of securing international recognition for Bangladesh. In the Cold War period, the principles of non-interference in internal affairs and the territorial integrity of states were deeply embedded in international law and practice. (The contending principle of humanitarian intervention gained international acceptance only after the end of the Cold War and the collapse of the Soviet Union, when the United States and its allies enjoyed a period of unchallenged supremacy.) As Haksar cautioned, an Indian military intervention in East Bengal in April 1971 would have been condemned by the international community as an unprovoked invasion. Without the assured support of a superpower, it would almost certainly have precipitated a UN Security Council resolution demanding immediate withdrawal. To appreciate the magnitude of the political challenge in 1971, we must recall that since the end of World War II, no secessionist movement had succeeded in breaking up a sovereign state. Katanga and Biafra provided vivid illustrations. The principle of territorial integrity posed a formidable obstacle, which could only be overcome if a rebellion succeeded in establishing control of the territory it claimed.

Elements of a Grand Strategy: Support for the Freedom Fighters

Operation Jackpot was put in motion by the end of April. The BSF had been informally providing such assistance as it could to the freedom fighters since 26 March. In view of the massive scale on which assistance was required for implementation of Operation Jackpot, it was decided on 30 April to transfer the task to the Indian army and to place BSF units in the border areas under the army's operational command. The army was tasked to train and equip 20,000 freedom fighters initially, and later raise the number to 1,00,000, if necessary. It was envisaged that the guerrilla operations would evolve through three stages. In stage one, the operations would be restricted to selected targets in areas where the Pakistani forces either did not have a presence, or where the state of communications prevented them from reacting in time. In stage two, the guerrillas were to attack Pakistani border outposts, patrols and convoys, and carry out major acts of sabotage. Stage three was to be the culminating stage, in which the guerrillas were to function as 'formed troops' cooperating with the Indian army in a war against Pakistan. To begin with, the Indian army and BSF were to keep the border 'hotted up' in order to tie down Pakistani forces. They were also tasked to provide artillery and mortar fire support to Bangladeshi freedom fighters attacking isolated Pakistani border outposts. Gen. Manekshaw issued operational instructions along these lines to Lt Gen J.S. Aurora, GOC-in-C, Eastern Command.[10]

Military planning

Planning for the final push was taken up in parallel with Operation Jackpot. By the end of May, Chief of Staff of the Eastern Command, Maj. Gen. (later Lt Gen.) J.F.R. Jacob, submitted a draft plan for the final operations on behalf of the Eastern Command. It called for a rapid advance on Dhaka, bypassing fortified towns, with the subsidiary objective of destroying Pakistani command and control centres en route.

Jacob regarded Dhaka, the provincial capital, as the 'geopolitical and geostrategic heart of "East Pakistan"'.[11] The plan formulated by Army Headquarters (AHQ) at the end of July drew substantially on Jacob's draft but departed from it on the crucial question of the principal target. Dhaka was not identified as the principal target. Rather, the objective was to liberate most of the territory, including the major ports – Chittagong and Khulna – thus bottling up the Pakistani forces in a few garrison towns that were cut off from supplies or replenishments. A siege would ensure withdrawal of all Pakistani forces from Bangladesh.

The aim was to establish an independent Bangladesh state as speedily as possible, in view of the possibility of a ceasefire imposed by a Security Council resolution. (As we shall see later, on the eve of the war, orders were issued to liberate the entire territory of Bangladesh, following a Soviet offer of unconditional support in the Security Council.)

Foreign policy

New Delhi's military and diplomatic initiatives were closely interrelated. Apart from promoting sympathy and support for the Bangladesh cause in the international community, the principal tasks of India's foreign policy in 1971 were to create a legal case for military intervention; to ensure timely supplies of military equipment; to deter possible Chinese intervention in support of Pakistan; and to prevent premature intervention by the Security Council before the military operations had been successfully concluded.

In the circumstances prevailing in 1971, it was essential to gain the support of at least one of the superpowers. Only this move would ensure timely military supplies, deter possible Chinese military moves on the border, and ensure that the Security Council did not impose a premature ceasefire before the military objectives had been achieved. The pursuit of these goals necessitated a major adjustment of India's foreign policy – entering into a Friendship Treaty with the Soviet Union.

From the end of March, India had facilitated the widest possible international press coverage of the brutal suppression of democracy in East Pakistan and the savage violation of their human rights. The aim was to win international sympathy for the liberation movement, even if governments were reluctant to extend political support. Public opinion would influence the policies of western democracies in important ways during the war that would take place in December 1971; it would also expedite recognition of Bangladesh in the weeks that followed.

While extending all possible support to the freedom struggle, the Indian government refrained from explicit support of calls for an independent Bangladesh, lest it should be charged with interference in the internal affairs of Pakistan. New Delhi only called for a solution acceptable to the freely elected representatives of the people.

India added a new dimension to this publicity campaign in the last week of May. Pointing to the rising tide of refugees from East Pakistan, it observed that Pakistan was 'exporting' its domestic problem to India by driving the refugees across the border. The repression in East Bengal was, therefore, not only an internal problem of Pakistan; it had an international dimension, affecting India's internal security. This implied a responsibility on the part of the international community to bring pressure on Pakistan to mend its ways. The implicit message was that if the international community failed to do its duty, India would be left with no option but to take action in self-defence. This was an innovative doctrine, designed to fill the legal lacuna we noted earlier.

Domestic policies

The strategic aim of ensuring the liberation of Bangladesh by the end of the year was supported by a panoply of domestic measures. While providing asylum to all refugees fleeing from the reign of terror let loose by the Pakistani army, New Delhi was clear from the outset that the refugees must return to their homes in an independent Bangladesh. Therefore, in contrast to earlier cases of refugee arrivals across India's borders, the Bangladesh refugees were concentrated in camps situated along the border, from which they could be speedily repatriated. With one or two minor exceptions, they were not shifted to other areas for resettlement (though, inevitably, some refugees did melt away to join the informal labour market in nearby areas). This policy was tacitly understood, right from 25 March. It stood in sharp contrast to the approach generally followed by India in respect of refugees from other neighbouring countries.

The new policy carried a political risk. The increasingly heavy concentration of refugees – whose numbers eventually reached an estimated 10 million – in the border districts carried the risk of tension and even conflict between the host communities and the refugees. There are few parallels in history for the profound sense of sympathy and solidarity with which the people of the border provinces received the hapless refugees from East Bengal. Nevertheless, as the stream of refugees rose to a tidal wave, the pressures on living space and supplies of essential goods and services carried the potential for discord. In the state of Tripura, the refugees actually outnumbered the local inhabitants. The small town of Bongaigaon in West Bengal, with a population of 5,000, received no less than 3,00,000 refugees over just a few months![12] Against this background, it was essential to ensure that goodwill – and, in particular, communal harmony – between the host and guest communities remained unimpaired. Strict instructions were issued accordingly to the local authorities.

The refugee exodus from East Bengal in 1971 was among the largest in recorded history. Providing shelter, food and basic healthcare for this massive refugee population entailed a huge strain on the budgetary and administrative resources of a developing country like India. International aid covered only a modest part of the total expenditure. No less than 1,500 refugee relief camps were set up. Schools and public buildings were vacated to accommodate the refugees. Fiscal planners had to somehow accommodate refugee relief in an already stretched budget.

Though the military crackdown was directed against all supporters of the Six-Point Demand, Hindus were a special target of the Pakistan army. US Consul General Blood reported to the State Department on 19 April 1971 that '. . . various members of the American community have witnessed either burning down of Hindu villages, Hindu enclaves in Dacca and shooting of Hindus attempting [to] escape carnage, or have witnessed after-effects which are visible throughout Dacca today'.[13] This developed into an undeclared military pogrom to drive out the Hindus from the province. Bengali Muslims abhorred this slaughter, Blood reported.[14] According to a CIA estimate, of the 8 million refugees who fled East Bengal in September, as many as 6 million were Hindus.[15] India was anxious to ensure that this Pakistani provocation did not trigger communal tensions in India. Under advice from New Delhi, state governments and local authorities took special care to prevent misperceptions and ensure communal peace and harmony.

Policy coordination

Under the prime minister's instructions, a special committee of secretaries was set up in April to monitor and coordinate policy on these multiple political and economic fronts. The committee was headed by Cabinet Secretary T. Swaminathan, and its core group included Foreign Secretary T.N. Kaul, Home Secretary Govind Narain, Defence Secretary K.B. Lall, Secretary to the Prime Minister P.N. Haksar and RAW Director R.N. Kao. The army chief and secretaries of other ministries were invited to attend sessions focusing on their respective jurisdictions.[16]

Infused with a sense of urgency, the special committee functioned with great efficiency. The speedy decision-making and flawless inter-departmental coordination during the 1971 crisis stood in sharp contrast to the stately pace at which government business was usually conducted. A glimpse into the committee's functioning is provided by its last report before the outbreak of war.

On 28 November 1971, the special committee was in a position to report that the '[moment] for decisive action has come'.

The defence ministry confirmed: '... as soon as a decision is taken, the defence Services are in a position to secure the defeat and surrender of the occupying forces in East Bengal in the shortest possible time'.

Keeping in view the role of the UN, the MEA suggested: '[w]e should provoke Pakistan into starting a war against us.'

The home ministry reported: '... [a]ll the States and particularly the border States have confirmed that necessary measures for maintenance of internal security have been taken ... The need for utmost vigilance to maintain communal peace has been impressed upon the State Governments.'

The cabinet secretary reported: '... our foreign exchange reserves are in a fairly comfortable position and no serious situation is likely to emerge in the short term.'[17]

By the end of April, India had developed a comprehensive approach encompassing all its national capabilities in the spheres of defence, foreign policy, economy and internal security, in order to achieve the goal of facilitating the emergence of Bangladesh as a sovereign state recognized by the international community. This grand strategy seamlessly combined military and political measures. Its details were further elaborated or modified in light of the changing situation, but its basic features remained intact. Implementation of its diverse components was coordinated and monitored at the highest official levels in the cabinet secretariat and the Prime Minister's Office. The outcome was a spectacular victory in the 1971 war, facilitating the early entry of Bangladesh into the comity of nations.

4

Mujibnagar

Tajuddin Ahmed's contribution to the liberation of Bangladesh is second only to that of Sheikh Mujibur Rahman. The charismatic Mujib provided the inspiration for the freedom movement. Tajuddin, the statesman and organizer, guided the struggle through its darkest months to a triumphal conclusion.

In the second week of April, Tajuddin was able to re-establish contact with other Awami League leaders. On his return to Kolkata from New Delhi, Tajuddin met with the senior Awami League leader, Kamaruzzaman, who had also arrived in the city. He then boarded a Dakota aircraft placed at his disposal by the Indian authorities to meet up with other Awami League leaders who had crossed into India at various border points. Picking up Syed Nazrul Islam, Mansoor Ali and Abdul Mannan en route, he arrived in Agartala on 11 April, where he found other senior Awami League members – Khondaker Mushtaque Ahmed and Col. Osmani – waiting for him. Two days of discussion and argument followed.

Tajuddin was acutely conscious of the urgent need to rally the masses and keep up the momentum of the popular resistance. Without waiting for the outcome of his meeting with other Awami League leaders, Tajuddin made a rousing broadcast from Agartala on 11 April on a small radio transmitter supplied by the BSF.

Speaking in the name of the 'President, Bangabandhu Sheikh Mujibur Rahman, and the Government of the People's Republic of Bangladesh', he saluted the people of Bangladesh, who 'have joined the ranks of the immortals among the freedom fighters of history', . . . 'To the world we were a peace-loving people, friendly, humane, fond of music and dance, imbued with an awareness of culture and beauty. War and violence were thought to be foreign to our nature. But today whilst we remain true to our heritage, Bengalis have shown that they are also a warrior people, with an unconquerable will and courage to face an aggressor who enjoys overwhelming superiority in the use of weapons . . . [today] a mighty army is being formed around the nucleus of professional soldiers from the Bengal Regiment and the E.P.R. [East Pakistan Rifles] . . . and now by thousands of Awami League and other volunteers.'

He appealed to the international community to suspend arms supplies to Pakistan, to provide arms for the liberation struggle, and to extend recognition to Bangladesh. To his fellow countrymen living abroad, he appealed for financial support for arms purchases for the liberation army.[1]

The Awami League leaders assembled in Agartala finally reached agreement on the constitution of a government on the lines proposed by Tajuddin.[2] It was decided to form a five-member government, led by Sheikh Mujibur Rahman as president and comprising Syed Nazrul Islam (vice president), Tajuddin Ahmed (prime minister), Khondaker Mushtaque Ahmed, A.H.M. Kamaruzzaman and Capt. Mansoor Ali. Khondaker Mushtaque Ahmed was allotted the foreign affairs portfolio. Col. Osmani was appointed commander-in-chief, with cabinet rank. The swearing-in ceremony of the new government was held in the presence of the Indian and foreign press on 17 April, in a mango grove in the village of Baidyanathtala – renamed Mujibnagar – in Bangladesh, just across the border from a BSF post. A 'Proclamation of Independence Order' was solemnly read out, stating that Sheikh Mujib had 'duly made a declaration of independence at Dhaka on March 26, 1971'; that the elected representatives of the people of Bangladesh had resolved to form a government headed by Mujib; and that, in his absence, Syed Nazrul Islam would serve as acting president. In order to lend credibility to Tajuddin's earlier broadcast of 11 April, the proclamation was pre-dated 10 April. In the presence of Indian and foreign journalists, a Mukti Bahini contingent presented a guard of honour to the acting president.[3]

After the ceremony, the government-in-exile shifted back to Kolkata, from where it conducted its operations. The ministers and their families were provided accommodation in various parts of the city. Tajuddin alone lived apart from his family in his office rooms, working tirelessly round the clock. Col. Osmani also set up his headquarters in the Theatre Road premises, spending his nights on a camp cot in the office. The government-in-exile rapidly expanded its activities, serviced by an office which soon grew into a full-fledged secretariat with the arrival of personnel who had left their posts in East Pakistan to seek refuge in India. Radio broadcasts over Swadhin Bangla Betar Kendra (Free Bangladesh Radio) had commenced from Agartala as early as on 2 April, employing a small transmitter supplied by the Indian authorities. This was soon replaced by a medium wave transmitter, and regular broadcasts commenced from Kolkata on 25 April.

With the defection of Bengali officers serving in Pakistani diplomatic missions worldwide, Bangladesh was able to build up a significant overseas presence. Two young diplomats serving in the Pakistan High Commission in New Delhi, K.M. Shahabuddin and Amjadul Huq, declared for Bangladesh as early as on 6 April. They were followed on the 17 April by the Pakistan deputy high commissioner in Kolkata, Hossain Ali, and other Bengali members of his staff. On 26 April, Mahmud Ali, a young diplomat posted in New York, became the first to declare for Bangladesh from a Pakistani mission outside India. A steady stream of 'defections' followed from other Pakistani diplomatic and consular offices, with some communications and logistical assistance from Indian embassies. Prominent Bangladeshis, such as Justice Abu Sayeed Chowdhury, were appointed as special emissaries of the Mujibnagar government to seek international sympathy and support for the liberation struggle. Bangladeshi resident communities in foreign countries also played an invaluable role in mobilizing international opinion.[4] Many Bengali diplomats who stayed on in Pakistani embassies contributed to the movement by passing on valuable information to Mujibnagar.[5] Thus, with Indian logistics and financial support, the Bangladesh government-in-exile was able to quickly establish an effective civil and military organization, as well as an unofficial presence in many countries.

Problems of an émigré regime

Despite these early successes, Tajuddin had to steer the ship of the state through stormy seas. Political exiles are subject to fits of doubt, depression and despair over the uncertain prospects of returning to their homeland. Many are haunted by the fear of being condemned to a life in exile. Émigré regimes tend also to be riven by deep personal jealousies and factional rivalries. Mujibnagar was no exception.

By mid-May, the advancing Pakistani army regained control of all the major towns in East Bengal. The last significant holdout, Belonia, fell on 10 June. The Mukti Bahini was obliged to fall back behind the Indian border and was left with virtually no presence on Bangladesh soil. The deteriorating situation on the battleground caused anxiety and despair among many exiles who had hoped for instant success. Not a few suspected that India would let them down. Soon after the swearing-in ceremony at Mujibnagar, Syed Nazrul Islam and Tajuddin Ahmed, in their capacities of acting president and prime minister, respectively, had addressed a formal letter to Indira Gandhi, seeking immediate diplomatic recognition. The absence of a response from the Indian prime minister caused much anxiety and concern to many Awami League leaders, including some members of the Mujibnagar cabinet. In a widely circulated report to Acting President Syed Nazrul Islam, Awami League General Secretary Mizanur Rahman Chowdhury complained bitterly of inadequate Indian support for the Mukti Bahini and attacked Tajuddin for placing his trust in India.[6] Tajuddin remained unmoved.

He never doubted New Delhi's intentions because he had grasped the fact that India's interests coincided with those of Bangladesh.

New Delhi was aware of the misgivings regarding its intentions. In mid-May, the acting president of Bangladesh, all cabinet ministers and Col. Osmani were invited to New Delhi for a meeting with Indira Gandhi. Several ministers expressed concern over the lack of clarity in India's policy, in particular the absence of diplomatic recognition. Responding on behalf of the prime minister, Haksar asked whether the absence of formal recognition had in any way hindered the activities of the freedom fighters. Was the demand for recognition based on the expectation that India would forthwith order its army to march towards Dhaka? If so, he wished to dispel any such expectation. These blunt words offered little comfort to the doubters in the audience.[7]

Tajuddin's assumption of the post of prime minister was resented not only by prominent Awami League members who had not found a cabinet berth (such as Mizanur Rahman Chowdhury) but also by his senior cabinet colleagues, Khondaker Mushtaque Ahmed and Kamaruzzaman. Hossain Towfiq Imam, who had had a ringside view of developments as cabinet secretary to the Mujibnagar government, says that both Khondaker (who had served as co-president of the Pakistan Awami League) and Kamaruzzaman (former general secretary of the Pakistan Awami League) had claims to seniority over Tajuddin in the party hierarchy. The mutual distrust between the government-in-exile's prime minister, Tajuddin, and its foreign minister, Khondaker Mushtaque Ahmed, ran so deep that the foreign minister chose to operate from a separate location in the city. Khondaker was kept out of most of Tajuddin's important meetings with the Indian prime minister and senior officials.[8] The foreign minister, on his part, had misgivings about Tajuddin's policies, including, in particular, his support for the Indo-Soviet Treaty. Incredible though it may seem, Khondaker and his foreign secretary believed that the treaty had adversely affected Soviet attitudes towards Mujibnagar! As we shall see below, Khondaker established links with US officials behind his prime minister's back.

There were deep differences also between the cabinet and the student leaders. The latter, as we saw earlier, were among the first to raise the demand for full independence in early 1971. They had tried hard to persuade Mujib to make an unambiguous declaration of independence on 7 March. On 23 March, they had marched in procession to Mujib's residence to raise the Bangladesh flag. They functioned as an autonomous power centre, reporting directly to Sheikh Mujibur Rahman. In April, the student leaders, led by Mujib's nephew Sheikh Fazlul Huq Moni, opposed the formation of the government-in-exile. They demanded that the government be dissolved and replaced by a Liberation Front or War Council in which they could play a major role.

Tensions between the Mujibnagar cabinet and the student leaders deepened when, in May, New Delhi decided to train and equip the Mujib Bahini, drawn from members of the Awami League–affiliated student group. The decision was taken in response to an earlier secret appeal made by Mujib. In a message to the Indian authorities shortly before his arrest on 26 March, Mujib had indicated that if he were to meet his death at the hands of the Pakistani army, the five student leaders – Sheikh Fazlul Huq Moni, Abdur Razzak, Tofail Ahmed, Sirajul Alam Khan and Shahjahan Siraj – would carry on the struggle as his 'khalifas' or true successors.[9] This was interpreted to mean that Mujib wanted the student leaders to play a major role in the liberation war. New Delhi took the decision to train and equip the Mujib Bahini after the proposal had been approved by the acting president, Syed Nazrul Islam. The latter, however, did not consult Tajuddin or Col. Osmani, both of whom were opposed to the creation of a separate force outside the control of the Mujibnagar government.[10] The training of the Mujib Bahini was entrusted to RAW and not to the Indian army, which was responsible for training the Mukti Bahini commander-in-chief, Col. Osmani. The operations of the Mujib Bahini, which functioned independently and without coordination with the Mukti Bahini, drew strong criticism not only from Osmani but also the Indian army. After several complaints from Osmani, New Delhi did eventually try to persuade the student leaders to function in coordination with the Mukti Bahini, but these efforts met with only limited success.[11]

The persisting factional rivalries within the Mujibnagar government were a cause of concern to the Indian government. An assembly of the elected representatives of the people of Bangladesh had yet to be convened. On 20 June, Asoke Ray, who now headed the external affairs ministry liaison office in Kolkata, touched on this question in a conversation with Tajuddin, hinting that the position of the Mujibnagar government might be strengthened if its policies were endorsed by the legislators – members of the national and provincial assemblies – elected from East Bengal in 1970. The suggestion met with Tajuddin's approval. The first assembly of the elected representatives of the people of Bangladesh was convened in the town of Siliguri in West Bengal in early July.[12]

The Siliguri conference was held at a time when the fortunes of the liberation war were still at a low ebb. A vast guerrilla army was being raised, but major operations would be launched only after the monsoons. Thus, at the Siliguri meeting, Tajuddin's competence was questioned and the Awami League general secretary, Mizanur Rahman Chowdhury, called for his resignation. Col. Osmani came under attack for the reverses suffered by the Mukti Bahini. Questions were raised about India's intentions, its failure to accord diplomatic recognition to Bangladesh, and doubts were expressed as to its continuing support. Foreign Minister Khondaker Mushtaque Ahmed seized the opportunity to fan discontent over Tajuddin's performance and at India's intentions. Acting President Syed Nazrul Islam and Prime Minister Tajuddin Ahmed rose to the challenge. Calling for patience and fortitude, the acting president stated that he firmly believed in the assurances received from India. He drew attention to India's help in organizing the massive Mukti Bahini training programme, which had already commenced. Calling for patience, he assured the audience that the results would become apparent in three or four months. In another moving speech, Tajuddin emphasized that the prerequisite for liberation was a capacity for prolonged struggle and sacrifice. Dispelling doubts about the outcome of the liberation war, he assured his audience that victory was certain. His inspirational speech was received with thunderous applause. The final outcome was an affirmation of confidence in the government-in-exile.[13]

The United Front and Moscow

The government-in-exile formed in April was a single-party regime composed exclusively of Awami League members. Indeed, all the elected representatives of the people present on Indian soil belonged to this party. However, all the major political parties in East Bengal also declared their support for the Mujibnagar government. These included the two branches of the National Awami Party (NAM) led, respectively, by Prof. Muzaffar Ahmed (NAP-M) and Maulana Bhashani (NAP-B), the pro-Soviet Communist Party of Bangladesh (CPB), and the Bangladesh Congress Party. Prof. Muzaffar Ahmed issued a statement declaring that the Mujibnagar government was the 'only legally constituted government of Bangladesh' and calling upon all 'democratic and progressive' nations to recognize and assist the new state. Maulana Bhashani appealed to world leaders to accord immediate recognition to Bangladesh and extend all possible help to the government of the People's Republic of Bangladesh. The CPB, aware of the Awami League's pro-west image, made a special effort to explain to 'fraternal parties' the background of the liberation war against a 'ruthless and barbarous enemy armed to the teeth by the imperialists and having the support of the Maoists of China'.[14]

With typical foresight, Tajuddin wanted right from the outset to involve these parties in the liberation struggle by bringing them into a United Front. Thus, in his broadcast on Swadhin Bangla Betar Kendra on 11 April, he invited 'all political leaders of all political parties of Bangla Desh to join us in a united struggle against the aggressor. Our struggle today rises above conventional political boundaries and must be seen as the struggle of the 75 million people of Bangla Desh for protecting their freedom.'[15]

At the end of May, Tajuddin sent his emissary, Mayeedul Hasan, to New Delhi to sound out Haksar's views on a United Front. He had in mind, particularly, the role the CPB could play to dispel Soviet misperceptions about the pro-west character of the Awami League. The Awami League had long maintained close contacts with the Indian and American missions in Dhaka, but it had had few interactions with the Soviet mission. Haksar was very supportive, and he encouraged the Mujibnagar authorities to establish regular contact with the Soviet embassy in New Delhi.[16]

With India's growing involvement in the Bangladesh liberation struggle, Haksar saw the need for regular liaison at the ministerial level. His choice fell on Durga Prasad Dhar, the suave, charming and shrewd politician-diplomat who had been active in Kashmir politics since 1946 and had been elected to successive terms in the state legislature from 1951 to 1967. A close confidant of Indira Gandhi, he was appointed as ambassador to the Soviet Union in 1969 and was responsible for negotiating the Indo-Soviet Treaty. To provide a suitable covering role for Dhar, who had just finished his term in Moscow, Haksar proposed to appoint him as chairman of the 'Policy Planning Committee' in the MEA, with the rank of minister of state. The proposal was opposed by Foreign Minister Dinesh Singh, but the minister was overruled by Indira Gandhi.[17] Dhar took up his new post immediately after the Indo-Soviet Treaty had been signed. In the final analysis, implementation of the treaty would depend on the extent of Soviet sympathy for the Bangladesh movement. Thus, in addition to liaising with Mujibnagar, Dhar also took the initiative in promoting mutual understanding between Moscow and Mujibnagar.

The question of a United Front assumed a new importance after the conclusion of the Indo-Soviet Treaty. Tajuddin, who had been in favour of a United Front even in April, realized that it had become all the more important, in the context of the treaty, to draw the pro-Soviet parties into a United Front. Initial soundings, however, elicited an unenthusiastic response from the foreign minister, Khondaker Mushtaque Ahmed. Tajuddin kept Haksar informed about the position through an emissary.[18] When Dhar visited Kolkata at the end of August, he encouraged the Mujibnagar government to form a United Front, explaining the importance of involving leftist parties for mobilizing Soviet support. On 6 September, an eight-member National Advisory Committee was formed, comprising Tajuddin, Khondaker Mushtaque Ahmed and two other ministers, as well as the leaders of the NAP(M), NAP(B), CPB and Bangladesh Congress parties.[19]

It remained to lift the ban on recruitment of CPB and NAP(M) followers to the Mukti Bahini. Tajuddin's envoy, Mayeedul Hasan, had mooted this idea in a discussion with Dhar in August. When Dhar visited Kolkata in September, prior to Indira Gandhi's crucial visit to Moscow, he informed Tajuddin that Mrs Gandhi hoped to persuade the Soviet leaders that involvement in the Bangladesh liberation war was in the nature of assistance to a 'war of national liberation' (permissible in Soviet eyes), rather than interference in a civil war and in the internal affairs of another state. Lifting the ban on recruitment and induction of some left-wing elements in the Mukti Bahini would help project an appropriate image in Moscow. As Col. Osmani was not present in the city, Tajuddin sought the opinion of the deputy chief of staff, Group Capt. A.K. Khondaker, before giving his formal assent. Khondaker, who had an astute understanding of the larger strategic picture, unhesitatingly supported the proposal.[20]

The Indo-Soviet Treaty was welcomed by Tajuddin, but not by his foreign minister. The foreign secretary, Mahbubul Alam Chashi, offered a curious assessment of the treaty, maintaining that the Soviet position had actually become colder since the conclusion of the treaty and that support was no longer readily forthcoming![21] Foreign Minister Khondaker's distrust of the Indo-Soviet connection and what he believed to be a growing leftist influence in Mujibnagar was to precipitate a dramatic confrontation at the end of October.

Mrs Gandhi shows her hand

Till late October, Indira Gandhi had held her cards close to her chest. Her government had made a herculean effort to provide shelter and sustenance to millions of refugees. It had helped to train and equip some 1,00,000 freedom fighters. It had provided all possible support and assistance to the Mujibnagar government. The Mujibnagar authorities were grateful to India for this support; yet many of them nursed doubts and fears about the limits of New Delhi's support. Would India let them down when it came to the crunch? There were deep misgivings about India's continuing silence on the appeal for diplomatic recognition and the absence of a clear indication of its intentions regarding a decisive military intervention.

The clouds of doubt and despair were finally lifted when Acting President Syed Nazrul Islam and Prime Minister Tajuddin Ahmed met with Indira Gandhi on 22 October, on the eve of her tour of Europe and the United States. For the first time, the Indian prime minister revealed her hand to her Bangladeshi guests. She informed them in the strictest confidence that her foreign tour was a final attempt at persuading the international community to throw its weight behind a peaceful and early solution to the Bangladesh problem. She was not optimistic, however, about the outcome. Should this last effort fail to produce the desired results, then a final solution would have to be found through other means. This was the first unambiguous indication given to the Mujibnagar government about India's ultimate intentions. New Delhi suffered some embarrassment when the elated Nazrul Islam, unable to contain his excitement, passed on the good news to several members of the Awami League hierarchy![22]

Joint planning for the final stage of the liberation war and post-war reconstruction began in mid-November, after Mrs Gandhi's return from her tour of Europe and the United States. But before this could be undertaken, it was necessary to deal with a security issue which could potentially put the plans at risk.

Khondaker and the United States

New Delhi had been receiving intelligence reports for some time concerning clandestine contacts between Khondaker Mushtaque Ahmed and the US consulate general in Kolkata. The full details of this shadowy affair have never been revealed, but declassified US documents show that at the beginning of July, a man named Qazi Zahurul Qaiyum approached a political officer of the US consulate in Kolkata, claiming that he was acting on specific instructions from the Bangladesh foreign minister. In two meetings with the political officer, Qaiyum stated that some Awami League leaders feared the devastating consequences of a war; they hoped for a peaceful settlement, even if that meant a retreat from the demand for full independence. He requested Washington to arrange a meeting between representatives of the Awami League, Pakistan, the United States and India. Qaiyum added that Mujib must be a participant in the negotiations. Any agreement negotiated with Mujib would be acceptable to the people of Bangladesh, even if it involved a compromise with the demand for independence. Qaiyum said that if the ground was prepared, Khondaker was ready to visit Pakistan for talks.[23]

The White House rejected the condition regarding Mujib's participation as unrealistic ('fat chance of Yahya agreeing,' commented Kissinger) but it was interested in the possibility of direct talks between Islamabad and the Awami League aimed at reaching a settlement *within the framework of united Pakistan*. The Kolkata office was accordingly instructed to meet discreetly with Khondaker and probe the accuracy of Qaiyum's account. Qaiyum, however, was either unwilling or unable to arrange a direct meeting. He questioned the need for a direct meeting and said that in any such meeting the foreign minister would be obliged to reiterate the official demand for full independence. Indeed, when the US consulate political officer finally succeeded in meeting directly with Khondaker on 28 September, the latter asked for American intervention to arrange a peaceful transition of East Pakistan into independent Bangladesh. Side-stepping the US suggestion for direct talks between the Awami League and Pakistan, Khondaker requested that Washington convey the Awami League's views to Islamabad. Khondaker did not report this contact to his cabinet colleagues.

On instructions from Washington, the political officer made another attempt to contact Khondaker in order to convey the US response – which, of course, was to press him to enter into direct talks with Pakistan. Khondaker, however, was not present in the city. In his absence, the US official chose to meet Hossain Ali, of the Bangladesh foreign office, to communicate Washington's response and request him to pass it on to Khondaker. Hossain Ali replied cautiously that he would pass on the message to the acting president and then – if necessary – to the foreign minister![24]

This is what we learn from declassified US documents. Details from Indian intelligence reports are not available. These developments caused serious concern to Dhar, even though Asoke Ray, the man on the spot in Kolkata, cautioned against reading too much into Khondaker's contacts with US officials.[25]

The fact that the foreign minister chose to conceal from his cabinet colleagues his contact with the US official in September raises questions about his intentions. Khondaker was known to have a negative opinion about the Indo-Soviet Treaty and, more generally, about what he saw as a left ward shift in Mujibnagar politics. His preference for a US connection reflected an astonishing diplomatic naivete, given the US stance in the Bangladesh crisis. This also gave rise to questions about his commitment to a fully independent Bangladesh. The foreign minister planned to be present at the UN during the General Assembly session. Tajuddin was concerned that Khondaker's statements in New York might create confusion and embarrassment for Mujibnagar.

New Delhi had not so far made an issue of Khondaker's reported secret contacts with US officials. At the end of October, however, as the war drew near, the Indian authorities decided it was time to take up the question with Mujibnagar. Mrs Gandhi had already shown her hand to the Bangladesh leaders. The die had been cast and preparatory moves for the final showdown had already begun. Unity of aim and maintenance of absolute secrecy regarding joint plans had become an absolute necessity for India's national security. On 27 October, D.P. Dhar flew down to Kolkata to apprise Tajuddin of India's concerns. India and Bangladesh were about to begin joint planning for the final stage of the liberation war. Could security be guaranteed while Khondaker occupied the post of foreign minister?[26]

Tajuddin himself was in favour of dismissing Khondaker, but the acting president, Syed Nazrul Islam, decided to simply shift the offender to another cabinet post.[27] From Hossain Ali's report, Islam must have had at least partial knowledge of Khondaker's contacts, but it is not clear how he interpreted these unauthorized initiatives. The acting president also had to bear in mind the need for maintaining party unity. In the event, Khondaker was shifted to another ministry, while Abdus Salam Azad replaced him as foreign minister. Khondaker's associate, Foreign Secretary Mahbubul Alam Chashi, was dismissed from office on disciplinary grounds.

With this, the decks were cleared for joint planning for a decisive war.

5

Mukti Bahini

Pakistan's Operation Searchlight sought to disarm and 'neutralize' all Bengali military and paramilitary units as well as police personnel. This was one of its objectives. To maintain maximum secrecy, senior Pakistani army officers flew out from Dhaka by helicopter to communicate these instructions directly to the local commanders. However, in the charged atmosphere prevailing in East Pakistan in the latter half of March 1971, Bengali officers had begun to suspect that action would be taken against them. In Chittagong, Bengali troops struck preemptively against West Pakistani personnel. In many other areas, Bengali troops dispersed into the countryside before the Pakistanis could move. They were joined by the civil guards (ansars and mujahids) with some basic training in the use of arms, and by large numbers of students and other youth anxious to join the liberation war. They received enthusiastic support from the local populace. Sangram Parishads (Struggle Committees) sprang up all over the country to resist the Pakistani army in every possible way. The Pakistani army was able to seize Dhaka, Chittagong and other cantonments, but many towns and much of the countryside remained outside their control at the end of March.

The liberation war began as a series of spontaneous and uncoordinated local resistance actions. It was against this background that a number of rebel East Bengal Regiment (EBR) officers assembled on 4 April in the Teliapara tea estate in Sylhet, just across the Indian border. They decided that the liberation war should be conducted under a central military command and an independent Bangladesh government. They chose as their military commander Col. (Retd) Muhammad Ataul Goni Osmani, a highly respected figure in the EBR and in EPR. Osmani, who had been commissioned as an officer in the British Indian army during World War II, had served in both these forces after the creation of Pakistan and had acquired a reputation for championing Bengali interests. He was a strong advocate of increasing military recruitment from the eastern wing. When serving in the 1st East Bengal Regiment, he not only introduced Bengali marching tunes, including Tagore songs, but insisted that the daily situation reports be submitted in Bengali. This enthusiasm for a secular Bengali culture did not endear him to his West Pakistani superiors. After retiring from service, Osmani joined the Awami League in 1970 and was elected to the National Assembly at the end of the year. As the constitutional crisis deepened in March 1971, Osmani acted as a channel of communication between Bengali officers and Mujib.

Osmani was not easily recognizable in Teliapara. He had been obliged to remove his signature handlebar moustache in order to escape detection by the Pakistani army when he left Dhaka! Under his guidance, the assembled officers drew up the Teliapara Document, which outlined their initial plans for the liberation war. This envisaged the raising of a large guerrilla force which would be tasked with destroying Pakistani communications facilities, engage in hit-and-run operations against isolated enemy outposts and convoys, and also liquidate 'collaborators' of the enemy. Regular forces would secure a 'lodgement area' or base, provide cover to the guerrillas and launch direct attacks on Pakistani forces as soon as possible. The size of the regular force would be raised partly by training new recruits and partly by inducting the best elements of the paramilitary and guerrilla forces. Indian assistance would be sought for the liberation war.[1]

Shortly afterwards, the Mujibnagar government formally appointed

Osmani as the commander-in-chief of the liberation army, with the rank of cabinet minister. The appointment, in effect, fixed an official seal of approval on the Teliapara action programme. On 18 April, the Mujibnagar cabinet formally '. . . decided that adequate arrangement [sic] should be made by the C-in-C in conjunction with the supporting [Indian] authorities for training of students and youth for various operational tasks in Bangladesh'.[2]

Operation Jackpot

On arriving at the border, rebel EBR and EPR officers approached India's BSF for assistance. The BSF director general, K.F. Rustomji, sought the prime minister's instructions and was advised that he could go ahead but that he must not be found out![3] Accordingly, the BSF provided such limited assistance as it could to the freedom fighters in the shape of arms and ammunition. In several cases, it also gave protective cover to Mukti Bahini operations, even crossing the border on occasion.

After Tajuddin's meeting with Prime Minister Gandhi and the formation of the Mujibnagar government in April, New Delhi decided to extend massive assistance to the Mukti Bahini. In view of the limited resources available to the BSF, the responsibility for training and equipping the freedom fighters was assigned to the army on 30 April. Accordingly, in May, Gen. Manekshaw issued instructions to the GOC-in-C, Eastern Command, Lt Gen. Aurora, to raise and equip a guerrilla force in cooperation with the Mujibnagar authorities. The plan, Operation Jackpot, envisaged that the guerrilla operations would develop in three stages.

In Stage 1, guerrilla operations were to be restricted to selected targets where the Pakistani army was not present, or where they would be unable to react in time for lack of communications. The objective was to disperse the Pakistani forces engaged in protective tasks. At this stage, the Indian army and the BSF, in conjunction with the Bangladesh forces, were to keep the border 'hotted up', in order to tie down Pakistani troops. Isolated Pakistani border outposts might also be eliminated by artillery and mortar fire, where Pakistani forces were not in a position to retaliate.

Stage 2 was in the nature of an extension of the first stage. Guerrilla forces were to be regrouped into smaller units capable of attacking border outposts, patrols and convoys. In addition, they were also to carry out large-scale sabotage operations, destroying rail, road and inland water transport infrastructure, with the aim of isolating Pakistani forces posted in forward areas from their main support areas, such as cantonments and other troop concentrations. Guerrilla units would have to be inducted inside Bangladesh, at safe havens where local support was available. Selected students were to be trained to lead these operations inside Bangladesh.

In Stage 3, the culminating stage of the campaign, the guerrillas would function as formed bodies of troops in the event of a war with Pakistan. This stage would see an intensification of sabotage operations targeted specifically at installations located in the major towns of Jessore, Rajshahi, Dhaka, Mymensingh, Sylhet, Rangpur and Dinajpur.[4]

The Indian army had originally envisaged training around 8,000 guerrillas through a three-month course. An additional period of specialized training was envisaged for the leaders. However, the Mujibnagar authorities pressed for a far larger force; they felt that a short three-week training course would meet the requirement.[5] Thus, the strength of the guerrilla force was placed at 20,000,[6] subject to expansion as required. In view of the emergent situation, the training period had to be limited to a mere four weeks. In the event, due to pressing demands from Mujibnagar, the intake was stepped up in July to 12,000 per month, and increased further in September to 20,000 per month; and the training period was reduced to three weeks. By the end of October, the Mukti Bahini guerrillas numbered over 61,000, and another 6,000 had been inducted into the Mujib Bahini commanded by the student leaders.[7] Under constant pressure from Mujibnagar, the number of Mukti Bahini – regulars and guerrillas – trained by India rose progressively to around

1,00,000 by the end of November. This was a considerable achievement in a six-month period, but a price had to be paid in terms of quality, as the training period had to be cut short. In retrospect, Manekshaw said, '. . . a more careful assessment ought to have been made by me of the numbers that could be properly trained and effectively used during the available six months'.[8]

The bulk of the guerrilla force was drawn from the ranks of students and other youth. To facilitate recruitment, youth camps were set up separately from the main refugee camps. Recruits were politically screened by Awami League representatives, but from late September, volunteers cleared by the pro-Soviet parties – the National Awami Party (M) and the Communist Party of Bangladesh – were also inducted as freedom fighters.[9] Special care was taken to exclude volunteers who might have links to Naxalite or pro-Chinese extremist groups. The Indian authorities were always conscious of the possibility that weapons supplied to the guerrillas might end up in Naxalite hands or in the clandestine arms market.

An important development was the raising in mid-May of a force of frogmen for sabotage operations to disrupt sea and inland river transport. Very early in the day, Tajuddin and Osmani appreciated the importance of these operations in the riverine terrain of Bangladesh. An Indian naval team under Lt Cdr Samant was responsible for training the force, which constituted the fledgling Bangladesh navy. Samant led from the front in operations within Bangladesh and would be awarded the Maha Vir Chakra for his role in 1971.[10]

In October, a small Bangladesh Air Force was established under Group Captain A.K. Khondaker. Their assets consisted of two aircraft (a Dakota and an Otter) and two helicopters.[11]

It is clear from Manekshaw's directive that India planned for a short guerrilla campaign, not a full-fledged drawn-out guerrilla war. India feared that in a prolonged guerrilla war, leadership would pass into the hands of pro-Naxalite and pro-Chinese elements. New Delhi planned the guerrilla operations as a short-duration strategy aimed at preparing favourable conditions for a quick and decisive conventional campaign. The guerrillas would play their part by destroying the communications and transportation infrastructure on which the Pakistani army was dependent, by forcing dispersal of Pakistani troops and isolating them from their support areas, and by undermining the opponent's morale. In the final stage of a classic guerrilla war, the guerrillas convert themselves into a regular army. In the last phase of the 1971 war, the guerrillas operated as an adjunct or auxiliary to the regular forces of India and Bangladesh.

Mukti Bahini (April–June)

Manekshaw's instructions were broadly consistent with the outline plan formulated by the Mukti Bahini commanders at their Teliapara meeting on 4 April, envisaging the raising of a large guerrilla force tasked with disrupting Pakistani lines of communication, carrying out hit-and-run operations on convoys and isolated posts, and eliminating local collaborators of the Pakistani army.

In view of the time required for recruitment and training, the guerrillas would be ready for operations only from the month of July, after the commencement of the monsoon. This was an auspicious season for commencing guerrilla actions: torrential rains and floods impeded movement of regular troops during the monsoon. Till the end of June, the Mukti Bahini forces were composed of regulars from the EBR, lightly armed border security forces (EPR), police and other law enforcement agencies (mujahids and ansars) who had some training in the use of arms, and untrained students and other youth.

In the spontaneous uprising that erupted on 25 March, these forces, actively assisted by the populace, had succeeded in seizing control of several major towns and much of the countryside. The Pakistani army had expected to be in control of the major urban areas by 10 April, but it met with unexpectedly stiff resistance as it fanned out from the cantonments to establish control over the major cities and communication centres.

The Mukti Bahini put up a gallant defence against a far more powerful foe, but was compelled to fall back step by step on every front. By mid-May, the major towns were under Pakistani control. The last Mukti Bahini stronghold, Belonia, fell on 10 June. With the loss of Belonia, the Mukti Bahini was left in control of no more than a few square miles of territory along the Indian border. Deprived of a base or 'lodgement area', the freedom fighters retreated across the border to seek shelter and sanctuary in India.

After this initial setback, the Mukti Bahini sector commanders convened in Kolkata for a week, 10 June to 17 June, to take stock of the situation and draw up a new strategy. The conference marked the end of the first phase of the liberation war and the beginning of its second phase. The first phase saw a conventional war between two vastly unequal forces. It was a war for control of territory, in which the Mukti Bahini, the weaker conventional force, was compelled step by step to retreat and finally seek sanctuary on Indian soil. The guerrilla force being trained would be ready for induction within a month. The Mukti Bahini was about to emerge as a composite force comprising both conventional forces (Nyomito Bahini) and a vast guerrilla force (Gono Bahini). How was this composite force to be organized? What tasks should be assigned to the Nyomito Bahini and Gono Bahini respectively? These basic questions needed to be resolved before the liberation war entered the next phase.

Inevitably, the commander-in-chief, Osmani, came in for criticism. On the eve of the Kolkata conference, a proposal was mooted to create a War Council composed of the sector commanders and to kick Osmani upstairs as defence minister, divesting him of the post of commander-in chief. Some commanders openly charged him with failing to coordinate operations from his Kolkata headquarters. Osmani saw the proposal for a War Council as an expression of a lack of confidence in his leadership and submitted his resignation. It was Tajuddin who saved the situation by persuading the commander-in-chief to withdraw his resignation and to chair the conference.

The Kolkata conference took a major step towards integrating guerrilla warfare in the strategy of the liberation war. This had become possible because the first batch of guerrilla trainees would soon be ready for induction. The conference decided to divide the battle-front into eleven clearly defined sectors. Each sector would organize guerrilla bases in its assigned territory. The 'sector troops' (mainly paramilitary EPR) were tasked to provide support to the guerrilla operations. Leadership at these bases would be provided by a small number of EBR regulars from the Nyomito Bahini (conventional forces), assisted by a political adviser to motivate the populace. The aim of guerrilla operations was to disrupt communications and logistics facilities, conduct economic warfare by destroying warehouses for export products in order to deny foreign exchange revenues to the Pakistani regime, conduct psychological warfare to break enemy morale, gather intelligence, and rouse public opinion against collaborators and eliminate them, if necessary.[12]

Osmani's critics accused him of having failed to coordinate Mukti Bahini operations from his headquarters in Kolkata and to arrange adequate supplies of arms and ammunition for the freedom fighters. He, in turn, held Lt Gen. Aurora responsible on this account. Tajuddin shared Osmani's concern. On 3 August, they conveyed their complaints to New Delhi through RAW channels. In a three- hour meeting with RAW Joint Director P.N. Banerji, Osmani and Tajuddin listed their complaints against Aurora. Osmani said that arms and ammunition were not being supplied to them on the required scale. (Osmani's demands were evidently based on the somewhat more generous scale on which the Pakistan army was equipped, in comparison to Indian army units.) The Bangladesh C-in-C complained that a proper operation room had not been set up for him, neither had he been provided with the communication and air transport facilities required for overseeing and coordinating operations in different sectors. This had given rise to dissatisfaction and discontent in the Bangladesh forces. Osmani also complained of interference in the conduct of operations, which bred indiscipline and disrespect for the C-in-C. Tajuddin emphasized that these problems had given rise to a great deal of unfair criticism against Osmani in the Bangladesh forces as well as in the Awami League.[13]

Whatever the merits of these complaints, it was evident that Osmani felt slighted by Aurora. All those who came into contact with Osmani were impressed by his integrity and deep dedication to the cause of an independent Bangladesh. Shunning every comfort, he led an austere life, sleeping on a camp cot in his office. Yet he could be touchy on matters of protocol. Osmani's predicament was that, as a colonel, he was outranked by the Indian generals whom he had to deal with, while he, understandably, insisted on being treated as a commander-in-chief, even though Bangladesh had yet to gain recognition as a sovereign state. Maj. Gen. Sukhwant Singh recalls an occasion when Osmani's plane circled over an airfield for about ten minutes till the Indian army commander he was to meet had arrived at the airfield to receive him.[14]

Mukti Bahini (July–September)

The first batch of 110 newly trained guerrillas was infiltrated into Bangladesh in July.[15] As planned, Indian troops provided artillery cover to facilitate this infiltration of the freedom fighters. According to an Indian estimate, almost 50 per cent of the Pakistani border outposts were neutralized by the end of July.[16] In the same month, Maj. Gen. (later Lt Gen.) B.N. Sarkar, an officer known for his fervent espousal of the Bangladesh cause, was appointed director of military operations (DMO), Eastern Command, and assigned the task of coordination with Bangladesh Forces Headquarters. Sarkar's appointment helped alleviate the personality conflicts between Osmani and Aurora. Tactful by nature and able to communicate with his Bangladeshi colleagues in their common mother tongue, Sarkar was able to develop a rapport with the Mukti Bahini leadership. The Bangladesh Forces Headquarters had not so far issued specific operational directives to the sector forces. In August, Sarkar instituted a system of regular meetings with the concerned Bangladeshi officers to jointly draw up monthly targets for Mukti Bahini operations. These targets were then circulated to the Bangladeshi sector commanders by Col. Osmani and to the concerned Indian officers by the Eastern Command.[17]

The initial guerrilla operations in July produced indifferent results. The Pakistan army's confidence about the success of its 'pacification' drive remained unshaken. It expected to resolve the internal security problem and to restore road, rail and riverine communications well before India was able to position itself to launch a military offensive.[18] However, after a shaky start, the guerrilla operations gradually gathered tempo, and by September Osmani was able to claim some spectacular successes. Culverts and bridges were blown up, disrupting Pakistani communications, and ambushes were carried out successfully. According to Lt Gen. Jacob, these operations were beginning to have an effect on Pakistani morale. In Manekshaw's assessment, by September the principal aim of the guerrilla operations – that is 'the creation of conditions in BANGLA DESH whereby operations by regular troops would be facilitated' – was being achieved, though not to the desired extent.[19] Guerrilla recruitment was raised in July to 12,000, and in September to 20,000 per month. To cope with demands for a further increase, the training period was reduced to three weeks from August onwards.

At the end of September, Osmani carried out a critical review of Mukti Bahini operations and drew up a new operational plan – '. . . though we have inflicted a degree of damage on the enemy, it is far short of what we should have achieved', was his general assessment. The aim of the operations had been to liberate and hold a 'lodgement area'. Excessive reliance had been placed on the role of regular army formations for the launch of an offensive to liberate and hold a 'lodgement area' or secure base within Bangladesh, from where a major offensive could be launched. This aim was to be achieved principally by regular army formations. With this aim in view, a brigade had been raised from three understrength East Bengal battalions by milking the paramilitary East Pakistan Rifles and the best elements among the mujahids and ansars.

This approach had proved unrealistic. 'Without armour, it [the regular army] is incapable of launching major offensives and therefore, the thought of liberating a lodgement area and to hold it, is not practicable.' The milking of 'sector troops' had only weakened them, while the EBR brigade could not be effectively utilized.

Osmani concluded:

> . . . we have to base our war strategy primarily on the unconventional war. It is therefore essential that the guerrilla ops is accorded the highest priority . . . Considering the limited time available at our disposal, we will be able to achieve this by inducting our regular forces into Coy Pl groups along with their commanders inside Bangladesh . . . This way, the guerrillas will be able to increase our area of influence, thus gradually liberating larger areas without resorting to set piece conventional battle . . . While the guerrillas will operate inside we must keep the border alive with ops so that the enemy is unable to pull out troops from the border for re-inforcement [sic] inside against our guerrilla ops . . . [the] overall plan should be should be to base our war strategy primarily on guerrilla ops.[20]

This review reflected the evolution of Osmani's thinking on the relative merits of conventional and non-conventional warfare. In Stage 1 of the liberation war, he had favoured a conventional war, with the guerrillas playing only a supporting role. Hence Jacob's criticism that Osmani's '. . . views were orthodox. He wanted to model his forces on the organization and tactics of the Pakistan army. He had reservations on the raising and employment of guerrilla forces, preferring to raise regular East Bengal Batallions, and devoted more time to organizing and training them than the Mukti Bahini'.[21] On his part, Osmani complained that at the outset of the liberation war itself Aurora had pressed for dismantling of the EBR and EPR and retraining of the troops in guerrilla warfare.[22]

Against the background of the increased tempo of Mukti Bahini operations, Pakistan revised its military plans for the defence of East Pakistan in September. The previous plan, drawn up in 1970, did not envisage defence of the entire East Pakistan border. The focus was on the defence of Dhaka, which had to be held at all costs until a massive offensive launched from West Pakistan brought India to the negotiating table. The plan envisaged engaging the enemy along three successive defensive lines in order to delay its progress till succour arrived from the western wing. The new plan appears to have been based on intelligence reports of the Mukti Bahini's intention of establishing liberated zones in border areas. It called for a forward posture of defence based on border outposts, fortified where necessary. The objective was to deny the Mukti Bahini control of a territorial base that might provide justification for India's recognition of Bangladesh.[23] The new forward posture entailed redeployment of troops to the border from the Dhaka bowl and other strongholds in the interior. This unwittingly served the Indian strategy of drawing Pakistani troops to the border and weakening the enemy's interior defences and reserves, so that the India–Bangladesh forces could bypass fortified defensive positions and close in on Dhaka with maximum speed. It also facilitated an impressive increase in Mukti Bahini guerrilla operations in the interior.

Mukti Bahini (October–mid-November)

The Mukti Bahini achieved further successes in October. According to a Pakistani account, 'reliable estimates' indicated that by October the guerrillas had set off 497 explosions, attacking 188 government offices and godowns (warehouses) and 281 police stations; 231 bridges had been destroyed or damaged, as well as 90 power installations. There were frequent raids and ambushes on Pakistani patrols and small bodies of troops.[24]

In his monthly report for October, Manekshaw noted with satisfaction:

> [The] tempo of guerrilla operations has picked up considerably . . . the concentration of our regular troops on the India–BANGLA DESH border has compelled the PAKISTAN army to move out from the interior . . . to the border opposite us: this action of theirs has denuded the heartland of BANGLA DESH of regular troops. This . . . will give the Freedom Fighters, of whom an increasingly large number are being inducted, an excellent opportunity to move about freely and hit targets wherever they should choose to do so.[25]

As Mukti Bahini raids, sabotage actions and ambushes gathered strength, the Pakistani army responded with artillery fire against the guerrillas, often causing destruction on the Indian side of the border. As a preventive measure, the Indian army was authorized in September to respond with cross-border fire and to occupy border areas from where the firing originated.[26] With the intensification of Mukti Bahini operations in October, the scale and intensity of the Pakistani response registered a corresponding increase. With increased shelling of Indian border posts by the Pakistani army, Indian forces were permitted in November to go into Bangladesh territory up to a distance of ten miles in order to silence Pakistani artillery. In carrying out these instructions, the Indian army also took care to secure specific positions that would improve its offensive posture, with an eye on the impending war.[27]

This led in many cases to major conventional battles between Indian and Pakistani troops, with the Mukti Bahini guerrillas playing a supportive role. Thus, on 20 November 1971, Indian forces launched a preliminary operation in the Boyra area, during the course of which Pakistan lost fourteen tanks and three aircraft, apart from losses of men. On orders from Manekshaw, an attack on the Pakistani defences at the border town of Hilli was launched on 23 November. In the heavy fighting that ensued, Indian losses included sixty-seven killed and ninety wounded. Indian forces were able to register some advances, but the Pakistanis held on to Hilli itself till 11 December – the eighth day of the formal declaration of war.

In Jacob's assessment:

> The Pakistanis were thrown off balance and our strategy of drawing the Pakistanis to the border began to work. We secured suitable jumping off places, particularly where obstacles had to be crossed, and such operations also gave our troops realistic initiation into battle.[28]

The stage was set for a swift victory in the war that was to follow in December.

6

Military Plans

Critics have argued that India won the war in 1971, but lost the peace because the Kashmir problem was left unresolved. This misses the point that the political aims underlying India's military plans for the Bangladesh liberation war were not focused on Kashmir. The 1971 war differed fundamentally from all other India–Pakistan conflicts. Its core political objective was unrelated to Kashmir or to any disputed territory such as the Rann of Kutch. India's objective was to bring the civil war in East Pakistan to an early conclusion before it gravely endangered India's own security. For the first and only time, the principal theatre of a war between India and Pakistan lay on the eastern – not the western – front.

Until March 1971, India's military contingency plans had been designed to respond to and repulse a Pakistani offensive in the west. The Indian armed forces had no plans for a major war in East Pakistan. Its contingency plans for the east envisaged only two limited tasks: repulsion of a Pakistani attack in the Siliguri–Cooch Behar ('chicken's neck') corridor connecting the north-eastern states with the rest of India; and defence of the city of Kolkata against aerial bombing raids.[1] Thus, planning for the Bangladesh liberation war had to begin from scratch. India's unpreparedness to fight a war in East Pakistan is vividly illustrated by the fact that when the Eastern Command began to draft operational plans in April, it discovered that the maps of East Pakistan in its possession were over fifty years old, dating back to the British Raj! One of the first tasks of the Eastern Command was to obtain up-to-date maps from the Mukti Bahini.[2]

The Eastern Command previously had two principal tasks: to protect the borders of India and Bhutan against possible Chinese aggression; and to counter insurgencies in Nagaland, Manipur, the Mizo Hills and, more recently, tackle the Naxalites in West Bengal. On 19 April 1971, it was given the additional and urgent responsibility of assisting the liberation of Bangladesh. The Eastern Command lost no time in addressing its new responsibility. Within the space of a month, it had not only commenced training and equipping a guerrilla force but had also drawn up a draft plan for the final push into East Bengal in November/December. The principal architect of the plan was the chief of staff of the Eastern Command, Maj. Gen. (later Lt Gen.) J.F.R. Jacob.

The plan was based on the following strategic outline.

(i) The final objective of the operations was to liberate Dhaka (which, in Jacob's words, was the 'geopolitical and geostrategic heart of East Pakistan').
(ii) The thrust lines would isolate and bypass Pakistani forces in order to race towards the final objective, Dhaka. Capturing towns would be time-consuming and would entail heavy casualties.
(iii) Subsidiary objectives would be to seize communication centres and to destroy Pakistani command and control capabilities, thus disrupting Pakistan's defence posture and forcing a retreat. Fortified strongholds would be bypassed and dealt with later.
(iv) Preliminary operations would aim to draw out Pakistani forces to the border, weakening the defence of key areas in the interior.[3]

The forces required for the purpose would be found partly from within the resources available to the Eastern Command and partly by additional allocations from other sectors. Since the operations were planned for the winter months, when most of the Himalayan passes would be snow-bound, some of the troops earmarked for defence of the India-China border could be diverted to the East Pakistan front. (Disagreements would arise later on the permissible extent of these troop diversions.) Likewise, some of the troops involved in counter-insurgency operations could be temporarily diverted for the Bangladesh operations. AHQ indicated that 9 Infantry Division, 4 Mountain Division, 340 Mountain Brigade Group and a battalion group of 50 Parachute Brigade would be allotted to the Eastern Command.[4]

A radically different approach was proposed by the Western Command. This envisaged liberating Bangladesh through a decisive war in the western sector, with only holding operations in the East! Lt Gen. K.P. Candeth, GOC-in-C, Western Command, argued that if the Pakistani armed forces were decisively defeated in West Pakistan, they would have no option but to surrender also in East Bengal, where they would find themselves surrounded by a hostile population and with no hope of reinforcements or supplies. The proposal was turned down, since its aims went far beyond India's overall political objective. Manekshaw clarified to the army commanders that it was no part of India's policy to humiliate Pakistan.[5]

AHQ drew up a draft plan in early July 1971. Its chief author was the highly regarded DMO, Maj. Gen. K.K. Singh. The plan drew on many elements of the draft received from Eastern Headquarters, but differed from it on a crucial question. Dhaka was not listed as a specific target. The main goals of the plan were to liberate the *major part* of Bangladeshi territory, including the ports of Chittagong and Khulna, and to facilitate the establishment of an independent Bangladesh government in the liberated territory. The Indian army was to join hands with the Mukti Bahini in the campaign. The DMO was less sanguine than Jacob about the prospects of a frontal assault on Dhaka *within the time available*. AHQ reasoned that the Pakistani army could not hold on to Dhaka for long if it was denied access to the 'entry' ports on which they depended for supplies and reinforcements. The presence of Pakistani forces in the city and other isolated outposts would thus become militarily unsustainable.[6]

The implicit assumption underlying the plan was that the war would be brought to an end by a UN resolution before an unconditional Pakistani surrender could be enforced in Dhaka. The aim, therefore, was to occupy the major part of Bangladeshi territory, and to place the Pakistani forces in an untenable position that would soon compel them to withdraw from the rest of the territory.

The plan met the minimum requirements for attaining India's political aim. This was to speed up the emergence of an independent Bangladesh, with the two fold objective of pre-empting pro-Chinese and pro-Naxalite elements from taking over the leadership of the Bangladesh liberation war, and of ensuring the voluntary return of the refugees to their homeland. In conformity with international law, recognition could be formally extended to a state that was in effective control of the major part of its territory. Though highly desirable, control of the capital city was not an essential requirement for recognition. It was reasoned that Pakistan, denied access to Chittagong and other ports, would in any case find itself compelled to surrender the beleaguered city shortly after a UN-imposed ceasefire.

The draft plan was shared with the air force and navy at the end of July 1971. Thereafter, in the first week of August, Army Chief of Staff Gen. Manekshaw, accompanied by DMO Maj. Gen. K.K. Singh, flew down to the Eastern Command Headquarters in Kolkata to discuss the details of the plan with Lt Gen. Aurora and Maj. Gen. Jacob. Lt Gen. Aurora was in agreement with the approach spelled out in the AHQ draft plan, but it elicited a spirited protest from Maj. Gen. Jacob, his chief of staff. Jacob argued that the task of denying Pakistan access to Chittagong and Khulna (or the downstream ports of Mangla/Chalna) could easily be accomplished by a naval blockade. The task should, therefore, be allotted to the navy. Jacob pressed the point that Dhaka was the 'geopolitical heart of East Pakistan' and its 'capture' should be the key objective of army operations. He dismissed the significance of Chittagong, which, he said, was 'well east of the main centre of gravity, almost peripheral'. Manekshaw explained that Dhaka would automatically fall if Chittagong and Khulna were liberated. Jacob remained unconvinced.[7]

Detailed planning began on the basis of the AHQ paper. War games were conducted, and their lessons incorporated in the plan. Close consultations were held between the three services to achieve coordination. In addition to its standard roles of protecting the coastline, sea lanes and merchant shipping and striking at Pakistani naval and economic targets, the navy was specifically tasked with imposing a blockade of East Pakistani ports. It was also tasked to train Mukti Bahini naval personnel for mining and sabotage operations. The role allotted to the navy called for a major redeployment of assets from the Arabian Sea to the Bay of Bengal. Despite protests from the navy's Western Command, the aircraft carrier *INS Vikrant* and *INS Brahmaputra* and *INS Beas* were transferred to the Eastern Fleet.[8] The Indian Air Force aimed to achieve total air supremacy in the eastern theatre, while maintaining sufficient reserves to meet a possible threat from China. The air force was given the new task of accelerating the army's advance by providing transport aircraft and helicopters, particularly for major river-crossing operations. Deficiencies in military equipment were identified and steps were taken to obtain the requirements from the Soviet Union in a timely manner. Transportation and military infrastructure was strengthened on an impressive scale to facilitate military operations.

An updated master plan was ready by October 1971. Its overall aims were: (i) to assist the Mukti Bahini to liberate a part of East Pakistan where the refugees could return to live under an independent Bangladesh government; (b) to conduct offensive-defensive operations in the western theatre to prevent Pakistan from capturing Indian territory; and (c) to defend the northern border in the event of Chinese intervention.[9]

The plan anticipated a powerful Pakistani attack on the western front. It expected Pakistan to launch a concentrated attack on Poonch and to attempt to disrupt the line of communication between Pathankot and

Jammu. Adequate forces were provided to meet the first contingency. To counter the second move, the plan provided for an Indian advance along two thrust lines – between the rivers Basantar and Beas in the north, and from Thakurpur on the river Ravi in the south. Further, with a view to consolidating India's defence positions, limited attacks were planned in Ladakh's Shyok valley and Kargil, and in the area lying west of Dera Baba Nanak Bridge in Punjab. In the secondary southern sector, stretching from Ganganagar in Rajasthan to the Arabian Sea, thrusts were planned towards Rahim Yar Khan in the south of Pakistan's Punjab province and Naya Chor in Sind.

The primary targets, of course, lay on the eastern front, where the aim was to liberate a major part of Bangladesh through a rapid advance bypassing Pakistani strongholds, while ensuring their isolation by seizing control of major communication centres. The eastern front was divided into four sectors. In the north-western sector, the army was to advance up to Bogra, the principal communication centre, where Pakistani forces were to be tied down. In the western sector, the main communication centres at Jessore and Jhenida were to be liberated. In the eastern sector, the Meghna bulge was to be liberated. In the northern sector, the army was to advance along the Jamalpur–Tangail line.[10] As in the earlier AHQ plan, Dhaka was not identified as a specific aim, though the option was left open for consideration, depending on the progress of the campaign. The updated plan assigned to the navy the task of blockading Chittagong and Khulna. This was based on an assurance from the Indian navy that it would deny Pakistan access to these ports.[11] Aircraft based on *INS Vikrant* were to bomb Chittagong and lay mines around ports in East Pakistan. The air force, as noted earlier, was to ensure total command of East Pakistani airspace right from the outset, and to provide support to army and navy operations. It was also tasked to equip and train a fledgling Bangladesh Air Force.

There were divergent opinions among the generals on the Dhaka question. Even within the Directorate of Military Operations, there were differences of opinion between DMO Maj. Gen. K.K. Singh and his deputy, Maj. Gen. Sukhwant Singh, who shared Jacob's conviction that Dhaka was a feasible goal. By September–October, the balance of opinion among the generals began to shift in favour of a march to Dhaka, even though this was not reflected in an updated AHQ plan. Under Maj. Gen. Sukhwant Singh's persuasion, Lt Gen. Sagat Singh, commanding IV Corps, fell in with the idea. The story is best told in Sukhwant Singh's own words.

> I suggested to Sagat Singh indirectly . . . 'Why don't you secure the Brahmanbaria–Ashuganj area, and then the road to Dacca will open itself for you to stage a triumphant march to the heart of Bangladesh polities [politics?].' 'But that is not my task,' he snapped back. 'I'm only suggesting,' I said with a smile. A glint came into his eyes . . . 'Tell me, does India mean business this time or are they wasting our time?' he asked. Assured that the government 'meant business' this time, Sagat Singh readily fell in with the proposal.[12]

Jacob, on his part, discussed the liberation of Dhaka with Maj. Gen. Gurbux Singh Gill, who commanded Headquarters 101 Communication Zone. The plan was to cross the Brahmaputra at Jamalpur and to airdrop a battalion of paratroopers at Tangail in the area controlled by the Bangladeshi freedom fighter Kader Siddiqui. The two groups were to link up and advance to Dhaka, together with Siddiqui's forces. In order to meet Gill's requirement of additional troops for the task, it was intended to move two brigades from the Himalayan border to the eastern theatre.[13] Jacob informed the new DMO, Maj. Gen. Inder Gill, about the plan and the intended move of troops from the northern border. Gill concurred with Jacob's plan. 'Chief of Staff Eastern Command and I were quite clear about the requirement and bent our efforts towards its accomplishment,'[14] he later recollected. Thus, well before the outbreak of the war, some of the leading generals on the Indian side had in mind a detailed plan that envisaged the liberation not only of the major part of Bangladesh but also of its capital city, Dhaka.

At the end of November 1971, New Delhi received an unambiguous assurance of Soviet support in the Security Council in the event of war. Moscow had earlier been reluctant to directly associate itself with an initiative that might be viewed as interference in a Pakistani civil war. (The evolution of the Soviet position is traced in Chapters 10 and 11.) The assurance of a Soviet veto meant that some more time might be available for completion of military operations, and it was now deemed feasible to liberate the whole of Bangladesh within the time available. Accordingly, AHQ issued an amendment to its earlier Operational Instruction, spelling out that the revised objective of the Eastern Command was to liberate the whole of Bangladesh. However, the amendment, which was received just a few days before the war, came too late to allow formal alteration of existing plans.[15]

India's military plans were formulated and implemented in an institutional framework that suffered from major flaws. The three services had separate headquarters that functioned autonomously and were not integrated with the defence ministry. Neither was there an institutional platform for regular interaction between the chiefs of staff and the principal civilian officers in the foreign, home and finance ministries. These institutional deficiencies were partly surmounted in 1971 through improvisation and informal coordination. Manekshaw represented the service chiefs at the meetings chaired by D.P. Dhar. The prime minister's closest advisers, including Dhar, Haksar and Kaul, also maintained regular informal contacts with Manekshaw, who, in turn, kept the other service chiefs informed of political developments.[16] The defence ministry highlighted these interactions in its annual report for 1971–72.

> The interaction between the civil and military leaderships was continuous and informal . . . As time passed, international, political and strategic factors, the evaluation of which called for careful analysis, had an increasingly important bearing on the choice of options open to us. Consequently, the scale, pattern and timing of our defence preparedness

were, of necessity, to be coordinated with a number of external developments.[17]

Coordination between the three services also reached unprecedented levels. The defence ministry's annual report stated:

> The coordination among the Chiefs of Staff was reflected at the command level and below. Based on our experience of 1965 operations, liaison officers from the Air Force were stationed at the command level with effective communication links with air formations and the operational Command structure to enable effective operational coordination. Similar coordination was achieved between the two Naval Commands and the concerned Air Commands.[18]

Air Chief Marshal P.C. Lal confirms that the IAF ensured close coordination with the army by locating an Advance Headquarters of the Western and Eastern Air Commands alongside the corresponding Army Command; a tactical Air Centre with each Corps HQ; and Forward Air Controllers further down the field.[19] Likewise, Vice Admiral Kohli, who headed the Western Naval Command in 1971, has recorded the following:

> A special feature of the preparatory stages was that, for the first time ever, the Chiefs of Staff of the three services jointly examined in the minutest detail the plans of the various commands of the three services. Like the other Commanders-in-Chief I made my presentation which was subjected to detailed scrutiny, and some very searching questions were asked about the legal aspects of the blockade and contraband control and the effects it would have on neutral and friendly merchant ships and their countries.[20]

The quantum leap in informal consultation and coordination stood in sharp contrast to the experience of the 1965 war. Air Chief Marshal

Lal recalls that in 1965, the Chiefs of Staff Committee mechanism was simply bypassed. Gen. Chaudhuri took the air chief into confidence informally about his discussions with the prime minister and defence minister, but the naval chief was excluded from these meetings on the ground that the navy could play no more than a modest role in the war. In 1965, no joint plans were prepared by the three services. The air force and navy were not even asked to define their respective roles in the event of war. As a result, there were shortfalls in the close support to ground forces provided by the IAF. Lal also makes the telling point that the absence of a joint navy-air force plan for defending naval bases enabled the Pakistan Navy in 1965 to bombard the Indian naval base in close proximity to the IAF's Jamnagar base.[21]

Thus, in 1971, coordination between the three services partly compensated for the absence of an integrated defence structure. Credit is due to the concerned military and civilian officers, but we should not lose sight of the fact that it was possible to put these informal or improvised arrangements in place only because several months were available for preparation for the war. Moreover, the improvisations could not completely close the gaps in coordination caused by institutional deficiencies. Coordination between the chiefs of staff and the leading civil servants was mostly effected through informal meetings. The political dimension of policy was often unclear to some others who should have been more fully in the picture. Even the cerebral air chief, Lal, recalled later that he had doubts in his mind about the objectives of the war.[22] The spectacular military success achieved in 1971 must not obscure the grave deficiencies in India's institutional structures, many of which persist to this day.

7

Mobilizing World Opinion

(April–October 1971)

India's diplomatic response to the Bangladesh crisis proceeded on two parallel tracks: a general drive to mobilize the widest possible international support for the cause of the people of 'East Bengal'; and the search for the support of a superpower in the expected event of a war. This chapter is an account of India's efforts on the first track to mobilize international sympathy and support for the victims of the reign of terror unleashed in East Bengal and to create conditions there that would enable the refugees to return to their homes.

India faced an uphill task in mobilizing international support for Bangladesh. As Haksar had pointed out, the principles of non-interference in the internal affairs of a sovereign state and the territorial integrity of states were deeply entrenched in international law and practice. Enshrined in Article 2 of the UN Charter, non-intervention was a foundational principle of international law. The doctrine of humanitarian intervention was yet to find a place in international law. That doctrine was to gain international acceptance in the closing decade of the century, when the collapse of the Soviet Union and the east–west balance of power created an environment in which it could be successfully invoked by the western powers. An equally formidable obstacle was the principle of territorial integrity, interpreted as excluding secession of any part of a sovereign state. This principle found particularly strong support among the new Afro-Asian states. Most of these comprised diverse linguistic, ethnic, tribal and religious groups, and had yet to develop an overarching national identity. They were still in the process of evolving into fully formed modern nation-states. Many of them faced the spectre of secessionism. In these countries, the principle of territorial integrity was powerfully reinforced by what was perceived as the national interest.

In the first two months of the crisis, the principal aim of India's diplomatic campaign was to focus the attention of the international community on the massive violation of human rights and democratic principles in 'East Bengal' and the urgent need for humanitarian assistance to the refugees fleeing to India. It emphasized that restoration of 'normalcy' was the essential condition for enabling the refugees to return voluntarily to their homes. India appealed to the international community to bring pressure on Pakistan to stop the massacres and outrages against human rights and to restore 'normalcy' in 'East Bengal'.

As the campaign unfolded, there was a seamless evolution of the Indian position. By mid-May, 'normalcy' was being defined with greater clarity, as a political settlement acceptable to the elected representatives of the people of East Bengal, that is, to Mujib's Awami League. Before the end of May, as the number of refugees approached the staggering figure of 3.5 million, another dimension was added to the drive. India maintained that the repression in East Bengal could no longer be regarded as a purely internal problem of Pakistan. Pakistan was 'exporting' its internal problem to India by driving millions of refugees across the border, thereby posing a threat to India's security and social stability. New Delhi maintained that it was incumbent on the international community and, in particular, the Great Powers, to help preserve peace in South Asia by prevailing on Pakistan to find an early solution to its political problem. This new line also implied that India had the right to act in self-defence if the international community was unable or unwilling to persuade Pakistan to halt the campaign of terror in East

Bengal and to reach an agreement with the elected representatives of the people of East Bengal.

Thus, the Indian diplomatic campaign evolved from a simple appeal based on human rights and provision of humanitarian assistance to victims of human rights violations, to a broader approach that also included a legal justification for intervention by India and the international community. And finally, it included an implied warning that India would be compelled to exercise its right of self-defence if the international community failed in its duty to persuade Pakistan to create conditions for the voluntary repatriation of the refugees by working out a political settlement with the elected representatives of the people of East Bengal.

End-March to early June, 1971

On 31 March, the Indian Parliament unanimously adopted a resolution moved by the prime minister. This expressed 'solidarity with the people of East Bengal in their struggle for a democratic way of life', reiterated India's commitment to the defence of human rights, and called upon the international community 'to prevail upon the Government of Pakistan to put an end immediately to the systematic decimation of people which amounts to genocide'.[1] Following the resolution, New Delhi launched a massive and sustained campaign to focus the attention of the international community on the political and human rights aspects of the savage military crackdown in 'East Bengal'.

India faced a herculean task. The principles of sovereignty and territorial integrity of states were powerful barriers to international involvement in this case. In the absence of an overriding national interest, these legal principles were the default policy option for most states. The problem was particularly acute in the case of the newly independent Afro-Asian states, as mentioned earlier. Few of them were democracies; many showed scant respect for human rights in their own countries. Many of these new states faced the spectre of secessionism in their own territories. This was particularly true of sub-Saharan Africa, which had been carved up by the European colonial powers in the latter half of the nineteenth century along arbitrary boundary lines that cut across tribal and ethnic divisions. In the decade before the launch of the Bangladesh liberation war, Africa had witnessed abortive secessionist movements in Katanga and Biafra. Ambassador Akwei of Ghana voiced the general sentiment of the African Group at the United Nations on 7 December:

> It is not for us to dictate to Pakistan what it should or should not do. We have to respect the sovereignty and territorial integrity of every State Member of this Organisation . . . The Organisation of African Unity knows that once intervention in the affairs of a Member State is permitted, once one permits oneself the higher wisdom of telling another Member State what it should do with regard to arranging its own political affairs, one opens a Pandora's box. And no continent can suffer more than Africa when such a principle is thwarted.[2]

India received a somewhat more sympathetic hearing in the western democracies. The massacres in East Bengal and the plight of the refugees received wide coverage in the major British, American and continental newspapers and TV channels. NGOs dedicated to human rights and humanitarian relief – Amnesty International, Oxfam and Action Bangladesh, among many others – were passionate advocates of the Bangladesh cause. A galaxy of celebrities in the artistic world – including such musical megastars as Ravi Shankar, Ali Akbar Khan, George Harrison, John Lennon, Bob Dylan and Joan Baez, and men of letters like Andre Malraux and Allen Ginsburg – appealed for support to Bangladesh. In an illuminating survey, Srinath Raghavan points out that the late 1960s saw the 'emergence of a new form of humanitarianism that was self-consciously transnational insofar as it refused to accept national governments as the sole source of authority and aimed to address a global audience'.[3] Raghavan observes that in 1971, there were thus two opposing trends at work: the new transnational humanitarianism and the entrenched principle of non-interference in the domestic affairs of a sovereign state. An advertisement inserted in the London *Times* on 13 May by Action Bangladesh captured the new spirit. It carried the caption 'This Is the Moment to Show that Man is More than "An Internal Problem"'.[4]

However, the new transnational humanitarianism was a significant factor mainly in open democratic societies. It found little response in the authoritarian states that accounted for a majority in the United Nations. Furthermore, even in the democracies where it played a major role in shaping public opinion, transnational humanitarianism had yet to breach the wall of state sovereignty in 1971. None of the western democracies issued an open condemnation of Pakistan, lest it should be construed as interference in Pakistan's internal affairs.

Even in Britain where, due to historical connections and the presence of a large Bangladeshi immigrant community, public sympathy for East Bengal was very strong, the government refrained from public censure, contenting itself with appeals in confidential communications for an end to the bloodshed and a return to negotiations. On 7 April, Prime Minister Edward Heath wrote to Gen. Yahya Khan, 'There must be an end to bloodshed and the use of force as soon as possible and a resumption of discussions. Political leaders, who received such massive support, must at some stage participate in these discussions.'[5] Australia and New Zealand were prepared to go one step further by voicing their views in public. Jack Marshall, the acting prime minister of New Zealand, issued a statement on 14 April, expressing his 'earnest hope that the present bloodshed in East Pakistan will soon cease and that with goodwill on all sides Pakistan's political and military leaders can renew their attempt to reach agreement by negotiation and compromise'.[6] Australia went further than any other western country, stopping just short of an open condemnation that might be construed as 'intervention'. Speaking in the Australian House of Representatives on 22 April, Prime Minister McMahon expressed the 'view' that ' . . . there should be no more loss of life' and that 'the leaders of the Awami League should be given full authority civilly to represent their people in the Constituent Assembly of Pakistan'.[7]

The Soviet Union was the only major power to respond positively to India's appeal in April. Though its message was couched in terms of human rights, the Soviet position was primarily based on political calculation. Hoping to draw India into a closer relationship, Moscow had decided in 1970 to end its earlier policy of balancing its presence in India and Pakistan. Thus, when the South Asian crisis erupted in 1971, Moscow immediately threw its weight behind India. On 2 April, President Podgorny wrote to Yahya Khan as a 'true friend', to make an 'insistent appeal' for an immediate halt of the 'bloodshed and repression against the population in East Pakistan and for turning to methods of a peaceful political settlement'. Podgorny said that the Soviet Union was guided by the Universal Declaration of Human Rights and concern for the 'friendly people of Pakistan'.[8] Significantly, the draft of the letter was shared with India before its dispatch and its text was made public immediately after its delivery to Islamabad.

India also received unexpected support from two states with which it had yet to establish diplomatic ties – the German Democratic Republic (GDR) and Israel. India maintained trade and consular ties with GDR but had refrained from establishing diplomatic relations, mindful of the sensitivities of the larger and more prosperous Federal Republic of Germany (FRG). Under the Hallstein Doctrine, the FRG proclaimed that it would regard recognition of the GDR by any foreign state (other than the 'occupying power', USSR) as an 'unfriendly act', with the implied threat of terminating diplomatic ties with that state. The GDR perceived an opportunity for expediting diplomatic ties with India (and establishing ties with a new Bangladesh state) in the South Asian crisis. Thus, in May, it extended an invitation to the foreign minister of the Bangladesh government-in-exile and received him with full protocol honours.

India had not established diplomatic ties with Israel, apprehensive of Arab reactions. However, India had extended formal recognition to the state of Israel as early as in 1950, whereas Pakistan had not. Unlike Pakistan, which questioned the right of existence of the Jewish state,

India bore no animosity towards Israel, and the two countries occasionally cooperated with each other through clandestine channels. In 1962 and 1965, India had used these channels to secure certain military supplies from Israel.

Towards the end of June, Israel issued a strongly worded condemnation of the Pakistani 'genocide' in 'East Bengal'. Speaking in the Knesset, Foreign Minister Abba Eban condemned the 'terrible acts perpetrated by the Pakistani army in East Bengal', which had resulted in a 'human tragedy amounting to genocide'. 'The Jewish people, which has suffered much sorrow and misery in its history,' he said, 'must be especially aware of and sympathetic to human suffering wherever it may be, and the State of Israel cannot stand aside inactive, when faced with a disaster engulfing masses of humanity.'[9]

These were not empty words. In August, India approached an international arms dealer with close connections to Israel, Shlomo Zabludowicz, in order to obtain urgently heavy mortars and ammunition required for supporting Mukti Bahini cross-border operations. The items were in short supply, and urgent deliveries could be made only by releases from Israel Defence Force stocks and by diverting production intended for Iran. Thanks to the benevolent interest taken by Prime Minister Golda Meir, the Israeli authorities provided the necessary clearances. The urgently required items were airlifted to India.[10]

United Nations

India had no great expectations of the United Nations. Nevertheless, on 29 March – within four days of the launch of Operation Searchlight – Ambassador Samar Sen, India's Permanent Representative at the United Nations, handed over a note to UN Secretary General U Thant, drawing his attention to the 'brutality with which the Pakistan army is suppressing the struggle for legitimate rights and aspirations of the majority of the people of Pakistan'. The note requested the secretary general to take an initiative to 'stop the mass butchery', arrange for sending an International Red Cross team to East Pakistan, and organize relief for the Bangladeshis who had fled to India, given the 'unexpected large-scale flight of refugees' to the country. U Thant replied that he was confronted by two 'insuperable obstacles' – the insistence of member states that the secretary general had no right to interfere in their internal affairs, and 'lack of authoritative information' concerning the situation. He advised Sen to directly approach the International Red Cross.[11] Thereupon, Sen circulated his demarche as a press release.

Sen, a highly skilled diplomat, could hardly have entertained any expectation that the secretary general would take initiatives that were certain to be viewed by Pakistan as interference in its internal affairs. An appeal to Pakistan to end the 'mass butchery', or the dispatch of an uninvited Red Cross team to the country, would clearly have attracted a strong reaction from Pakistan. Nor could the secretary general be expected to organize relief operations in India for what was still a *prospective* problem, by Sen's own account. Sen's real purpose was to give the widest possible *publicity* to the Indian appeal, and he achieved this aim by circulating his demarche as a press release.

As the stream of refugees turned into a torrent, the prospective problem soon became a grim reality. On 23 April, India requested the UN secretary general for international assistance to ease the immense refugee burden which had been suddenly thrust on the country as a result of the brutal Pakistani crackdown in East Bengal. In response to the request, U Thant designated Prince Sadruddin Aga Khan, the UN high commissioner for refugees, to act as the 'focal point' for relief operations by UN agencies in India and East Pakistan. With the secretary general's concurrence, Sadruddin expanded his mandate to include a 'good offices' role for the purpose of facilitating repatriation of the refugees. Sadruddin went to great lengths to ensure that the relief operations involved no implicit criticism of Pakistani actions. He determinedly turned a blind eye to the political root cause of the refugee exodus, arguing that it 'may be difficult to assess what precisely made these people leave. There may be people who are fleeing because they are afraid of famine . . . it would be absolutely futile to determine whether or not people left because of well-founded fear of persecution and therefore come under the mandate [of the UN high commissioner for refugees].' Replying to questions from the press as to whether the governments he had contacted were prepared to intervene with Islamabad in order to create an atmosphere of security that would enable the refugees to return to their homes, the high commissioner replied: 'There is one fundamental problem: that is respect due to state sovereignty . . . It is not for me to talk about any means which might be employed to influence a sovereign government.'[12] Sadruddin did not explain how he could facilitate repatriation of the refugees without ascertaining why they had fled from their homes in the first instance.

At the end of May, India drew the attention of the UN Economic and Social Council to the 'violation of human rights on an unprecedented scale' in 'East Bengal'. 'Unless . . . the international community is prepared to examine violations of such obligations undertaken by States and take whatever remedial measures may be necessary, all that we have said for the protection of human rights and fundamental freedoms becomes a mockery,' declared Ambassador Sen. He appealed to the international community to address the violation of human rights in East Bengal, to call upon Pakistan to restore normalcy, and to assist in humanitarian relief operations for the refugees in India. He emphasized that the '. . . subject is of international concern and international action alone will solve it. It is not an Indo-Pakistan problem, although India is immediately affected by the large influx of refugees.'[13] Despite Sen's eloquent appeal, the UN Economic and Social Council kept its attention narrowly focused on the question of humanitarian relief and on the report submitted to the body by the UN high commissioner for refugees.

Mid-May to October 1971

Until mid-May, the aim of the Indian campaign was to draw international attention to the 'genocide' and massive violation of human rights by

Pakistan, call for restoration of 'normalcy' in 'East Bengal', highlight the plight of the refugees and seek international support for refugee relief measures, pending their voluntary return to their homeland. By mid-May, as the refugee influx approached 3 million, India began to bring into focus a new dimension of the problem – the threat to India's security resulting from the massive inflow of refugees.

On 13 May, the Indian prime minister wrote to several world leaders, drawing their attention to the security dimension of the crisis. In her letter to President Nixon, for example, she pointed to the 'grave security risk' posed by the presence of nearly 3 million refugees in 'politically the most sensitive parts of India', areas that 'can very easily become explosive'. She pointed specifically to the 'dangers of a link-up between the extremists in the two Bengals'. The refugee influx, she stated, 'constitutes a grave security risk which no responsible government can allow to develop'. She concluded by appealing to Nixon to persuade the Pakistani military junta to give up its policy of repression.[14]

On 24 May, Indira Gandhi spelled out the security implications in an important statement in parliament:

> What was claimed to be an internal problem of Pakistan, has also become an internal problem for India . . . Pakistan cannot be allowed to seek a solution of its political or other problems at the expense of India and on Indian soil . . . [Pakistan's reign of terror in "Bangla Desh" is] threatening the peace and stability [of India] . . . Conditions must be created to stop any further influx of refugees and to ensure their early return under credible guarantees for their future safety and well-being . . . If the world does not take heed, we shall be constrained to take all measures as may be necessary to ensure our own security . . . The Great Powers have a special responsibility. If they exercise their power rightly and expeditiously then only can we look forward to durable peace in our sub-continent. But if they fail – and I sincerely hope they will not – then the suppression of human rights, the uprooting of people, and the continued homelessness of vast numbers of human beings will threaten peace.[15]

India had previously confined its position, in its international appeals, to the violation of human rights and democratic principles and the need for humanitarian assistance. Indira Gandhi now brought up the question of peace and security and the need to prevent Pakistan from 'exporting' its domestic problems to India. If the international community, and the Great Powers in particular, failed to meet their responsibilities, India would have the right to deal with the threat, in self-defence.

This political message was elaborated as a legal doctrine later in the year. On 3 November, the Indian representative in the UN Sixth (Legal) Committee, the distinguished jurist Nagendra Singh, called for a comprehensive definition of 'aggression' and 'self-defence':

> [A] definition of aggression excluding indirect aggression would be incomplete and, therefore, dangerous . . . There could be a unique type of bloodless aggression resulting from a vast flow of millions of human beings forced to flee into another country. If this vast invasion of unarmed men in totally unmanageable proportions were to not only impair the economic and political well-being of the receiving victim but to threaten its very existence . . . it would have to be categorised as aggression . . . [W]hat would be the concept of self-defence [in] such an eventuality?[16]

In June and July, cabinet ministers were dispatched to all the continents to explain and seek support for India's position that the refugee exodus had precipitated not only a humanitarian crisis but also a threat to its peace and security; that the refugee flow must be urgently halted and reversed; and that this required restoration of normalcy and a political resolution acceptable to the people of 'East Bengal'. The envoys emphasized the responsibility of the international community to press Pakistan to move in this direction. They called for a halt to arms supplies as well as economic aid to Pakistan, with the exception only of humanitarian relief under international supervision. Foreign Minister Swaran Singh instructed Indian diplomats to 'plug this once, twice, three, four times. Start from the lower rung. Go up to the higher levels.

Come to the lower level and try at all levels . . . We have [a] very definite objective and you have to prepare the ground.'[17]

Foreign minister's tour of the western capitals

In June, Swaran Singh himself visited the most important western capitals – Washington, London, Paris, Bonn and Ottawa. Two parallel developments had a bearing on the outcome of his tour. By June, public opinion in the major western democracies was strongly critical of Pakistan, thanks to the ceaseless efforts of human rights activists and regular press and TV exposure of the atrocities committed by the Pakistani army in East Bengal. Public opinion in several western countries favoured suspension of economic aid and military sales to Pakistan – though, as we shall see, the impact on official policy differed widely on the two sides of the Atlantic.

The second development was a World Bank-International Monetary Fund (IMF) team report on economic aid for Pakistan. By the end of April 1971, Pakistan was confronted by a severe economic crisis. Operation Searchlight had resulted in massive economic disruption in the eastern wing. Jute exports, which accounted for almost half of Pakistan's foreign exchange earnings, came to a near-total halt. By the end of the month, Islamabad was obliged to declare a moratorium on debt servicing and to request a meeting of the Aid Consortium for Pakistan to discuss plans for long-term rescheduling of its debts. A joint World Bank–IMF team visited Islamabad and Dhaka in June to form an assessment. A senior Pakistani civil servant provides a vignette of the situation prevailing in Dhaka on the night of the governor's dinner in honour of the team.

> While drinks were being served in the drawing room . . . sounds of bomb explosions, which did not seem to be very far off, were heard at regular intervals . . . By the time we had moved to the dining-table, shooting had been added to the bomb explosions and the chatter of machine-gun fire almost drowned the polite conversation.[18]

Not surprisingly, the team arrived at a negative conclusion. They found that an 'all-pervasive fear' and a 'severely damaged' infrastructure stood in the way of economic revival; that Islamabad had 'little understanding' of the problems of reviving growth.[19] When the Aid Consortium met on 21 June, it declined to provide new aid to Pakistan, except for humanitarian food aid to stave off famine in East Pakistan.

Britain

When Mrs Gandhi's letter of 13 May was received in London, the Foreign Office offered the pragmatic advice that 'our interest lies in retaining with Mrs. Gandhi as close and satisfactory a working relationship as we can'.[20] The British government was also under strong public and parliamentary pressure to take a strong stand against the brutal suppression of the people of East Bengal. Britain had already banned export of lethal military supplies to Pakistan in April (though exports of non-lethal items continued). In June, ahead of the Aid Consortium for Pakistan meeting, London decided to suspend further economic aid to Pakistan. Prime Minister Heath wrote to Gen. Yahya warning that 'there can be no future for a united Pakistan unless you can resume the process [negotiations with the Awami League] which you started'.[21] Replying to Mrs Gandhi's letter, the British prime minister said that he had impressed on Yahya the importance of halting the refugee exodus and the need for 'early political advance'. He promised assistance for the refugees in India – but then introduced a discordant note by referring to the need for 'arranging, *if possible*, for their ultimate return home [emphasis added]'.[22]

Swaran Singh's principal objective in London, therefore, was to disabuse the British of the notion that India might agree to permanently host the refugees. When he met Heath on 21 June, he explained the strain on India's security caused by the presence of the refugees and stated emphatically that India insisted that all the refugees must return to their homes. This required a political settlement acceptable to the

Awami League. It was essential that Mujib be released from prison and talks be held with him. Heath's response was positive. He said he 'fully understood' India's position and asked Swaran Singh to assure Mrs Gandhi that Britain '. . . would continue to do all we could to persuade President Yahya Khan to bring about a political solution as quickly as possible'. Within a day of his meeting with Swaran Singh, the British prime minister told the Pakistani high commissioner that Islamabad 'should understand the real fear felt in India about the instability that could be caused by the refugee problem'.[23]

France

In Paris, too, Swaran Singh achieved significant results. France had earlier adhered to a very narrow interpretation of the principle of non-interference. Thus, when Swaran Singh took up the question of the refugees with Foreign Minister Schumann on 12 June, the latter took the position that while the humanitarian question of refugee relief was an international concern, the question of a political solution was an internal problem of Pakistan. Undeterred by this setback, Swaran Singh seized the opportunity offered by the presence of President Pompidou at an official luncheon. He was able to persuade the French president to take a more sympathetic view of the Indian position. The outcome was reflected in the official French statement issued after the talks, which said that Schumann had 'expressed the wish that no effort be neglected to provide a political solution to this crisis which stops the flood of refugees and enables their return to their homes'.[24] Paris had earlier informed New Delhi that France had not entered into any new contracts for arms supplies to Pakistan after its crackdown in its eastern division. Towards the end of June, France also conveyed its decision to suspend arms deliveries even on old contracts.[25]

Federal Republic of Germany

When Swaran Singh took up his brief with his German counterpart in Bonn, he ran into the usual wall of 'non-interference'. Foreign Minister Scheel readily agreed that it was necessary to normalize the political situation in East Pakistan, but he insisted that this was an internal matter for the Pakistanis. Bonn was ready to work within the Aid to Pakistan Consortium to suspend further economic assistance, but not to exert 'political pressure'. Chancellor Brandt lent a more sympathetic ear to Swaran Singh's representation and assured him of his government's willingness to contribute to a solution 'within the scope of our possibilities'.[26] As promised, Bonn voted in favour of suspending fresh aid to Pakistan in the Consortium. Under pressure of public opinion, it also imposed an arms embargo in September, but blurred its political implications by applying the embargo to *both* Pakistan and India!

Canada

The Indian foreign minister found little comfort in Canada, a country that faced its own secessionist problem in the French-speaking province of Quebec. The Quebec problem appears to have influenced not only Canadian policy but also Ottawa's comprehension of the East Bengal situation. A foreign ministry memorandum prepared on the eve of Swaran Singh's visit summed up the Canadian appreciation of the situation. 'Our judgment is that the precipitate withdrawal of the Pakistan Army would probably turn East Pakistan over to chaos . . . What is needed from the Pakistan Government is a resumption of the search for an agreed political solution and we have been encouraged by recent indications that they are moving in this direction.'[27] Based on this grotesque assessment, Canadian policy not only eschewed any criticism of Pakistan but even insisted that 'aid [to Pakistan] should be without strings'.[28] This was the line taken by Foreign Minister Sharp in his meeting with Swaran Singh on 13 June. Ottawa refused to budge from its inflexible interpretation of 'non-interference'.

United States

In June 1971, a strange situation prevailed in Washington. Through Byzantine manoeuvres, the White House was keeping the State Department in the dark about its most important foreign policy initiative – its opening to China. Unknown to Secretary of State William Rogers, Nixon had been sending secret feelers to the Chinese leaders since 1969 through Yahya Khan and President Ceausescu of Romania. Finally, on 27 April 1971, at the end of a long-drawn-out exchange of secret messages, the Pakistani ambassador in Washington, Agha Hilaly, met Kissinger to deliver a verbal message from Zhou to Nixon. Zhou conveyed China's 'willingness to receive publicly in Beijing a special envoy of the President of the US'.[29] At the time of Swaran Singh's visit in June 1971, unknown to the State Department, preparations were in progress for Kissinger's secret trip to Beijing in the following month, via Pakistan. Rogers and his officials were unaware of the White House's China initiative and its fallout (for real or imaginary reasons) on US policy towards Pakistan.

As we saw in Chapter 2, Kissinger drew the attention of senior officials in early March to Nixon's 'special relationship' with Yahya, terminating a discussion on the question of advising the Pakistan president to exercise restraint. In April, in the face of strong media and Congressional revulsion at Pakistan's brutal military crackdown, the Senior Review Group chaired by Kissinger decided only to place a hold on military supplies and new loans to Pakistan, pending a decision by the president. The State Department was also aware of Nixon's strong dislike of the Indian prime minister. A senior State Department official recalls, 'When Mrs Gandhi's actions ran counter to White House desires, Nixon's customary sobriquet of "that bitch" was replaced by more unprintable epithets.'[30] The officials were, however, still in the dark about the implications of opening to China.

Against a background of mounting criticism of Pakistani atrocities in the media and Congress, the State Department took two provisional measures, subject to subsequent presidential approval. The first concerned military supplies. In 1968, Nixon had granted Pakistan a 'one-time exception' to the embargo on military sales to India and Pakistan imposed after the 1965 war. The employment of US-supplied tanks against unarmed Bengali civilians was strongly condemned in the US media and Congress. In April, the State Department imposed a temporary 'hold' on military supplies for Pakistan under the 'one-time exception', pending a White House decision. This infuriated the White House, and the State Department's efforts to close loopholes in the matter were thwarted by Nixon and Kissinger. The State Department also planned to cut economic aid and PL 480 foodgrain shipments to Pakistan for projects that could no longer be implemented because of the prevailing conditions in East Pakistan. Interim measures were taken towards this end, subject to subsequent presidential approval. These provisional measures aroused fury in the White House. Kissinger took strong exception to these measures, pointing once again to the president's 'special relationship' with Yahya.[31]

On 28 April, Kissinger obtained Nixon's approval for a policy that would: (a) allow shipments of non-lethal items to continue, while holding back shipments of 'controversial items in order not to provoke the Congress to force cutting off all aid'; (b) continue to process development loans for projects that had not been disrupted by the civil war; and (c) continue PL 480 assistance without stipulating whether it was destined for the eastern or western wing of Pakistan. This package was supposedly designed as 'an effort to help Yahya achieve a negotiated settlement'. Nixon's approval came with a handwritten note that read: '*To all hands. Don't squeeze Yahya at this time.*' '*Don't*' was underlined three times.[32]

In June 1971, it was, indeed, necessary for the White House to keep Yahya in good humour, since he was still its principal channel of communication with China. This was, however, only a secondary consideration. The primary factor was Nixon's personal dislike of the Indian prime minister and his regard for the Pakistani military dictator. This is evident from the fact that the White House 'tilt' in favour of Pakistan became even more marked after July, by when a direct channel of communication had been established between the White House and Beijing.

Swaran Singh met with Rogers and Nixon on 16 June. In his meeting with Rogers, Swaran Singh offered a 'reasoned and restrained analysis', in the words of his American interlocutors.[33] He emphasized that the first requirement was to end the military crackdown. The movement of refugees to India must be brought to a halt and all of the refugees must return to their homes. This required a political solution reflecting the will of the people, as distinct from a civilian regime deriving its authority from the Pakistani army. Asked if this would entail an independent Bangladesh, Swaran Singh replied reassuringly that India was not committed to any particular outcome. He urged Washington to use its influence with Islamabad to make it see that it was in Pakistan's own interest to install a government reflecting the will of the people. This offered some prospect of preserving the unity of the country.

Rogers said that the US could encourage Yahya to seek a political solution, but it could not ask him to accept secession. He said that the US had made no military shipments to Pakistan and would keep this matter under careful review. He observed that economic aid should not be used to gain political leverage. Countering him, Swaran Singh pointed out that in the case of Pakistan, economic aid strengthened the military; it therefore amounted to interference in its internal affairs. Swaran Singh urged the US to 'postpone' economic aid to Pakistan until Islamabad had taken corrective political action. Summing up the discussions, Assistant Secretary of State Sisco observed that the US and Indian views were 'very close'. The US would help India to cope with the refugee problem, while recognizing that this was only a palliative and that the real answer was a political accommodation.

Later, when discussions continued over a working lunch, Sisco mentioned that the US had been very careful about economic aid to Pakistan and there had been a substantial holding operation in this respect. During the conversation at the table, Swaran Singh briefly alluded to the possibility of an alternative track. He said that though India was pursuing the international diplomatic route, he feared a situation might be created necessitating some other means of persuasion. This was his only reference to a possible armed conflict. The Indian foreign minister created a favourable impression of restraint and sobriety on his State Department interlocutors.[34]

If the discussions between Rogers and Swaran Singh were marked by relative candour, the same cannot be said for the latter's meeting with Nixon. Briefing Nixon before the meeting, Kissinger told the president, 'I am just trying to keep them [the Indians] from attacking for 3 months' (presumably because the Pakistani channel to China would become redundant by then). He advised Nixon to give the Indians a pleasant surprise by announcing a major new contribution to refugee relief and to assure Swaran Singh that he was working on Yahya in his own way to encourage a political resolution, but overt US pressure would be counterproductive. 'It's a little duplicitous,' explained Kissinger, 'but these bastards understand that.'[35]

Concealing his 'tilt' towards Pakistan, Nixon listened to the Indian foreign minister's presentation with feigned sympathy. He said he was 'keenly aware' of the problem and the 'enormous agony' it had caused. Public pressure on Pakistan would be counterproductive, but other methods were also available. He asked the foreign minister to convey to Mrs Gandhi 'on a completely off-the-record basis' that 'I will use all the persuasive methods that I can [with Yahya Khan], but I must use them in the way that I think is the most effective.' He also informed Swaran Singh that he had decided to provide seventy million dollars for refugee support, adding that he recognized this was only a temporary palliative and that it would not solve the basic problem of getting the refugees to return to their homes.[36]

Nixon succeeded in misleading even such a shrewd and experienced statesman as Swaran Singh. Addressing a group of Indian diplomats in London at the end of his tour, Swaran Singh was upbeat about his talks with Nixon. '[The] present position is that we have got greater support in the White House as compared to the State Department.' he said.[37] Swaran Singh was soon to be disillusioned. In July, after Kissinger's dramatic visit to Beijing, the outlines of a Washington–Islamabad–Beijing nexus became evident.

The Indian foreign minister's itinerary included all the three western countries that occupied permanent seats in the Security Council. His discussions in London and Paris proved fruitful; in Washington, he drew a blank. London and Paris were receptive to public opinion. They also saw the Bangladesh crisis as a regional, South Asian issue and took into account the fact that their interests in India outweighed their interests in Pakistan. In Washington, media and Congressional opinion was similar to that of the British press and parliament. State Department perspectives, too, were not dissimilar to those of the Foreign Office. At least in the early months of the crisis, the State Department saw the question as essentially a regional issue and recognized that US interests in India outweighed those in Pakistan.[38] However, the White House was determined to pursue a very different policy, partly due to Nixon's personal prejudices and partly because it perceived – or misperceived – the problem as a Cold War issue.

United Nations

Meanwhile, the UN high commissioner for refugees, Prince Sadruddin Aga Khan, sought an expanded role for himself, beyond that of mobilizing refugee relief. On a visit to India and Pakistan in June 1971, he proposed establishing a United Nations High Commissioner for Refugees (UNHCR) presence in the border areas – in some of the refugee camps on the Indian side as well as in some refugee reception centres on the Pakistan side. Sadruddin asserted that a UNHCR presence at the border would help facilitate repatriation of the refugees. Pakistan agreed to accept the presence of a few UN officials in Dhaka, but not outside the provincial capital, fearing that the officials might witness scenes of oppression and brutality. New Delhi rejected the proposal outright, since it was unclear how the presence of these officials in the Indian border areas could facilitate repatriation. Indeed, the proposal seemed to imply that India was obstructing the refugees from returning home! India pointed out that New Delhi–based UNHCR officials were in any case permitted to visit the camps.

Sadruddin took great pains in his public statements to affect the neutral posture appropriate to a UN official, but he revealed his bias in favour of West Pakistan during a visit to Washington at the end of June. In a meeting with Secretary of State Rogers, Sadruddin said that India was providing full support to the 'Mukti Fauj' (Mukti Bahini) and insisting that a political solution involving Mujibur Rahman was a necessary condition for the voluntary return of the refugees. He urged applying pressure on India to moderate its position on the need for a prior political settlement, to force it to control and crack down on the Bangladesh elements, and stop infiltration of the Mukti Bahini across the border. He surmised that India's desire to protect this infiltration from foreign eyes explained the country's rejection of his proposal to station his officers in the border camps. He said he was not discouraged by the Pakistani response; Pakistan, he said, would agree to his proposal if India agreed to accept UNHCR personnel on its side of the border.[39]

Despite India's outright rejection of Sadruddin's suggestion, his proposal was revived in a modified form by the UN secretary general. On 19 July, U Thant suggested to India and Pakistan that UNHCR representatives be accepted on a trial basis in two or three selected areas on each side of the border, in order to 'ascertain whether in practice it would serve a useful purpose in facilitating the process of repatriation [of refugees]'. India rejected the proposal, pointing out that UNHCR officials based in New Delhi were provided every facility for visiting the refugee camps. The proposed induction of UNHCR representatives on the Indian side of the border would therefore serve no purpose and would only deflect attention from the urgent need to restore normalcy in East Bengal.[40]

The secretary general himself had few illusions about the effectiveness of the proposal. He did not share Sadruddin's bias and he recognized that the root cause of the problem lay in the failure of the Pakistan government to seek a political reconciliation with the Awami League. U Thant had become deeply concerned about the resultant threat to international peace. However, he felt bound by Article 2(7) of the UN Charter, which debarred the United Nations from intervening in 'matters which are essentially within the domestic jurisdiction of any state'. Hence, on 20 July – the day after he suggested to India and Pakistan the stationing of UNHCR representatives on both sides of the border – he sent a memorandum to the president of the Security Council, drawing his attention to the international security dimension of the issue. It was unusual for the secretary general to address the Security Council on a subject that did not figure on its agenda, but U Thant explained that he had 'reluctantly come to the conclusion that the time is past when the international community can continue to stand by, watching the situation deteriorate and hoping the relief programmes, humanitarian efforts and good intentions will be enough to turn the tide of human misery and potential disaster'. He drew attention to the 'lack of substantial progress toward a political reconciliation and the consequent effect on law and order and public administration in East Pakistan'. U Thant pointed out that the 'conflict between the principles of territorial integrity of States and of self-determination has often before in history given rise to fratricidal strife . . . In the present case there is an additional element of danger for the crisis is unfolding in the context of the long-standing and unresolved differences between India and Pakistan.'[41]

By characterizing the issue as a question of self-determination, U Thant sought to overcome the obstacle posed by the principle of non-intervention. The secretary general's appeal failed to move the Council. His invocation of the principle of self-determination led to a piquant situation. It drew a negative response from Pakistan, the traditional champion of the principle in the context of Kashmir, while it was endorsed by India. New Delhi observed that the 'conflict between the principles of territorial integrity of States and self-determination is particularly relevant in the situation prevailing in East Pakistan where the majority of the population is being suppressed by a minority military regime which has refused to recognise the results of the elections held by them only in December last year and had launched a massive campaign of massacre, genocide and cultural suppression'.[42] India formally invoked the principle of self-determination in December, after it had accorded formal recognition to the People's Democratic Republic of Bangladesh.

Failing to activate the Security Council, the secretary general ill-advisedly embarked on an initiative which he had himself previously rejected. On 20 October, he offered his 'good offices' to India and Pakistan. Yahya Khan promptly accepted the offer, inviting him to visit the subcontinent to discuss mutual troop withdrawals and the stationing of UN observers along the border to oversee these withdrawals and ensure the maintenance of peace. Equally predictably, Indira Gandhi rejected the offer – and not without a trace of asperity. 'The root of the problem,' she wrote, 'is the fate of the seventy-five million people of East Bengal and their inalienable rights . . . To side-track this main problem, and to convert it into an Indo-Pakistan dispute, can only aggravate tensions.'

The annual session of the UN General Assembly opened in the third week of September, in accordance with tradition. By then the Pakistani army had slaughtered hundreds of thousands of unarmed civilians and driven several million people across the Indian border. The reaction of the international community to these outrages may be judged from the General Debate in the Assembly, in which member states survey global developments from their perspective. Of the 117 countries that participated in the General Debate, less than half (fifty-five countries, excluding India and Pakistan) thought it necessary to refer to the events in East Bengal. Of these, twenty-four dwelt only on the humanitarian problems, excluding any reference to the political dimension. No more than eight countries referred specifically to the human rights question, and only four called for a political solution in consultation with the elected representatives of the people.[43]

The international community was ready to respond to appeals for refugee aid, though not on a scale commensurate with requirements. In some of the major western democracies, public opinion reinforced by Indian diplomacy led governments to impose an arms embargo and suspend economic aid to Pakistan. Even Nixon was unable to openly resume military supplies and had to seek recourse to clandestine means of evading the arms embargo. Most Third World countries looked on with indifference while a military dictatorship slaughtered hundreds of thousands of innocent men and women and drove out several millions from their homeland. The human rights of the people of Bangladesh, including their basic right to life and the right to self-determination, would gain recognition only after the success of the armed struggle.

8

A 'Geopolitical Revolution'

The Bangladesh liberation struggle coincided with a radical transformation in US policy towards China. This change – described as a 'geopolitical revolution' in Kissinger's memoirs – would have unpredictable implications for Nixon's policy in the South Asia crisis, posing a severe challenge for Indian diplomacy.

The 'geopolitical revolution' had its origins in the imperatives of an American withdrawal from Vietnam, combined with the opportunities thrown up by the sharp increase in tensions between the Soviet Union and China following bloody clashes on their disputed boundary in the Ussuri River in March 1969. Nixon and Kissinger discerned a double opportunity in the deepening Sino-Soviet confrontation. It gave the United States potential leverage with both Moscow and Beijing and an opportunity to construct a triangular relationship, in which each of the communist powers had an important stake in closer relations with the United States. 'Policy emerges when concept encounters opportunity,' Kissinger reflects in his memoirs. 'Such an occasion arose when Soviet and Chinese troops clashed in the frozen Siberian tundra along a river of which none of us had heard . . . From then on . . . we moved without further hesitation toward a momentous change in global diplomacy.'[1]

In China too, the Sino-Soviet confrontation precipitated a reappraisal of foreign policy. In the chaotic conditions prevailing during the Cultural

Revolution, Mao had set up an advisory committee on international affairs composed, strangely, of four celebrated marshals whom he had sent into political exile. The marshals – Chen Yi, Ye Jianying, Xu Xiangqian and Nie Rongzhen – had been consigned to 'investigation and study' in industrial factories in the capital. When their advice was sought after the Sino-Soviet clashes on the Xinjiang border later in 1969, Chen Yi and Ye Jianying recommended that China should play the 'card of the United States' to meet the Soviet threat. In September, the marshals suggested revival of the suspended Sino-US ambassadorial talks in Warsaw when the 'time was ripe'. Chen Yi also confided to premier Zhou En-lai his 'unconventional thought' that in addition to reopening the Warsaw talks, China should also take the initiative to propose Sino-US talks at a ministerial or even higher level, '... so that basic and related problems in Sino-American relations can be solved'. These views seem to have coincided with Mao's own thinking. His personal physician, Dr Li Zhisui, recalls Mao's observation in August: 'Didn't our ancestors counsel negotiating with faraway countries while fighting with those that are near us?'[2]

In the words of the historian Margaret MacMillan: 'The times were ripe for each side [the US and China] to make a move toward the other. In both countries there were influential voices saying that the advantages of a relationship, even a cool one, outweighed continuing non-recognition. For each the other was a card to play against the common enemy, the Soviet Union.'[3]

Thus, by the end of 1969, the United States and China decided to reopen ambassadorial-level talks in Warsaw. On 20 January 1970, the first round of Sino-US talks under the Nixon administration was held in Warsaw. At the next meeting, on 20 February, the Chinese charge d'affaires, acting on instructions from premier Zhou En-lai and with Mao's approval, informed the US ambassador to Poland, Walter Stoessel, that Beijing was willing to receive a minister or high-level envoy representing the president in order to explore solutions to the 'fundamental questions' in Sino-US relations. The Chinese charge d'affaires emphasized that a resolution of the Taiwan issue was fundamental to improvement of bilateral relations, but he added that the Chinese side was also prepared to consider any ideas and suggestions that the US might wish to offer.[4]

Though there was general agreement in Washington on the need for an opening to China, Kissinger and the State Department did not see eye to eye on the preconditions for a high-level visit. The State Department view was that a high-level visit should be undertaken only after the Chinese had provided some indication that they were prepared to meet US concerns in Asia. In the absence of such an indication, there was a 'serious risk of our being used by Peking for its own purposes in its relations with the Soviets without any compensating gains [for the US]', particularly in South-east Asia. Moreover, an unprepared visit could create serious complications in US relations with friendly Asian countries.

Kissinger held a contrary view. 'The visit of an American emissary to Peking was bound to spark a geopolitical revolution; the effect on Hanoi alone would be traumatic,' he believed.[5] Kissinger was dismissive of the Warsaw channel, which he regarded as unproductive – a view that ignored the fact that the channel had yielded the sought-after invitation for a high-level visit. The real problem with the Warsaw channel was that it was operated by the State Department. In the ensuing inter-departmental power play, Secretary of State Rogers was no match for Kissinger. Nixon fell in with Kissinger's proposal to set up a secret channel of communication with Beijing, leaving the State Department in the dark. The choice of channel was to have momentous consequences for South Asia.

The White House launched its China initiative in the deepest secrecy in October 1970. On 25 October, Nixon asked Yahya Khan to convey a message to the Chinese leadership during his scheduled visit to Beijing in November. The US president's message was that he regarded a Sino-US rapprochement as essential, that the United States would never join hands with the Soviet Union in a condominium directed against China, and that it was prepared to send a high-level emissary to China. A similar message was sent through President Ceausescu of Romania the next day. The State Department was kept in ignorance. Secretary of State Rogers had no inkling of the move for the next nine months, till July 1971.

Zhou's response first arrived through the Pakistani channel on 8 December. China would welcome a visit by a special envoy of President Nixon to discuss 'vacation of Chinese territories called Taiwan'. A month later, the Romanian ambassador conveyed a similar message from Zhou, with an important additional element – Beijing was also prepared to receive President Nixon himself. The White House replied through the same two channels. The US was prepared to send a special envoy to discuss the entire range of outstanding issues, including Taiwan. On 27 April, Washington finally received the Chinese response through the Pakistani channel. Beijing was willing to 'publicly receive' a special envoy of the president, or even the president himself. Zhou suggested that arrangements for the visit could be made through the good offices of President Yahya Khan. On 10 May, Kissinger conveyed the US response to Pakistan's ambassador to the US, Agha Hilaly. Nixon was ready to accept Zhou's invitation to visit China, following a preparatory visit by Kissinger.[6] Yahya's role as an intermediary powerfully reinforced Nixon's pro-Pakistan leaning.

India and the superpowers (March–July)

A central element of India's grand strategy was the search for the support of at least one, and preferably both, of the superpowers. New Delhi hoped that pressure from the two superpowers would compel Pakistan to accept the legitimate demands of the elected representatives of the people of the eastern wing. Failing this, support from at least one of the superpowers would be needed to ensure adequate and timely delivery of military supplies, avert an unfavourable or untimely decision of the UN Security Council, and deter China from military intervention in support of Pakistan.

By the end of the 1960s, the Soviet Union had emerged as the principal supplier of military equipment to India. Shared concerns about Chinese intentions were one of the pillars on which Indo-Soviet relations rested. Relations were temporarily ruffled when the Soviet Union decided in June 1968 to sell arms to Pakistan in an effort to draw Islamabad away from its close ties to China, but Moscow soon came to recognize the futility of the exercise. Vigorous Indian protests elicited a Soviet assurance in October 1970 that arms sales to Pakistan would be discontinued.

While India relied on the Soviet Union for its defence requirements, it looked to the United States for economic aid. The United States was by far its principal source of economic aid. By 1971, however, India's economic development had reached a level where foreign aid, though important, was no longer a critical requirement, at least in the short term. Additionally, by 1971, the Green Revolution had freed India of its acute dependence on US PL 480 foodgrain deliveries. The intelligence agencies of the two countries had a modest programme of cooperation to monitor Chinese military movements in Tibet and nuclear tests in north-western China. Political ties came under strain in 1970, when the Nixon administration announced that it would provide armoured personnel carriers and replacement aircraft to Pakistan in a 'one-time exception' to its post-1965 policy of suspending arms sales to both India and Pakistan. Nevertheless, New Delhi expected Washington to maintain its traditionally supportive attitude in the event of a Chinese attack.

Moscow showed its hand without being asked. As we noted in Chapter 7, President Podgorny wrote to Yahya Khan on 2 April to convey his 'great alarm' over the use of armed force against the population of East Pakistan and the arrest of Mujibur Rahman and other Awami League leaders. The Soviet president appealed to Yahya to immediately stop the 'bloodshed and repression' in East Pakistan and seek a peaceful political settlement. Significantly, the Soviets consulted D.P. Dhar, then Indian ambassador in Moscow, before sending the letter.

Encouraged by this development, Indira Gandhi decided to take the Soviet leaders into confidence. Ambassador Dhar called on Kosygin to convey an oral message from the Indian prime minister. She was facing a 'terrible dilemma'. She was resisting heavy pressure from members of parliament and the general public to accord immediate recognition to the newly proclaimed state of Bangladesh. The leaders of the Bangladesh movement, who had appealed to her for help, were basically nationalists, but she feared that the leadership of the movement, with the passage of time, might slip out of their hands and pass into the hands of pro-China factions. China was 'playing a double-faced game', offering public support to Islamabad while working clandestinely to increase its influence in East Pakistan. India was 'deeply concerned about what China might do'. Thus, it was a 'matter of the highest importance' that the struggle in East Pakistan be brought to an end as soon as possible.

Dhar was instructed to sound out the Soviet leadership on two questions. Was there any possibility of a joint Soviet–US initiative to bring the East Pakistan conflict to an early conclusion? If this was not possible, were the Soviets prepared to share with India the burden of sustaining the freedom struggle in East Pakistan?[7]

The Soviet response, delivered by its ambassador in Delhi, Nikolai Pegov, simply ignored the suggestion of a joint Soviet–US initiative. It expressed high appreciation for the 'friendly sincerity' of Mrs Gandhi's message and commended her for resisting domestic pressures for according diplomatic recognition to Bangladesh. It asserted that 'there are still some possibilities for inducing the military administration in Pakistan to abandon the use of arms in East Pakistan'. Moscow shared with New Delhi the draft of another appeal from Podgorny to Yahya Khan, and invited Indira Gandhi to offer suggestions regarding the text. Referring indirectly to India's concerns about China, Moscow stated that it was 'extremely important not to allow the development of a situation in which the events in East Pakistan would expand beyond the territory of Pakistan, harm the interests of peace in the region and lead to interference of third countries'. Finally, Moscow expressed its great satisfaction with the development of Indo–Soviet relations, adding cryptically that 'there are unused possibilities' for further strengthening these ties.

New Delhi was disappointed with this enigmatic reply and did not quite know what to make of it.[8] Though friendly in tone, it ignored the suggestion of a joint initiative by the two superpowers. Neither did it offer any reassurance of support against Chinese designs. Indian officials failed to read the hint in 'unused possibilities' for raising the level of bilateral ties. Moscow was referring to a proposal it had made in 1969 for a treaty of mutual cooperation between the USSR and India.

On 27 March, just before the last flicker of hope for a united, democratic Pakistan was extinguished, Foreign Secretary T.N. Kaul shared with US Ambassador Kenneth Keating his profound concern about the evolving situation. Kaul said that refugees had already begun to come across the border. He apprehended that the trickle would soon grow into a massive flood, imposing a huge burden on India. Would the United States agree to share the economic burden of providing relief to the refugees? Kaul also said that he feared the situation developing across the border might precipitate a security threat to India. He drew Keating's attention to the presence of extremist pro-Chinese elements in East Pakistan. China might decide to fish in troubled waters. The foreign secretary suggested that it might still not be too late for the United States to convey to the Pakistan government its hope for a peaceful solution to the East Pakistan problem.

Keating parried the question concerning refugee relief with the observation that it related to a hypothetical situation. He responded to Kaul's second question on the lines of the instructions sent to his colleague in Islamabad. He said that Washington viewed the conflict in East Pakistan as a domestic issue that should be resolved internally by the Pakistanis themselves.[9]

This negative response did not extinguish Indian hopes of attracting US support. As we have seen, in its first feelers to the Soviet Union, India broached the possibility of a joint US–Soviet initiative to bring the

East Pakistan conflict to an end as soon as possible. Moscow's response to this suggestion was a deafening silence.

Declassified US documents reveal what appears to have been a surprisingly optimistic Indian initiative. (Available Indian records provide no confirmation of this report, but it deserves notice nevertheless.) On 9 April, Kissinger chaired a meeting of the 40 Committee, the group of senior US officials responsible for overseeing clandestine operations, to consider an Indian request to the CIA for provision of unmarked small arms for the East Bengal freedom fighters. (The request, presumably from RAW, might have been prompted by the intelligence agency's knowledge of the Awami League's hopes for securing US support.) CIA Deputy Director General Cushman said the CIA had a secure channel through which deliveries could be arranged but, in his opinion, the operation could not be kept secret for very long. He added that the CIA director, Richard Helms, was not in favour of the project. When Kissinger commented that he assumed the Indians had sufficient stocks of small arms to meet the requirement, a CIA official explained that India did not have the required unmarked and unattributable weapons. Under Secretary of State John Irwin was 'reluctant' to accept the Indian request, and Assistant Secretary Joseph Sisco thought that the Indians were 'testing' the US. It was one thing, Sisco said, for the US to close its eyes to clandestine Indian support for the East Pakistan resistance movement, but quite another to actively collude with the Indians. Kissinger brought the discussion to an end by observing that the president would never approve the project.[10]

The American response to India's appeal for support to the refugees was more positive. Partly in order to counter Congressional and media criticism of its political inaction, Washington supported India's request for UN humanitarian assistance for the refugees and contributed to it through international relief agencies. Nixon ruled out direct assistance to India to avoid giving offence to Pakistan.[11] At the same time, Washington instructed Ambassador Keating to warn New Delhi that US aid for the refugees would be called into question if reports of Indian intentions of training and equipping Bangladesh freedom fighters on Indian soil turned out to be true. When Keating met Foreign Minister Swaran Singh on 3 May to convey the US decision to support international relief efforts, he also raised the question of India's reported involvement with the freedom fighters. Swaran Singh dismissed the reports as 'absolutely incorrect'.[12]

As we noted earlier, Mrs Gandhi had written to Nixon on 13 May, drawing his attention to the South Asian crisis. She had pointed out that the presence of almost 3 million refugees from 'East Bengal' on Indian soil posed not only an enormous economic burden but also a grave security risk for India. The stifling of democracy in East Bengal would inevitably strengthen extremist political elements there, posing the real danger of their linking up with their counterparts in West Bengal. She had appealed to the US president to use his influence with the rulers of Pakistan to stop the repression that had driven their citizens across the border and to ensure the safety of Sheikh Mujibur Rahman.[13] In reply, Nixon had informed the Indian prime minister of his decision to step up humanitarian assistance for the refugees. On the political issue, he said disingenuously that he was engaged in 'quiet diplomacy' to encourage Pakistan to seek a peaceful political accommodation and to restore conditions under which the refugee flow would stop and the refugees enabled to return to their homes.[14]

By the time this misleading response was composed, the Nixon–Kissinger 'tilt' towards Pakistan had hardened. Until 27 April, when Ambassador Hilaly delivered Zhou's message inviting the president or his envoy to visit Beijing and suggesting that the modalities could be worked out through the Pakistani channel, Pakistan had been only one of the two channels used by the White House for communicating with China. After 27 April, Pakistan became the sole channel of communication with China for the US. It was to provide the secret embarkation point for Kissinger's flight to Beijing. This strengthened the case for the 'tilt', if only temporarily. The Pakistani channel would become redundant after Kissinger's visit, during which he would establish a direct line of contact with Beijing.

This explains why Kissinger told Nixon, 'I am just trying to keep them [the Indians] from attacking for three months,' while briefing the president before meeting with Swaran Singh.[15] As recommended by Kissinger, Nixon took a 'duplicitous' line in his conversation with the Indian foreign minister and succeeded in seriously misleading him.

The illusion was shattered within a few days. On 22 June, the *New York Times* reported that despite the American embargo, two freighters were set to sail from New York with a cargo of military supplies for Pakistan. The quantities involved were modest, and in fact the shipments originated from a loophole in the export control regime, but they came as a shock to New Delhi, which had only a few days earlier received assurances that no arms were being delivered to Pakistan.

Kissinger in India

An Asian tour culminating in New Delhi and Islamabad provided the cover for Kissinger's secret trip to Beijing. In Islamabad, Kissinger would announce that he had developed a stomach ailment in the subcontinent – a mishap not uncommon here among visitors from the western world – and then disappear from public view for a few days. A Pakistan Air Force plane would fly him to China in the greatest secrecy.

During his brief sojourn in India (6–7 July), Kissinger met the prime minister, the ministers of external affairs and defence, as well as Indira Gandhi's chief aide, P.N. Haksar. His principal aims were to assuage Indian outrage over the US arms shipments to Pakistan; to assess Indian intentions in East Pakistan; and to gently prepare his interlocutors for the impending breakthrough in Sino-US relations. Kissinger informed the Indian leaders that the Nixon administration aimed to gradually establish a relationship with China and that some developments might be expected in the coming months.

When Swaran Singh complained that he had been given the impression that no military supplies would be delivered to Pakistan, Kissinger said that he himself was under the same impression! He explained that the shipments had resulted from some lacunae in administrative controls. The foreign minister responded that he should have been informed of these lacunae. Kissinger expressed regret for the 'lackadaisical' manner in which the issue had been handled in Washington, but Swaran Singh remained sceptical. Haksar was more cutting. When Kissinger ascribed the shipments to a 'bureaucratic muddle', Haksar responded that if that was indeed the case, then an assurance should be given that the mistake would not be repeated. Kissinger shifted ground, stating that the supplies were only of marginal importance and that the US needed some leverage with Yahya Khan. 'You cannot explain the arms supplies as a bureaucratic muddle and yet argue that such supplies give you leverage,' Haksar observed sharply.[16]

Mrs Gandhi, in her meeting with Kissinger, highlighted the enormous and increasing burden imposed on India by the refugee influx. She said she did not want to use force and she sought US suggestions on how the refugee problem might be speedily resolved. When Kissinger asked how much time was available before the problem became unmanageable, the prime minister replied that it was already unmanageable. 'We are just holding it together by sheer willpower,' she said. Kissinger asked if Mujib had to be an essential part of a settlement. Mrs Gandhi side-stepped the question, stating that this was not an India–Pakistan problem; a settlement had to be reached between West and East Pakistan.

Kissinger touched on the international implications of an Indo-Pakistan conflict in his discussions with Haksar. He said that in the event of such a conflict, China would certainly react, and this would lead India to rely on Soviet assistance. This would cause complications for the United States. Haksar replied that India wanted a peaceful solution; if China were to intervene, India expected and hoped that US sympathies would lie with India: 'I am a bit puzzled by your saying that if we get involved in a conflict which is not of our choosing and the Chinese intervened in one way or other, the United States, instead of assisting us, would feel some sort of discomfiture.' Haksar requested a clarification on the broad framework within which the United States viewed its policies towards the Soviet Union, China and India. Kissinger replied reassuringly that it would be folly for the United States to seek to improve relations with China in such a manner that it jeopardized Soviet interests. 'Also, if the Chinese seek to dominate . . . India, we cannot connive in this. In this global view, Pakistan is only of regional significance.'[17]

The China theme was explored further in Kissinger's meeting with Defence Minister Jagjivan Ram. Defence Secretary K.B. Lall asked Kissinger if he thought China might 'start something'. Kissinger replied, 'We think it highly unlikely. I might also tell you that we would take a very grave view of any Chinese move against India.' Probing a little further, Lall inquired: 'Is it possible that China might be in some doubt in this regard?' Kissinger replied: ' . . . we will leave them in no doubt.'[18]

From India, Kissinger flew to Pakistan for discussions with Yahya, after which he and his hosts enacted their elaborate plan of deception to provide cover for Kissinger's secret trip to Beijing. (Secretary of State Rogers was informed about Kissinger's China visit shortly before the flight took off!) The plan was implemented flawlessly, and the world was taken by total surprise when it was revealed that the Nixon's assistant for national security affairs had visited Beijing and that the US president himself would soon visit China. For India, it came as a double surprise. The revelation of a Pakistani role in the US–China breakthrough raised questions about its implications for US policy in the South Asia crisis.

The Jha telegram

Nixon chaired a meeting of the National Security Council on 16 July to consider the implications of the breakthrough in Sino-US ties for US policy in South Asia. He opened the meeting by stating that the situation in the subcontinent posed enormous risks for America's China policy. It was imperative that the Pakistanis not be embarrassed at this time. World opinion was on the side of the Indians, but they were 'a slippery, treacherous people'. The US could not allow a war in the region until 'we take this journey' to Beijing. Acknowledging that he had 'a bias', he said he would cut off all economic aid to the Indians if 'they mess around in East Pakistan'. Kissinger agreed that India seemed bent on war. By linking a solution to the refugee problem with an overall political solution, India appeared to be using the refugees for a political purpose. Kissinger said that he thought China would intervene if war broke out. If that came to pass, 'everything we have done [with China] will go down the drain'.[19]

It might be noted that by this time the United States no longer required a Pakistani channel for communicating with China. A direct channel had been established at the conclusion of Kissinger's trip. Kissinger's original justification for keeping Pakistan in good humour had ceased to be valid, but the president obviously had other reasons for humouring Yahya. Secondly, Kissinger's assessment of Chinese intentions was wide of the mark. We now know that China did not at any stage commit itself to direct military intervention in support of its Pakistani client. Nixon's insistence on accommodating Yahya's and Kissinger's misreading of Chinese intentions was to have a major impact on the unfolding South Asian crisis.

The very next day after the National Security Council meeting, Kissinger sent for the Indian ambassador, L.K. Jha, to deliver a pointed message. Jha's telegram to Foreign Secretary Kaul reported what Kissinger had conveyed:

> Please tell Foreign Minister and others with whom I talked in Delhi that [the] assurances I gave them about China on the eve of my visit stand and have the full approval of the President. Of course, if you decide to invade Tibet, we would not be able to help, but that is unlikely. *A more pressing danger when we would be unable to help you against China is that of an Indo-Pakistan conflict in which China comes to Pakistan's support* [emphasis added].[20]

Nixon's 'tilt' towards Pakistan had acquired a new and more

dangerous dimension. Kissinger's message suggested an incipient quasi-alliance between Pakistan, China and the United States. Indira Gandhi's response to the 'geopolitical revolution' was prompt and sure-footed. On 9 August 1971, India and the Soviet Union concluded a Treaty of Peace, Friendship and Cooperation. To Kissinger, the treaty came as a 'bombshell'.[21]

9

The Indo-Soviet Treaty

An Indo-Soviet Treaty was first mooted by Marshal Andrei Grechko, the Soviet defence minister, during a visit to India in March 1969. The marshal's visit coincided with armed clashes between the Soviet Union and China on the contested Sino-Soviet border along the Ussuri River. The hostilities took relations between Moscow and Beijing to new depths. In his discussions with Indian leaders, Grechko dwelt on the danger posed by Beijing to neighbouring states and held out an assurance of Soviet support in the event of a Chinese attack on India. In this context, the marshal proposed a treaty to strengthen mutual cooperation between the USSR and India in the political and military fields.

The primary aim of the Soviet initiative was, of course, to counter Chinese military adventures. However, there was a further dimension to Grechko's proposal of a treaty. A parallel Soviet objective was to build on Moscow's role as a reliable arms supplier in order to enhance its political and strategic ties with a wider group of Asian and Middle Eastern states. These included not only countries facing a potential military threat from China (such as India and Vietnam), but also others that did not lie on China's periphery or face a Chinese military threat. Thus, in the 1970s, the Soviet Union was to conclude treaties of friendship and cooperation with Egypt (1971), India (1971), Iraq (1972), Vietnam (1978), Yemen Arab Republic (1979) and Syria (1980).

In a related move, the USSR also proposed the creation of an Asian collective security system at an international conference of communist parties in Moscow on 8 June 1969.

In 1969, there was a broad convergence of Indian and Soviet interests in regard to China, but also nascent divergence over Pakistan. India–China relations were deeply strained as a result of the 1962 war. On New Year's Day in 1969, Prime Minister Indira Gandhi had taken an exploratory step towards an opening with China when she stated at a press conference that India was prepared to hold talks with China *without preconditions*, thus resiling from the earlier position that talks could be held only after Beijing's acceptance of the Colombo Proposals advanced by a group of non-aligned countries in 1963.[1] Mrs Gandhi's offer elicited no response from China, and relations between the two countries continued to be tense. The Chinese threat loomed large, especially against the background of a growing Sino-Pakistani military relationship.

At the same time, however, India was deeply concerned about a recent development in Soviet policy towards Pakistan. In 1968, the USSR agreed to supply arms to Pakistan, in an attempt to wean it away from China. It became a major aim of Indian policy to seek restoration of its position as the exclusive recipient of Soviet arms in South Asia. Moscow, on the other hand, sought to deepen its ties with both India and Pakistan, with the aim of drawing them into some sort of an Asian collective security system.

This became clear when Indian Ambassador to Moscow D.P. Dhar called on Marshal Grechko at the end of March 1969 to seek further elucidation of the Soviet proposal of a treaty. Referring to Grechko's assurance of Soviet support in the event of a Chinese attack, the ambassador inquired about the concrete shape of cooperation in the political and other fields. Dhar also dwelt on India's apprehensions of a Pakistani invasion, referring pointedly to the Sino-Pakistani collusion during the 1965 war. Grechko replied that Indo-Soviet cooperation in the military and political fields should be given a more concrete shape. 'Thinking aloud', he wondered if such cooperation could not be translated, as a first step, into a treaty of friendship and cooperation. At the next stage, the two countries could think in terms of closer military cooperation. Turning to Pakistan, the marshal said that he did not think Pakistan could pose a threat to India since it was weak and divided. However, if Pakistan did commit aggression, the Soviet Union would be on India's side. Moscow would side with the victim of aggression.[2]

The same message was conveyed by the Soviet ambassador to India, Pegov, who informed Romesh Bhandari, Dhar's second-in-command, that a major Soviet objective was to promote friendship between India and Pakistan so that they could jointly tackle China. Pegov also said that an Indo-Soviet Treaty of friendship would provide insurance against any possible aggression by China or Pakistan.[3]

At this stage, Moscow had only proposed a treaty in general terms; it had yet to present the concrete text of a draft agreement. This proposal evoked mixed reactions in New Delhi. Haksar, viewing the proposal in the context of the threat posed by China, was 'fully favourable as such a treaty will reflect coincidence of our interests at present'.[4] Ambassador Dhar, too, was enthusiastic. Highlighting Grechko's assurance that the USSR would come to India's assistance in the event of aggression by China or Pakistan, he said that if India agreed to consider the marshal's proposal, the Soviet Union might also be more forthcoming in meeting India's requests for sophisticated weapons, bombers and other military equipment, as well as in helping to accelerate the process of achieving self-sufficiency in defence production. He urged the government to explore these possibilities. If the Soviets proved sufficiently forthcoming, India could agree to conclude a Treaty of Friendship and Cooperation that was consistent with non-alignment. Foreign Minister Dinesh Singh reacted more cautiously. While accepting Dhar's proposal for exploratory talks, he raised questions about the purpose of the proposed treaty and its wording. Did we have similar treaties with other countries? Uneasy about its compatibility with India's non-alignment policy, Dinesh Singh asked for an examination of the implications of signing a Treaty of Friendship and Cooperation with the Soviet Union.[5]

Indira Gandhi conveyed her initial response to the Soviet proposal in a letter to Kosygin. She began by expressing India's 'great anguish' over the loss of Soviet lives caused by the Chinese attack, recalling in this context the Chinese aggression against India in 1962. 'Therefore, it is natural for the Government and people of India to feel that a new bond, forged by our common suffering and grief, is added to the friendship between our two peoples and Governments.' In this context, she proposed a detailed examination of the 'several suggestions' that had emerged in the 'exchange of ideas' between Dhar and Grechko. The prime minister made it clear, however, that her concerns were not limited to China. She brought up once again the question of Soviet military sales to Pakistan and concluded by expressing her appreciation for the assurance given by Marshal Grechko that the Soviet Union would support India in the event of *Pakistani* aggression.[6]

New Delhi's intention at this stage was to engage in exploratory talks on the Soviet proposal with the aim of seeking an early harvest in the form of termination of Soviet military sales to Pakistan and enhanced access to sophisticated Soviet weapon systems and military technology. Dhar was expected to conduct the talks without making any commitment that might raise questions about India's non-alignment. This general approach was not translated into specific negotiating instructions.

In the absence of instructions, Ambassador Dhar allowed himself to be carried away by his own enthusiasm. He called on Kosygin and told him that India's response was 'both positive and constructive'; however, there were 'questions of pure mechanics which have to be resolved before we can progress towards the stage when the practical implications of such a treaty can be considered'. Dhar mentioned in this connection questions such as venues, interlocutors, lists of subjects, etc. Kosygin was not taken in by Dhar's evasive rhetoric. Well aware of India's deep concern over Soviet–Pakistan ties, he invited the ambassador's comments on the subject. Dhar made a forceful presentation of the

Indian case, concluding that 'no single act has caused greater harm to the image of the Soviet Union in my country than your policy of arms aid to Pakistan'. The Soviet premier replied, 'I deeply appreciate your frankness, Mr. Ambassador, but you have not resolved my dilemma in policy. I suggest you should consider all these matters during your forthcoming discussions with our representatives . . . We must review the whole question, the question of our arms aid to Pakistan, the question of Indo-Soviet relations and find an effective answer . . . Will it not be possible to make an appropriate provision in the treaty itself which will completely remove the question entirely?'[7]

Dhar's report on this conversation caused consternation in New Delhi. The foreign minister, Dinesh Singh, minuted, 'I am afraid the Ambassador has gone too far on the treaty. I have also ascertained with P.M. [prime minister] he did not have the authority to [go?] to this length.'[8] New Delhi ignored Kosygin's hint linking the treaty to cessation of Soviet military supplies to Pakistan. India was prepared to carry on a general discussion on an Indo-Soviet agreement but not to accept a treaty which might be construed as a deviation from the path of non-alignment. Dhar made a course correction as instructed, during a meeting with Deputy Foreign Minister Firyubin, and was congratulated by the foreign secretary 'for the skilful manner in which you carried on the discussions without making any commitments'.[9]

The problematic article

Meanwhile, the Soviet proposal had acquired greater clarity when Ambassador Pegov handed over to Dinesh Singh on 22 April 1969 a draft Treaty of Friendship and Cooperation. The ambassador emphasized that the document was a 'very preliminary' draft that could serve as a basis for discussion. The core of the Soviet draft lay in Article 6, which had this provision:

> In case either of the Parties is subjected to an attack or a threat thereof, the Parties will immediately initiate mutual consultations with a view

> to arriving at agreement on, and implementing, appropriate effective measures to ensure peace and security of their peoples.

Moscow was mindful of India's attachment to non-alignment. With this in mind, Article 4 stated:

> The Soviet Union respects the policy of non-alignment with military groupings pursued by India, a policy that constitutes an important factor in the struggle for universal peace and international security.[10]

This was a welcome reassurance, but it did not still New Delhi's misgivings about Article 6 and its compatibility with non-alignment. The prime minister candidly mentioned her reservations to Kosygin when he visited India in May. She said that she was mainly concerned about two issues regarding the draft treaty: first, that it should contain no phraseology that might be misunderstood as a shift in India's policy of non-alignment; and second, it should contain no provision that might be misconstrued as being directed against a third party. Kosygin tried to reassure her on both points, but Mrs Gandhi was not fully convinced. Thus, when Kosygin referred to possible treaty provisions concerning economic and political cooperation, the Indian prime minister asked him pointedly what he meant by 'political cooperation'. The Soviet leader replied that he meant cooperation in the field of foreign policy; however, this would be dropped if it was not acceptable to India. At another point, when Mrs Gandhi expressed her apprehensions concerning China, Kosygin offered to incorporate in the treaty a clause on 'mutual assistance'. Indira Gandhi responded that this would amount to a military agreement. Kosygin said that the Soviet Union would not insist on such a clause, but he believed that India would probably resort to such consultations if the threat arose, regardless of any treaty.

Indira Gandhi spoke frankly about India's concern over Soviet arms supplies to Pakistan. Soviet assistance to Pakistan had an impact on the regional balance of power. Apart from this, the Soviet equidistance from

India and Pakistan caused irritation in India. Moscow should refrain from any action that suggested parity of treatment between India and Pakistan. The Indian prime minister permitted herself to muse that this point would be met to some extent if there was an Indo-Soviet Treaty. The talks ended on an inconclusive note, and the two leaders agreed to continue discussions on the treaty in Moscow, through the diplomatic channel.[11]

In Moscow, the ingenious Ambassador Dhar continued to spin out the 'exploratory' talks with only the sketchiest of instructions. Haksar himself expressed his dissatisfaction over the absence of instructions and drew the prime minister's attention to the need for clarifying India's ideas on the Soviet proposal.[12] Dhar, too, complained about being left without instructions.

Finally, at the end of August 1969, an Indian counter-draft was ready. Prepared by Kaul in association with Dhar and Kewal Singh, secretary in the MEA, it bore the title 'Treaty of Peace, Friendship and Cooperation'. The problematic Article 6 of the Soviet draft was replaced with a new formulation that read:

> Each High Contracting Party undertakes to abstain from providing any assistance to any third Parties that engage in conflict with the other High Contracting Party. In the event of either High Contracting Party being subjected to an attack or a threat thereof by a third Party, the two High Contracting Parties shall immediately enter into mutual consultations.

The first part of the new article was fashioned in the context of Soviet military sales to Pakistan. The latter part was a truncated version of the Soviet Article 6. It dropped the reference to 'appropriate effective measures to ensure peace and security' in order to distance the treaty from a military pact. As a 'peace' agreement, it included a pledge to 'respect the boundaries, independence, sovereignty and territorial integrity of each other and to refrain from interfering in the internal affairs of the other party'. It even included an undertaking to refrain from entering into any military alliance directed against the other signatory and to 'abstain from any aggression against the other High Contracting Party'! Furthermore, with the aim of giving the treaty the appearance of a general agreement on cooperation, a mass of new provisions was introduced, covering cooperation in such diverse spheres as the economy, science and technology, art, literature and education. Finally, the reference to India's policy of non-alignment was retained, with the addition of a reciprocal expression of India's respect for the Soviet policy of promoting detente.

In seeking ministerial approval, Kaul emphasized that the draft treaty was in full conformity with non-alignment. Like the Soviet draft, it specifically recognized India's non-alignment and eschewed any provision that permitted the presence of foreign troops or bases on Indian soil. Second, it could be construed as a non-aggression treaty; this was consistent with non-alignment. India could offer to sign similar treaties with any other country. The treaty would meet India's immediate objective of halting Soviet arms supplies to Pakistan. The deletion of the reference in the Soviet draft to the object and outcome of the consultations would enable the Indian side to differentiate the agreement from a military pact, while making it serve as a warning to both Pakistan and China.[13]

After six months of evasive and 'purely exploratory' discussions, the Indians finally handed over their counter-draft to the Soviet side in September 1969. When detailed discussions began on this draft, Deputy Foreign Minister Firyubin politely indicated some basic objections. He observed that the title of the treaty was inappropriate; peace treaties were signed by warring states on the conclusion of hostilities. It had no place in a friendship treaty. A non-aggression clause was not appropriate in the context of the close ties between India and the Soviet Union. Non-aggression pacts, he said, were in fashion in the pre-World War II era, before the UN Charter prohibited the use of force. A friendship treaty reflected a far higher level of ties between the signatories. Firyubin also inquired why the reference to 'appropriate effective measures' had been dropped from the Soviet formulation and why the Indian draft was confined only to 'consultations'. Dhar gave a hint of India's reasons, replying that the intention was to avoid 'unfair criticism and preventing people from reading too much of belligerency and militancy' in the agreement.[14] The discussions led to a certain narrowing of differences and agreement on some peripheral issues, but not to the crucial Article 6 of the Soviet paper.

New Delhi now reverted to two other issues on which it had lodged repeated protests in the past. Dhar was advised in October that the draft treaty could not be finalized until Moscow provided an assurance that it would not supply any offensive weapons to Pakistan. The second condition was that Soviet maps should correctly depict India's boundaries.[15] India had earlier lodged protests on these issues.

At this stage, a new factor came into play. Moscow came to accept the failure of its efforts to persuade Pakistan to break away from its close military and political ties to China or even to participate in Soviet-sponsored schemes of Asian economic cooperation. When Kosygin visited Pakistan in May 1969, he had put forward a proposal for a transit agreement to facilitate trade between the USSR, Afghanistan, Pakistan and the rest of South Asia. Yahya Khan, not the most astute among statesmen, initially accepted the proposal, but retracted later when his military colleagues and the foreign ministry forcefully drew his attention to the implications for Pakistan's trade policy vis-à-vis India, as well as for Sino-Pakistani relations.[16] Yahya paid a reciprocal visit to Moscow in the following month. When he raised the question of additional military supplies, Kosygin seized the opportunity to inform him in blunt terms that Pakistan could not be on friendly terms with both China and the Soviet Union.[17] Yahya remained unmoved. These exchanges brought home to Moscow the lack of realism in its policy of dangling arms sales in the hope of drawing Pakistan away from its intimate military and political ties with China.

Thus, by October 1969, the Soviet Union was ready to meet the Indian request regarding arms supplies to Pakistan. Kosygin at last offered a categorical assurance regarding cessation of arms supplies to Pakistan. The assurance was repeated by Marshal Grechko and Firyubin. An indication was also received that action would be taken on the question of revising Soviet maps depicting India. In a 'Strictly Personal & Top Secret' letter to Foreign Minister Dinesh Singh in November 1969, the Indian charge d'affaires in Moscow, Romesh Bhandari, pressed for immediate finalization of the treaty. 'I would now submit that the time has come for us to arrive [at] a decision on this matter. Any delay in doing so would cause doubts in the minds of the Soviet leadership regarding our sincerity. This could in turn lead to a rethinking on their part in respect of the assurances they have now given.'[18]

Bhandari's letter was shown to Indira Gandhi, but she had no intention of concluding the agreement. She valued the Soviet assurance of support in the event of Chinese or Pakistani aggression against India; however, India did not face an immediate threat. She was concerned also about domestic and international perceptions regarding the compatibility of the treaty with non-alignment. Her government enjoyed only a small majority in parliament, and inside her own party she faced a mounting challenge from the right wing. New Delhi simply pocketed the Soviet assurance regarding arms supplies to Pakistan – its immediate aim in the negotiations – and decided to put the proposed treaty in cold storage, to be taken out should the need arise in the future. Ambassador Dhar advised his Soviet interlocutors that the domestic political situation in India was not conducive to an early conclusion of the treaty. He highlighted the threat posed by 'rightist reactionary' elements to Indira Gandhi's leadership and suggested that the negotiations be placed on hold until a more propitious moment. Once again, the Soviets were ready to oblige, and the proposed treaty went into hibernation.

At the end of 1970, Indira Gandhi decided to break free from the right-wing party bosses and force a formal division of the Congress party. Reduced to a minority in parliament, she sought a fresh electoral mandate. The Lok Sabha was dissolved and general elections held in

March 1971, more than a year ahead of schedule. The result was a resounding victory for Mrs Gandhi's Congress (I) party, which won 350 out of a total of 515 seats, obtaining more than a two-thirds majority in the Lok Sabha. The prime minister's right-wing opponents were decimated. The electoral verdict removed the domestic political constraint that Ambassador Dhar had advanced as the reason for putting Moscow's treaty proposal in cold storage. However, Indira Gandhi showed no interest in reviving the talks – until the summer of 1971, when the logic of events left her with no other option.

Compulsions of 1971

India had hoped, until July, to obtain support from both superpowers in dealing with the East Bengal crisis. New Delhi had greater expectations of the Soviet Union, but it also sought US sympathy and support. As we saw in the previous chapter, in early April, Indira Gandhi appealed to the Soviet leadership to consider a joint initiative with the United States. Moscow was prompt in extending diplomatic support, but it maintained a polite silence on the appeal for a joint initiative with the United States. New Delhi had failed to understand the cryptic reference in the Soviet reply to 'unused possibilities' for developing bilateral ties.

The enigmatic phrase acquired clarity when Swaran Singh, who had recently replaced Dinesh Singh as the foreign minister, visited Moscow in early June 1971 to obtain an urgent assurance of Soviet support in the event of Chinese intervention. Towards the end of May 1971, the Indian army had drawn up a draft outline plan for military intervention in Bangladesh.[19] The operation was to be launched not earlier than mid-November, after winter conditions had closed the passes on the China border, thus minimizing the risk of Chinese intervention. Indian policymakers were, however, concerned about a possible preemptive Pakistani strike, supported by China, before the onset of winter. Swaran Singh's purpose was to seek an urgent assurance of support from Moscow in such a contingency. He did not have a treaty or any other specific arrangement in view. As Kosygin had shrewdly observed as early as in 1969, India would turn to the Soviet Union for support if it feared a Chinese threat – treaty or no treaty.

On the eve of Swaran Singh's visit, Marshal Grechko reiterated his call for an Indo-Soviet Treaty to a sympathetic Ambassador Dhar. The Chinese, he said, 'were aware that India was relatively militarily weak. They could, therefore, afford to be aggressive, even insolent and arrogant.' Grechko made a forceful case for a treaty of mutual assistance, which would act as a strong deterrent against aggression by China or Pakistan.[20]

Swaran Singh deliberately ignored this strong hint and tried to skirt the question of the treaty when he met Soviet Foreign Minister, Gromyko on 7 June. He briefed Gromyko about the latest developments in East Bengal, concluding that 'a situation may arise which may demand the entry of the Soviet Union into it in order to counter the difficulties which may be created by Chinese support to Pakistan. Perhaps even now you will have to consider some appropriate steps by which the Chinese support to Pakistan can be counter-balanced.' The Soviet foreign minister seized on this appeal to bring up the question of the treaty. He observed: 'You have made a very important and very useful statement . . . Some time ago we had an exchange of views regarding the desirability of signing some sort of a treaty . . . What do you think of the feasibility or otherwise of resuming the exchange of views and ideas regarding the draft Document?'

Swaran Singh reluctantly agreed that talks on the treaty could be resumed, but he tried to separate the two issues, urging that priority be given to his request. 'While we are discussing and considering this Document, we may be too late, events may overtake us. Can we think of something quickly?' he asked. Gromyko was unmoved, only expressing his satisfaction over India's readiness to resume discussions on the treaty.

When he met Kosygin on the following day, Swaran Singh repeated his request for Soviet support. India, he said, looked to the Soviet Union to neutralize a Chinese military intervention in support of Pakistan. Kosygin agreed that it was very possible that China would want to fan tension and conflict, but was silent on the appeal for assistance. Swaran Singh was not a man to give up easily. He continued to dwell on the Chinese threat and on India's determination to defend itself if attacked. He concluded by observing, '. . . we have no doubt that we can count on your help and understanding'. Finally, Kosygin offered some words of assurance. 'You can depend on us as your friends,' he said.[21] It was a general assurance, but not the specific commitment sought by the Indian foreign minister.

It was clear from these conversations that the Soviet Union was ready to come to India's assistance in the event of a Chinese attack but that it wanted to base this on a formal treaty. The Indian side tried to evade this issue, but did not offer a specific suggestion regarding an alternative form of commitment, such as a simple verbal understanding or a secret exchange of letters.

Foreign Secretary Kaul examined the options and concluded that a formal treaty would be preferable. A mere verbal understanding was inadequate. A secret exchange of letters would not serve as a deterrent to China in the current developing situation. The best option was a formal treaty providing for mutual consultations in the event of a threat to national security, alongside a clause endorsing India's policy of non-alignment. He recommended that a treaty with the Soviet Union be concluded at an early date, in order to deter China from military intervention in the event of an Indo-Pakistan conflict. Kaul submitted a revised Indian draft. This incorporated a few minor amendments based on a comparison with the text of the recently concluded UAR-USSR Treaty of Peace and Friendship, as well as a major change (unacknowledged as such) reflecting India's heightened threat perception. At the end of the reference to 'consultations' in the crucial provision concerning response to an attack or a threat against one of the signatories (Article 9 in the new draft), Kaul now proposed to add the words 'with a view to removing the threat that may arise and ensuring peace'. This amendment would go a long way in removing the most important difference between the Indian and Soviet drafts.[22]

Thus, by June 1971, Swaran Singh had reluctantly agreed to resume negotiations on a treaty that had been languishing in cold storage for over a year and a half. In preparation for the negotiations, senior officials had drawn up a revised Indian draft that partly bridged the most important difference with the Soviet position. However, even at this stage, with the possibility of an early preemptive Pakistani attack in collusion with China, Indira Gandhi withheld her approval. Unlike her father Jawaharlal Nehru, she rarely spelled out her thoughts at length on official files. One can only infer that she was reluctant to take a step that might adversely affect India's non-aligned image and her ties with the west. The prime minister was still hopeful of securing US understanding and support in the impending crisis.

White House reveals its hand

The situation changed radically on 15 July, with the dramatic announcement of Kissinger's secret trip to Beijing, via Pakistan, and President Nixon's planned visit to China. The Pakistani role added a new dimension to the US–China entente. The Soviet ambassador in Delhi met Foreign Secretary Kaul on the following day to urge him that it had become more necessary than ever before to finalize the treaty as a deterrent against Chinese, Pakistani or American designs against India.[23] Kaul needed no persuasion. On 17 July, he made out a powerful case for the treaty in a note submitted to the foreign minister and prime minister.

> In light of the continued supply of American arms to Pakistan, the secret visit of Kissinger to Peking from Pakistan and the possibilities of normalization of relations between USA [and] the People's Republic of China and the likely entry of PRC into UN in the forthcoming session of the General Assembly, the close alliance between Iran, Turkey and Pakistan, and the support given by Algeria, Saudi Arabia and some other Muslim countries to Pakistan on Bangladesh and the possibility

> of Pakistan provoking a conflict with us in August or September, I would suggest that we give immediate consideration to the Document and finalize it by the 15th August, if not earlier.[24]

The last straw came in the form of the Jha telegram, reporting Kissinger's warning that '[a] danger when we would be unable to help you against China is that of an Indo-Pakistan conflict in which China comes to Pakistan's support'.[25]

After intensive discussions, a broad consensus emerged in New Delhi. This was captured in a memorandum prepared by Kaul.

> We had been stalling this idea [the proposed treaty] so far by prolonging informal discussions between our Ambassador and the Soviet Government . . . [O]ur Ambassador in USA has reported that there is every possibility of America increasing arms supplies to Pakistan. Dr. Kissinger told him after his return from Peking that America would not intervene in any conflict between India and Pakistan even if China did so. This has changed the whole perspective in which the Soviet proposal has to be considered . . .
>
> [I]f the Sino-American detente works out successfully, there is no other alternative left to us but to have a reliable friend in case of necessity. The charge that non-alignment has left us friendless would be disproved. The present Treaty does not conflict with our concept of non-alignment and reaffirms the Soviet Government's respect for our policy of non-alignment. Non-alignment does not mean that if one's security and territorial integrity are threatened we cannot enter into any arrangements we may consider necessary to meet and avert such a threat.[26]

On Mrs Gandhi's instructions, the Indian draft underwent a final revision. It was handed over to the Soviet side on 2 August by Ambassador K.S. Shelvankar, who had recently replaced D.P. Dhar in Moscow. Dhar himself, now the coordinator of India's Bangladesh policy, arrived in Moscow on 3 August. The treaty was finalized the very next day in meetings between Dhar and Gromyko. The revised Indian draft already accepted the Soviet wording on the central clause (Article IX). The Soviets gave up their earlier reservations concerning the incongruous non-aggression clause in the Indian text and its reflection in the title by the insertion of the word 'peace' before 'friendship and cooperation'. Soviet Foreign Minister Gromyko flew to India on 8 August and signed the treaty the next day with his Indian counterpart, Swaran Singh.

A senior Indian diplomat who had been involved in the drafting exercise at an earlier stage offered his professional appraisal of the final text. 'Article 9 has just the right amount of substance and shadow to confound our enemies and hearten our friends.'[27]

10

Working the Treaty

(August–October 1971)

Following the conclusion of the Indo-Soviet Treaty, Swaran Singh began detailed discussions with Gromyko extending over four sessions, from 9 August to 11 August 1971. He shared India's thinking about the crisis and spelled out his expectations from the treaty with great candour.

In the opening session, Swaran Singh referred to the Pakistani announcement that Mujib would be brought to trial on charges of treason. Gromyko promptly agreed to do everything possible to restrain Pakistan from proceeding on this course. He said the Soviet Union fully understood and supported the steps taken by India in international forums. It condemned the military repression in East Pakistan and held the military junta responsible for the massive influx of refugees into India. While assuring India of Soviet understanding, Gromyko said he was confident that India would show the utmost restraint and take all possible steps to prevent a war. Swaran Singh replied that India wanted to prevent a war but the possibility could not be ruled out, given the encouragement Pakistan was receiving from China and the United States. He concluded the first session by expressing the hope that Indo-Soviet consultations might succeed in averting the tragedy of a war.[1]

Expanding on this theme in the next two sessions, the Indian foreign minister said that Pakistan was likely to launch an attack against India sometime between mid-September and mid-October. Pakistan was well aware that it could not prevail against India without Chinese intervention. Pakistan was thus likely to strike before snowfall closed the Himalayan passes in November. A second factor was the success achieved by the Bangladeshi freedom fighters. The Mukti Bahini might be able to secure permanent control over some areas. If this came to pass, the hawks in Pakistan might treat it as justification for launching a war against India. Intelligence reports indicated that the Pakistani junta was thinking in terms of a war of two to three weeks' duration. They had stopped all leave to armed forces' personnel, recalled their reservists and had set up anti-aircraft defences around their airbases in West Punjab. Information had also been received about the presence of around 1,20,000 Chinese troops along the India–China border.

Swaran Singh said that in this situation, India expected the Soviet Union to make prompt deliveries of required military supplies. India also required assured supplies of oil and certain non-ferrous materials needed by the defence industries. Iran had informed India that it would cut off oil supplies to India in case of an Indo-Pakistan conflict; other Gulf countries might follow suit. Since the Soviet Union was buying Iraqi oil, it could easily ship this oil to India. Second, Swaran Singh strongly urged Moscow to consider how it could counteract Chinese military pressure on India's borders. He suggested this might perhaps be achieved by exerting countervailing pressure on the Xinjiang border. This was particularly important, since information had been received that the Chinese had diverted three divisions from Inner Mongolia to Tibet. Swaran Singh also proposed closer cooperation between the Indian and Soviet intelligence agencies. Lists of Indian requirements for military equipment, petroleum products and non-ferrous metals were handed over to the Soviet side.[2]

In the final round of talks on 11 August, Swaran Singh went to the heart of the problem. Taking Gromyko into confidence about India's contacts with Mujibnagar, he revealed that the latter felt they could take control of substantial areas in the north and north-east of the country by the end of August or, at the latest, by September. When Gromyko inquired about the extent of the territories under Mukti Bahini control, Swaran Singh pointed out certain areas on the map, adding that some areas west of the Padma River might also come under the control of the freedom fighters. The Soviet foreign minister sought more details about the percentage of East Pakistan territory under actual Mukti Bahini control. Defence Secretary K.B. Lall clarified that though large areas were controlled by the Mukti Bahini, continuous control of these areas had yet to be achieved by them. The freedom fighters felt that full control would be achieved by the end of September, but Lall himself felt that this was too optimistic an assessment.

Swaran Singh observed that more substantial help would obviously have to be given to the freedom fighters. This might even make it necessary to accord recognition to Bangladesh. India's recognition of Bangladesh as an independent state would lead to a rupture of diplomatic ties with Pakistan and also, perhaps, to a Pakistani attack on India. Before taking such a step, India would like to know the Soviet reaction. The Indian foreign minister explained that he was raising these issues so that the two countries could carefully study the implications of such a step and draw the necessary conclusions. Swaran Singh emphasized the dangers of a long-drawn-out liberation war. The longer it continued, the greater would be the danger of power passing into the hands of pro-Chinese extremist elements – an outcome that would not be in the interests of India, the USSR or Bangladesh.

The Soviet foreign minister observed that this was the first time India had presented the problem in such a frank and forthright manner. He 'understood' the importance India attached to the question, but he could not express an opinion since the question required closer examination. Gromyko said that in order to make an assessment of the situation, it was important to know whether the Mukti Bahini was strong enough to prevail against the Pakistani army. He asked some searching questions. Would the freedom fighters be able to get control over sufficiently large areas? Would they be able to prevent the Pakistani army from retaking these areas? Had India sounded out friendly neighbours in South-east Asia to ascertain whether they would support India on the question of recognizing Bangladesh? Swaran Singh replied that India did not want to sound out other countries without first consulting the Soviet Union. Regarding the prospects of the Mukti Bahini, he said it was difficult to give a detailed answer, but India believed that the 75 million people of Bangladesh were united in their freedom struggle and that the Pakistani army would be unable to retain control of the nation.[3]

These discussions revealed the extent, as well as the limits, of Soviet support. Moscow was more than ready to make sure that the treaty acted as a deterrent against a Pakistani attack or Chinese intervention; indeed, it had been pressing for such a treaty for more than two years. The Soviet Union was also prepared to attach top priority to Indian requests for military supplies. It was ready to provide diplomatic support in the form of public criticism of Pakistani repression in the eastern wing, holding Pakistan responsible for the flight of the refugees to India, and demanding that Islamabad release Sheikh Mujib and negotiate a political solution with the elected representatives of East Pakistan. However, Moscow envisaged a political solution *within the framework of a united Pakistan*. It was not ready – as yet – to support a secessionist movement.

An immediate result of the Indo-Soviet Treaty was stepped-up diplomatic support for India, coupled with a hardening of Moscow's attitude towards Pakistan. Jamsheed Marker, the Pakistani ambassador in Moscow, recalls that in August '. . . a new and ominous element began to emerge in our relations with the Soviet Union . . . the Soviets had begun to take the view that Pakistan was likely to initiate hostilities with India in order to divert world opinion from the internal disorder in East Pakistan'.[4] Gromyko forcefully put across the new Soviet stance when the Pakistani foreign secretary, Sultan Mohammed Khan, visited Moscow in the first week of September. Expressing regret over Pakistan's failure to take steps to solve the refugee problem, Gromyko underlined the point that the 'refugees have spilled over the national border: the situation has thus spilled over the normal framework of Pakistan–Indian relations'. The refugee problem could not be solved unless the Pakistan government stopped its policy of repression and persecution. 'In this situation, any steps against Mujibur Rahman would create new difficulties . . . a severe sentence on Mujibur Rahman would be denounced by the Soviet people and world public opinion.' Referring to Yahya's statement that he would go to war if even a morsel of East Pakistan territory came under Indian control, Gromyko said he got the impression that 'certain circles in Pakistan are not against war'.[5]

The most powerful message delivered by Gromyko concerned the Indo-Soviet Treaty. Ambassador Marker provides a vivid first-hand account:

> Speaking in Russian, Gromyko said that the Soviet leadership had taken note of Yahya Khan's statement and warned, 'please do not take any action that would oblige us to fulfil our obligations to a country with whom we have a Treaty of Friendship'. At this point Gromyko stopped the interpreter, and looking long, hard and directly at Sultan Khan, he said in English, 'The interpreter did not interpret me correctly. I did not use the word "please". I think you understand my meaning'.[6]

The Moscow Summit

True to their treaty obligations, the Soviets spared no effort to meet India's arms requirements and to dissuade Pakistan from embarking on a military adventure. Soviet diplomatic support for India became much more forceful after the conclusion of the treaty. However, Moscow continued to visualize a political solution within the framework of a united Pakistan. It turned a blind eye to Indian involvement in the Bangladesh freedom struggle, but it was not ready to support a secessionist movement. This posed a major challenge to Indian diplomacy, what with the looming prospect of a war before the end of the year.

Moscow's principled opposition to intervention in a civil war was subject to certain caveats. The Soviets took a more flexible position in the case of a 'war of national liberation'. This, in turn, was related to their assessment of the political orientation of the freedom fighters. Here, the Awami League was at a disadvantage: it was not a pro-Soviet, left-wing party. Before 25 March, it had been in regular touch with American diplomats and had relatively few contacts with the Soviets. The Mujibnagar government was composed exclusively of Awami League members; it offered no role for pro-Soviet parties like the CPB and NAP(M), even though these parties were totally committed to the freedom struggle and offered unconditional support to Mujibnagar.

Indira Gandhi visited Moscow at the end of September 1971 with the aim of changing the Soviet perception of the liberation war. The message she wanted to convey was that war might be expected by December, that the Bangladesh freedom struggle had the characteristics of a 'national liberation' war and that its inevitable outcome was the emergence of an independent state of Bangladesh. It was in this context that she sought Soviet support under the friendship treaty.

In advance of the Moscow summit, D.P. Dhar flew to Kolkata for talks with the Mujibnagar authorities. As we saw in Chapter 4, Dhar was able to strengthen Tajuddin's hand and to persuade other Awami League leaders to constitute a United Front with three 'progressive' parties – the CPB, NAP (M) and the Bangladesh Congress Party. Recruitment to the Mukti Bahini was also opened up for members of these parties. It was hoped that these changes, desirable in themselves, would also produce a more benign Soviet perception of the Bangladesh freedom struggle.

Dhar flew to Moscow in the last week of September to prepare the ground for the prime minister's visit. In his talks with Deputy Foreign Minister Firyubin on 23–24 September, he left no doubt that India expected war to break out before the end of the year. The Soviet Union and India, he said, needed to consider what steps they should take to deal with the situation. Firyubin was not prepared to accept the inevitability of war. The Soviet position, he emphasized, was to 'preserve peace by all means'. Moscow was 'trying to influence Pakistan to prevent a situation from developing into a catastrophe. So I would pose your question [as to] what is to be done in a different form. Are all possibilities exhausted for an alternative to the solution which leads to a catastrophe? . . . Is there even a very small possibility for a positive solution?' Holding his ground, Dhar replied, 'By all means let us pursue the paths of peace . . . If you are ready to build on a small piece of hope, I am ready to build on practically nothing. But I would not be your friend if I were not to tell you frankly and sincerely that we do not see any hope and that we must prepare for the worst.'[7]

Firyubin would not be dislodged from his advocacy of a peaceful solution. When the talks were resumed on 24 September, he firmly reiterated the Soviet position that the national interests of India and Pakistan could be served only by a peaceful solution of their problems. After contrasting India's consistent pursuit of peace with Pakistani bellicosity and its atrocities in East Bengal, Dhar emphasized that 'portents of a conflict are writ large over the subcontinent'. Turning the broader geopolitical picture, he argued that the United States and China were acting in concert to ensure that India was contained as an insignificant nation, that the Soviet Union was ousted from Asia and the Indo-Soviet Treaty reduced to nought. Would such an outcome help the cause of peace, he asked, or would it only help the 'forces conspiring against us'?

Firyubin sought clarification of India's views on three questions. First, how would events develop till December? Second, would East Pakistan break away from Pakistan? Third, what role did India visualize for the Soviet Union in bringing about the 'quick solution' of which Dhar had spoken? Dhar replied that with the onset of the dry season, the Pakistani army would move out of its cantonments and resume its severe repression in East Bengal. The refugee flood would increase in intensity, vastly aggravating India's problems. Intelligence reports also indicated that Pakistan was planning a preemptive attack in the western sector. Second, all objective observers had come to the conclusion that East Bengal would not remain a part of Pakistan. The real question was whether India and the USSR would help the new nation to be friendly to them. Did India and the Soviet Union possess the political wisdom to ensure that in the new configuration of forces in South Asia, they are able to assist in the birth, however painful, of the free and friendly nation of Bangladesh? Regarding Firyubin's last question, Dhar said it would be presumptuous of him to attempt an answer. It was for the Soviet Union to decide on its course of action. However, in his personal capacity as a student of Soviet political philosophy and policy, he would humbly say, 'Support the oppressed!'[8]

On 28 September 1971, Indira Gandhi had two sessions of meetings with the full Soviet troika – party General Secretary Brezhnev, Supreme Soviet Chairman Podgorny and Chairman of the Council of Ministers Kosygin. The presence of all three members reflected the importance Moscow attached to the visit of the Indian prime minister. In the plenary forenoon session, Mrs Gandhi appears to have been constrained by the presence of the full delegations on both sides. The Soviet leaders tried, without much success, to draw her out in a frank discussion of India's intentions. Brezhnev invited her to share her thoughts about what should be done to solve the problem confronting India. What were the options, and what solutions did she suggest? Reluctant to show her hand in the presence of a large number of officials, Mrs Gandhi only stated that it was difficult to say what could be done at this late stage. The situation might have been different if the international community had pressured Pakistan at an earlier stage and if the United States had withheld open support to Yahya Khan. One thing was clear: the refugee exodus must be halted and conducive conditions must be created for the return of the refugees to their homes. In this connection, she rejected the UN secretary general's proposal to place UN observers on the Indian side of the border.

Brezhnev inquired if the UN could play a useful role. Indira Gandhi replied that Pakistan was trying to raise the question in the UN in order to convert its domestic crisis into a bilateral Indo-Pakistan dispute. Pakistan wanted to divert international attention from the Bangladesh freedom struggle. Indo-Pakistan talks could serve no purpose; only the 'Bangladesh government' was competent to negotiate with 'West Pakistan'. Fruitful talks could be held if Mujibur Rahman was released unconditionally.

Agreeing with Mrs Gandhi on the last point, Kosygin said that the civil war was Pakistan's problem. India had 'only the one problem of refugees and they must go back'. How would the situation develop? As he understood it, India supported the Mujibnagar government. Kosygin suggested: '. . . maybe we should work for a federation [of the two wings of Pakistan] and independence could come later?' Mrs Gandhi said that it was for the people of East Bengal to decide if that idea was acceptable; however, her impression was that the Pakistani rulers had alienated these people so completely that it would be difficult to persuade them to accept a federation.[9]

The leaders met again later in the day in a restricted session, where the only officials present were Foreign Secretary Kaul on the Indian side and two Russian interpreters. This permitted a freer discussion. Mrs Gandhi now said she greatly feared that in spite of all her efforts, India might be drawn into a conflict. The country had to be fully prepared to face the situation. This led Brezhnev to observe, '. . . we have a more grave picture before us than we had before'. An important point that had emerged from her observations was that the 'provisional Government of Bangladesh' would not accept anything less than independence. Brezhnev, who seemed to be the most sympathetic of the troika, conceded that the conflict in East Pakistan 'may be, in some respects, a war of national liberation', but he added that since the Soviet Union recognized Pakistan as a single entity, it could only view the conflict as a civil war. Kosygin urged that India should not get involved in the Pakistani civil war. The East Pakistanis, he warned, wanted to 'shove on' to India's shoulders their national conflict.

When Mrs Gandhi referred to the increasing domestic pressure on her to recognize the provisional government of Bangladesh, each member of the troika cautioned her against taking this step. Brezhnev said that 'rendering practical assistance to the guerrillas is quite another question', but extending formal recognition would close the door to a political or negotiated solution. The reactions of Pakistan, China, the US and other western countries had to be considered. Formal recognition would precipitate a war and cause an increase in the influx of refugees. Podgorny added that recognition would not be timely if the freedom fighters were not in a position to ensure their independence. Kosygin warned, '. . . once you are drawn into it, it will be difficult to get out of such a conflict.' He proposed an alternative course of action: Soviet and Indian diplomats could jointly work out measures to put pressure on Pakistan to desist from assuming 'provocative postures'.

'Thinking aloud', Brezhnev suggested a meeting between Mrs Gandhi and Yahya Khan to discuss the return of refugees, stopping of atrocities, etc. World public opinion, he added, would favour such an initiative. The Indian prime minister rejected the proposal. 'I doubt if I could return to my country if I did this,' she said. This was not an Indo-Pakistan problem, she pointed out firmly.

Summing up the discussions, Brezhnev sought to distil some 'common points' that had emerged. He said that the two sides shared a common desire to find a peaceful solution, though they differed on the question of high-level Indo-Pakistan negotiations. He assured the Indian prime minister of his 'complete political support'. He warned that it would be undesirable to recognize Bangladesh 'at present', as this might create further complications, but this did not mean that 'our two countries will be at different poles'. He proposed that the two foreign ministries should coordinate concrete measures. The Soviet Union also needed some time to consider what measures it could take to influence Pakistan and world opinion.[10]

The summit did not bridge the basic difference between the two sides. The troika continued to insist on a negotiated settlement, warning against the consequences of a war. The Indian prime minister rejected outright Soviet suggestions concerning Indo-Pakistan negotiations, insisting that negotiations on the future of East Bengal could only be held between Pakistan and the Awami League led by Mujibur Rahman. She warned that war seemed imminent. However, despite these persisting differences, the summit proved fruitful. The first chinks had begun to appear in the Soviet diplomatic armour. Brezhnev had made a significant concession when he acknowledged that 'in some respects' the Bangladesh freedom struggle was a war of national liberation. (The sharp-eyed Dhar took note that Podgorny had nodded in assent at this point.[11]) This hesitant half-step opened up important new possibilities. Second, the Soviet leaders were left in no doubt that India was determined, one way or another, to ensure that the millions of refugees who had fled across the border would be enabled to return to their homeland. Moscow did not question this aim, even though it was not yet ready to accept the inevitability of war.

These outcomes were reflected in the skilfully drafted joint statement issued after the talks. In its English version, it spoke in more than one place of 'East Bengal', while the Russian version continued to refer to 'East Pakistan'.[12] (American diplomats did not fail to notice the discrepancy. When Ambassador Keating inquired about it, Foreign Secretary Kaul explained that it was mutually agreed with the Soviets.[13]) The joint communique also called for a solution 'paying regard to the wishes, the *inalienable rights* and lawful interests [emphasis added]' of the people of East Bengal. Self-determination is an 'inalienable right' in international law. To eyes trained to read between the lines of diplomatic documents, the joint communique hinted at a nuanced adjustment of the Soviet position that the civil war in 'East Pakistan' was a purely domestic question. Finally, the Soviet side 'took into account' the Indian prime minister's statement that 'India is fully determined to take all necessary measures' to ensure the early return of the refugees to their homeland, while reaffirming at the same time their own position as expressed in Podgorny's 2 April letter to Yahya Khan. The reference in the joint statement to Mrs Gandhi's position prompted the Pakistani ambassador in Moscow, Jamsheed Marker, to speculate whether the 'Kremlin and New Delhi had arrived at a tacit understanding that . . . armed Indian intervention, with full Soviet material and diplomatic backing, was a possibility to be considered'.[14]

Reassessment in Moscow

Indira Gandhi had made it clear to the troika that a peaceful solution to the East Bengal crisis could only be found through direct negotiations between the Pakistan government and Mujibur Rahman or his representatives. Wanting to leave no stone unturned in its quest for peace, Moscow decided to explore this unpromising option. An opportunity presented itself in mid-October, when the Shah of Iran held a grand celebration in Persepolis to mark the 2500th anniversary of the founding of the Persian empire. A meeting was duly arranged between Podgorny and Yahya Khan. The Soviet president suggested to Yahya that he should release Mujib – 'an essential factor in any peace process' – and secure his agreement on future plans for the eastern wing. Everything would then fall into its proper place. Yahya angrily rejected the proposal, stating that he would never talk to the 'traitor'. He referred to his own plans to bring back normalcy in a few months. Podgorny replied sharply that the next few months would only see more bloodshed: 'Please, Mr President, do not base your hope on plans which may not materialize. You do not have unlimited time.' It was an appeal as well as a warning. Yahya dismissed it outright. 'From then onwards,' recalls Pakistani Foreign Secretary Sultan Khan, 'Moscow became increasingly hostile and its communications were openly threatening in tone and content.'[15]

After Yahya's rebuff, Moscow moved closer to New Delhi's assessment. Towards the end of October, Soviet Deputy Foreign Minister Firyubin arrived in India for consultations. The agenda covered specific issues of military supplies as well as general considerations bearing on war and peace. During Indira Gandhi's Moscow visit, the Indian delegation had handed over to the Soviet side a list of military equipment – including such items as armoured personnel carriers, GRAD rocket launchers, heavy mechanical bridges and Mi8 helicopters – that were originally scheduled for delivery in 1972. The Indian delegation had requested that these deliveries be expedited and the items supplied in 1971 itself with a view to increasing India's deterrence capacity.[16] Firyubin brought a favourable response to these requests, confirming that the most urgent requirements would be airlifted if necessary.[17]

On the East Bengal question, Firyubin urged his hosts to pursue their objectives by assisting the liberation movement but without getting directly involved in a war with Pakistan. After Firyubin's discussions with Mrs Gandhi, Swaran Singh and Dhar, Counsellor Purushottam, a shrewd analyst of Soviet policy, hazarded this opinion:

> Soviet support to us in the event of war may be expected to consist of (a) the maintenance of essential supplies . . . (b) the maintenance of a regular channel of communications between the two countries and (c) close coordination with India at the United Nations . . . No clear idea seems to have been given of possible Soviet action in case of involvement of third countries in the situation . . . What I feel, however, is that . . . [the] Soviet response to any third party involvement would be determined in full realisation of . . . [the treaty] commitment.

In Purushottam's view, Firyubin's assurance of support was 'unequivocal and explicit' Firyubin's discussions in New Delhi reflected the ongoing evolution of Soviet thinking. After Persepolis, Moscow had shed its hopes of a negotiated settlement between Islamabad and the Awami League, but it had yet to accept the full implications of the impossibility of a peaceful resolution. It took that final step at the end of November.[18]

11

Indira Gandhi Visits Western Capitals

It was evident by October 1971 that the international community was not prepared to exert the pressure required to compel Yahya Khan to seriously address the refugee problem and come to terms with the Awami League. The United States, the country exercising the greatest influence in Islamabad, not only refused to press Yahya Khan to adopt any measure that he might find unpalatable but failed even to condemn the brutal suppression of human rights in East Bengal. The flow of refugees into India continued unabated, imposing intense economic and social stress in India's eastern provinces. In September, with the end of the rainy season, there was a sharp rise in tensions along India's eastern borders. Mukti Bahini operations expanded dramatically, precipitating frequent border clashes, while Pakistan began to strengthen its troop deployment along India's western borders.

On 12 October, US ambassador Kenneth Keating called on Foreign Minister Swaran Singh to convey Washington's concern over the increasing risk of war between Pakistan and India. He said the United States had specific information that 40,000 Mukti Bahini fighters were poised to cross the border by mid-October, with another 20,000 following at the end of the month. Mukti Bahini operations on this scale could not be achieved without Indian support. If this report was correct, Pakistan would make a military response in the west. Nobody could accuse India of initiating the problem, but India had a responsibility – of preventing it from escalating into war. Keating warned that if war were to break out, it would have a serious impact on Indo-US relations. Therefore, in order to reduce the danger of an Indo-Pakistan conflict, the United States proposed that both India and Pakistan should (a) pull back forces from the border; and (b) place curbs on parties involved in cross-border operations on the eastern and western borders.

Swaran Singh asked if he had understood Keating correctly to say that Indo-US relations would be adversely affected if Pakistan were to attack India in retaliation for the success of the freedom fighters and India were to defend itself against the Pakistani attack. He rejected the description of Mukti Bahini actions as 'cross-border' operations, pointing out that most of these actions took place deep inside East Bengal. 'When history judges these events, it will attribute to you the greatest responsibility for this situation, for your military and political support to the [Pakistani] military junta . . . To start at this point without going into the chain of events is to distort reality,' he said.[1] The US proposal failed to address the root cause of the crisis – the brutal suppression of the people of East Bengal by the Pakistan army.

Such was the state of play when Indira Gandhi embarked on a tour of the major western capitals of London, Paris, Bonn, Vienna, Brussels and Washington. She offered a bland, low-key explanation for her tour. 'Our country is facing danger,' she declared in a national broadcast. 'Yet, after much thought, I decided to undertake the journey. The invitations were of long standing and it seemed important in the present situation to meet leaders of other countries for an exchange of views and to put to them the reality of our situation.'[2]

As we saw earlier, on the eve of her departure, she confided her aim to the Bangladesh leaders, Syed Nazrul Islam and Tajuddin Ahmed. She informed them that she was going to make a final appeal to the international community to push for a peaceful and urgent solution to the crisis but that she was not optimistic about the outcome. A final solution, she confided, might have to be found through other means.

In each of the capitals she visited, the Indian prime minister would explain why the East Bengal crisis could only be resolved through negotiations between Islamabad and Mujib's Awami League and why India rejected proposals that treated the question as an Indo-Pakistan issue. These included proposals for mutual troop withdrawals, stationing of UN observers on the border, and offers of 'good offices' between India and Pakistan. She would highlight the threat to India's security resulting from Pakistan's policy of 'exporting' its internal political problem by driving millions of refugees into India. She would seek international support for India's stand, while indicating that India would not be deterred from defending her security.

Apart from projecting India's stand on the crisis, Indira Gandhi also had a specific objective – to dissuade America's European allies from toeing the US line at the United Nations.[3] This applied particularly to the two permanent members of the Security Council, the UK and France. Mrs Gandhi had few expectations from her Washington visit, but she needed to reciprocate Nixon's 1969 visit to India. Moreover, after her visits to Moscow, London, Paris and other capitals, exclusion of Washington from her itinerary would have caused undesirable speculation.

United Kingdom

In London, Mrs Gandhi had a one-to-one meeting with Prime Minister Edward Heath on 31 October. Heath broached the question of mutual withdrawal of troops and posting of UN observers in border areas to prevent a conflict. Indira Gandhi explained why India rejected these suggestions, emphasizing that an agreement between Islamabad and the Awami League was required to resolve the crisis peacefully. Asked about the possible outcome of such talks, she said that she was not sure if Mujib would settle for anything less than independence. She also indicated that she did not see how she could continue to hold back the great domestic pressures she faced and said she feared that war might break out. Heath asked the Indian prime minister to keep him informed if the situation deteriorated.[4]

The British side explored the question of a dialogue and political settlement in greater detail the next day, when Foreign Secretary Douglas-Home called on Mrs Gandhi. Douglas-Home inquired what sort of a political solution would suit India best. The Indian prime minister began by recalling that Islamabad had used East Pakistan as a base for Naga, Mizo and other anti-India insurgencies. 'However, the situation in East Bengal is now so chaotic that it causes us serious concern which we cannot tolerate. Naxalites on our side have taken advantage of the situation.' Referring to the 1938 Munich Agreement with Hitler, she observed that no lasting solution could be found by 'buying peace'. 'We feel that had the world community taken greater interest in matters as they developed, they could have helped to bring the situation under control, but its failure to take positive action only made matters worse.' When the British foreign secretary raised the question of a dialogue, Mrs Gandhi replied that a dialogue could take place only between Yahya and the Bangladesh leaders.[5]

Following these candid discussions, Foreign Secretary T.N. Kaul and his counterpart, Sir Dennis Greenhill, met to analyse the implications of the talks that had taken place at the higher political levels. Greenhill said that some of Mrs Gandhi's statements indicated that war was perhaps now inevitable. He asked what role India expected third countries to play in the event of hostilities and what position India would take on any intervention by the United Nations. To the first question, Kaul gave the guarded reply that India did not want war, but that if it was attacked India would be compelled to fight. He was blunt in his answers to the other questions. If war broke out, India would not be in a position to accept a return to the status quo in East Bengal. India saw no reason why other countries should get involved. 'We would also react very strongly against any attempt to equate India and Pakistan. We hope that the

British government would not react in the manner it did in 1965,' he observed pointedly.[6] (This was a reference to Prime Minister Wilson's pro-Pakistan tilt during the 1965 Indo-Pakistan war, which he later acknowledged was a misstep.)

These candid discussions proved fruitful. Heath wrote to Yahya Khan on 9 November asking him to consider releasing Mujib and holding negotiations with the Awami League. (Yahya rejected the appeal, stating that it was impossible for him to negotiate with Mujib.) At the end of the month, Heath told members of the Cabinet Committee on Defence and Overseas Policy that '. . . in the long run our interest probably lay more with India than Pakistan', adding, '. . . we should take care not to repeat our 1965 experience when . . . we had suffered maximum disadvantage without compensating benefit from either side'.[7]

France

In Paris, too, the Indian prime minister found a positive response. President Pompidou went through the motions of sounding her out on mutual troop withdrawals along the Indo-Pakistan borders, the UN secretary general's offer of his good offices, and direct talks between Mrs Gandhi and Yahya Khan. He did not press these suggestions after Mrs Gandhi explained India's firm position. The discussions in Paris proved very productive. The French side agreed that a peaceful resolution could be found only if Mujib were released from prison and negotiations held with him. Pompidou offered to write to Yahya in this sense. Paris also agreed that the emergence of an independent Bangladesh was only a matter of time.[8] The French president kept his word. On 18 November, the French ambassador in Islamabad handed over a letter from Pompidou to Yahya Khan calling for Mujib's release and suggesting that negotiations be held with the Awami League. Yahya angrily rejected these suggestions.[9]

Federal Republic of Germany

In her talks with Chancellor Willy Brandt in Bonn, Indira Gandhi went over the same ground on the questions of mutual troop withdrawals and mediation between India and Pakistan. Brandt was sympathetic when Gandhi emphasized that a peaceful solution could be found only if Mujib were released from prison and negotiations resumed with the Awami League. The chancellor agreed to write to Yahya seeking Mujib's release.[10] Haksar and Kaul took up with West German officials the question of their bracketing India with Pakistan in the matter of the arms embargo. They asked that the embargo on exports to India be lifted and that all previous commitments to India be honoured. Following Mrs Gandhi's visit, Brandt issued orders for resumption of arms deliveries to India, while keeping in place the embargo against Pakistan.[11]

Austria and Belgium

The visits to Vienna and Brussels were of less consequence. The Austrian president and chancellor both expressed great sympathy and understanding the Indian position, but pleaded their inability to take a public position in view of their former Foreign Minister Kurt Waldheim's candidature for the post of UN secretary general.[12] In Brussels, Mrs Gandhi's talks with Prime Minister Gaston Eyskens commenced on unexpected lines. Eyskens, a former economics professor, launched on a lengthy discourse on international economic issues, taking up most of the available time. This was not the subject at the top of the Indian prime minister's agenda, but she took the opportunity to seek and obtain Belgian support for expediting a pending economic and commercial agreement between India and the European Economic Community (EEC). Finally, Eyskens turned to what he described as the 'refugee problem'. This gave Mrs Gandhi an opportunity to explain that, apart from the economic burden of coping with the refugee influx, the continued presence of millions of refugees imposed unbearable social and political stresses on India. 'I am sitting on a volcano,' she said. She gave a negative reply when the Belgian premier asked about the possibility of the UN organizing repatriation of the refugees. This led Eyskens to reflect that the 'only way out is to grant greater autonomy but, of course, this is an internal problem of Pakistan'. When Mrs Gandhi pointed out the implications for India's security, Eyskens modified his position, and said, 'Although theoretically it is an internal problem for Pakistan, there have been examples where the UN has intervened in similar circumstances, as for example, in Angola, Mozambique, the Portuguese colonies and South Africa. Perhaps the UN can consider some action.'[13] The Belgian prime minister's observations on East Bengal ended on that erratic and inconclusive note.

United States

Writing to Kaul in mid-August, L.K. Jha reported:

> The most significant feature of Indo-American relations in the recent past has been that in terms of public opinion, Press and media response and Congressional support, we have reached an unprecedented high water mark, while in terms of relations with the Administration, we have reached a particularly low ebb . . . The attitude of the Administration is based largely on the President's personal reaction to India. He has a feeling that he is personally not liked by Indians and that supporters of India in this country have always worked against him . . . He is pleased with the kind of homage the Pakistanis always pay him.[14]

In the course of preparations for Mrs Gandhi's US visit, Jha alerted New Delhi to the state of affairs in the Washington bureaucracy:

> In the higher echelons of the State Department, there is no particular knowledge or experience of South Asia. The lower echelons, both on the India Desk and on the Pakistan Desk, have supported our view-

point, i.e., cut off military supplies to Pakistan, suspend economic aid, pressurize Yahya Khan to end military action and negotiate a political settlement with Sheikh Mujibur Rahman. As early as May-June 1971, they had argued that the old Pakistan would be hard to put together. The Pentagon had independently formulated the same judgement.

The President brushed these views aside. His senior political advisers (Kissinger, Rogers, Sisco and Irwin) had neither the expertise nor the inclination to try to mould the President's judgement. The continuance of the military supply pipeline and economic assistance to Pakistan was personally ordered by him in late May and reaffirmed in June and again in August.

Leakages of confidential information were taking place from the Pakistan desk of the State Department and the entire personnel of that desk was changed beginning with July.[15]

Both Nixon and Mrs Gandhi approached their encounter with some apprehension. Nixon confided to British Foreign Secretary Douglas-Home his fear that the Indian prime minister might 'come in here and, frankly, pull our legs'.[16] Mrs Gandhi had similar concerns. After meeting her, John Kenneth Galbraith told Kissinger that she was uncertain about the reception she would get in Washington. One of her aides had told him that she was apprehensive about some kind off 'brush-off' in the US capital.[17]

When the two leaders commenced their discussions on 4 November, they concealed their mutual distrust behind an elaborate screen of courtesies. Nixon addressed Mrs Gandhi as an 'old friend'. (He commonly described her as a 'bitch' in conversations with close associates.) Indira Gandhi reciprocated with equally insincere expressions of admiration for Nixon's China and Vietnam initiatives.

Getting down to business, Nixon made a skilful presentation of his Pakistan policy, emphasizing that initiation of hostilities between India and Pakistan was 'unacceptable'. For this very reason, he argued, it was imperative for the United States to retain influence with Pakistan. His policy was shaped by this factor. The US military assistance progamme had been retained in a 'most limited fashion' in this context. Regarding the refugee problem, the United States aimed to be as 'helpful as possible without interjecting itself into the internal affairs of the parties'.

Nixon proceeded to outline the positive impact of US initiatives. First, in June–July, it had 'persuaded' Pakistan that a famine would occur in East Pakistan unless massive preventive steps were taken. Also, as a result of US pressure, Yahya Khan had given up his initial opposition to an international relief presence in East Pakistan. US–Pakistani and UN efforts had succeeded in preventing a widespread famine, which might have further exacerbated the exodus of 'Moslem refugees' and added to India's burdens. Second, at the US urging, Yahya had appointed a civilian governor in East Pakistan and had announced an amnesty for persons of all creeds. Third, the US had obtained an assurance from Yahya that Mujib would not be executed. Fourth, at US's urging, Yahya had agreed to pull back some troops from India's western border as a first step to de-escalation. Finally, word had just been received from Yahya that he was prepared to hold direct 'discussions' with 'cleared' Awami League leaders, to meet a Bangladesh leader from Kolkata and to consider the US suggestion that Mujib be allowed to designate the representative.

Nixon said he recognized that 'in the long run Pakistan must acquiesce in the direction of greater autonomy for East Pakistan', but the US could not urge Yahya to accept policies that would result in his overthrow. He asked rhetorically whether Mrs Gandhi believed Yahya could really survive if he were to release Mujib at this point in time. Nixon said the greatest danger would arise if either India or Pakistan were to consider military action to seek a solution that 'only an historical process can settle'. He concluded by warning the Indian prime minister that an Indo-Pakistan conflict might not be limited to just the two countries; it would have 'implications and possibly great dangers for the whole framework of world peace. The American people would not understand if India were to initiate military action against Pakistan.'

Indira Gandhi had no intention of either negotiating with Nixon

or confronting him. Her plans were already drawn up. Avoiding a specific reply to the points raised by Nixon, her response took the form of some general observations on South Asian developments since the partition of British India. Pakistan had attacked India in 1947 and again in 1965, employing, on the latter occasion, arms provided by the US. Since then, US arms shipments to Pakistan had become a very sensitive issue in Indian politics. Despite the government's attempts to restrain public outrage, this factor could not but affect the stand of the Indian government towards the US. She contrasted the repressive policies of Pakistani governments in response to demands for greater autonomy in Baluchistan and the North-West Frontier with the forbearance shown by India towards its own separatist elements. West Pakistan had dealt with the people of East Bengal in a treacherous and deceitful way and had always confined them to an inferior role. She went on to describe in detail the atrocities inflicted on the people of East Bengal. Despite all these oppressive measures, the Pakistani army had been unable to re-establish control over the area and it was no longer realistic to expect East and West Pakistan to remain united. The prime minister stressed the crucial role of Mujib in any search for a settlement. Finally, the prime minister referred to the threat to India's security resulting from Pakistani actions. She said her main concern was the impact on India itself.[18] Mrs Gandhi deliberately chose not to engage on the specific points raised by Nixon.

There were no further discussions on the East Bengal crisis between Mrs Gandhi and Nixon. As previously agreed, the agenda for the final session meeting on 5 November dealt with global developments, including the US opening with China, Vietnam, the Middle East and US–USSR relations. However, officials of the two sides, led by Kaul and Undersecretary of State Irwin, met to seek further clarification of each other's positions. Mrs Gandhi had chosen not to respond to Nixon's suggestion regarding talks between Islamabad and 'cleared' Awami League representatives. Irwin explored with Kaul the possibility of a dialogue between Islamabad and an Awami League representative.

When Kaul inquired which Awami League leader Irwin had in mind, a State Department official replied that Khondaker Mushtaque Ahmed might fit the role. Kaul dismissed the suggestion, saying that he doubted whether Mushtaque had the authority to negotiate on behalf of Bangladesh. Kaul showed greater interest in a dialogue between nominees of President Yahya and Sheikh Mujib, though he emphasized that only the Bangladesh government-in-exile could take a decision on this question. India could not speak for the people of Bangladesh. The Bangladesh government insisted that Sheikh Mujib must be released from prison. Kaul inquired whether Mujib's nominee would be allowed to meet the incarcerated Bangladesh leader. What faith could the Bangladesh authorities have in negotiations, he asked, when Islamabad had announced that fresh – and obviously fraudulent – elections would be held in December to replace the freely elected representatives of the people of East Bengal? (Since Kaul had not rejected the proposal for talks between nominees of Yahya and Mujib, the State Department instructed US ambassador to Pakistan Farland to explore the proposal with the Pakistani president. Farland reported on 18 November that Yahya had rejected the proposal.[19]) Kaul, on his part, sought clarification on a point of critical interest to India. Stressing the urgency of a political settlement, he inquired about the time frame Washington had in mind. Irwin replied, 'We have no time schedule in mind.'[20]

The dazzling brilliance of Kissinger's memoirs obscures its factual errors. Kissinger claims in *White House Years* that the United States '. . . accepted autonomy as inevitable and independence as probable . . . Bangladesh would come into being by the spring of 1972 if procedures were given a chance'. He suggests that Washington was ready to work with India on issues like securing Mujib's release. He says that in the talks with Mrs Gandhi, Nixon '. . . stressed his conviction that the outcome was bound to be autonomy for East Pakistan leading to independence'.[21] The archival records, however, suggest that Kissinger is parsimonious with the truth. The White House memorandum recording the discussions between Nixon and Mrs Gandhi does not support any of these claims.

Far from offering to work with India to secure Mujib's release, the record shows that Nixon rejected the idea, saying that he could not be expected to propose a step that might lead to Yahya's fall from power. Nixon did not indicate that Bangladesh would become independent at any stage; he spoke only of 'greater autonomy' in the 'long run' and suggested that a resolution of the problem should be left to a 'historical process'. Irwin confirmed to Kaul that the United States had no particular time frame in mind for a political settlement of the East Bengal crisis.

Kissinger also omits to mention that within days of Mrs Gandhi's visit, he and Nixon came to recognize the bankruptcy of their Pakistan policy. On 5 November, US Aid Coordinator for Pakistan Maurice Williams filed a devastating report on his recent visit to that country:

> The reality is that Army policies and operations – behind the façade of a civilian government – are progressively and seriously alienating the Bengali population in East Pakistan . . . As Military Advisor, he [Major General Rao Farman Ali Khan] sits in the Governor's house and runs the province on behalf of the Governor. My call on General Farman Ali Khan October 25th interrupted a meeting with some ten of his military colleagues. They were, he said, selecting the men who would be elected in the next Provincial elections . . . Pakistan Army commanders continue to carry out terror raids against the population and villages.

Williams' final conclusion was:

> All official American suggestions are immediately taken seriously and lead to major policy statements by President Yahya Khan in Islamabad. The result is 'public relations diplomacy', but it is important not to confuse the form with the substance of policy. Elections, political accommodation, welcoming the return of all refugees, amnesty – these are fine policy pronouncements, but their implementation is in the hands of Army commanders who govern the Eastern Province, and these Army commanders do not as yet appear to be subject to foreign influences.[22]

Shaken by the report, Kissinger drew the president's attention to its highlights, suggesting that 'it may be time to add a new chapter in our strategy toward Pakistan . . . If President Yahya's own electoral process and the practices of his army will not win wide enough support to defuse the guerrilla campaign, the question then arises what other political steps he might take to establish a viable political alternative to the guerrilla's demand for independence.' Nixon recorded a marginal note: 'K – This is now imperative give me a recommendation.'[23] In the event, however, there was no policy change. The White House remained committed to a policy that it knew was doomed to fail.

On her return to India, Mrs Gandhi made a statement in parliament on 15 November concerning her foreign tour. She made no exaggerated claims of success. The prime minister said that she had put across to heads of government and makers of public opinion the threat posed to India's stability and regional peace by the situation prevailing in Bangladesh. Her discussions had helped to highlight the 'root cause' of the problem – the refusal of the Pakistani military regime to respect the electoral verdict, the reign of terror let loose on the people of Bangladesh by the Pakistani army, and the resultant influx of refugees into India. The countries she had visited realized that a political solution should be found through negotiations with the elected leaders of the people of Bangladesh. 'Most' of them also realized the importance of securing Sheikh Mujib's release, and they intended to convey this to Pakistan. The prime minister also said that she had 'exposed' Pakistan's efforts to sidetrack the basic issue by seeking to involve the United Nations, so as to convert the Bangladesh struggle into an Indo-Pakistan confrontation. Making a special reference to the UK, the prime minister said, 'I think my visit also helped to restore our relations with Britain which had suffered a serious setback in 1965.'

'We cannot depend on the international community . . . to solve our problems for us,' she emphasized. India appreciated moral and political support from other countries, but the 'brunt of the burden has to be borne by us and the people of Bangladesh, who have our fullest sympathy and support'. There was no chest-thumping or striking of theatrical postures in her speech. The prime minister exuded an air of quiet resolve. 'Calmness of spirit and strength go together,' she said. 'India is calm and we are capable of taking decisions in defence of our security and stability.'

By this time, Mrs Gandhi scarcely bothered to conceal her conviction that a solution based on a united Pakistan was no longer on the cards. Thus, in an interview to *Newsweek* magazine, she said, '. . . it is our assessment that East Bengal cannot remain united with Pakistan ever again in the same way it has been'.[24]

Right from the beginning of the crisis, Indira Gandhi had made a special effort to take leaders of the opposition parties into confidence and, by and large, they had reciprocated her trust. Their calls for immediate action were not designed to force her hand; rather, they strengthened her hand in international negotiations. In her speech in parliament on 15 November, the prime minister thanked '. . . all the political parties who have shown wisdom and restraint and kept the nation united against any external threat'.[25]

12

Prelude to War

By mid-November, most of the pieces on the chessboard of India's grand strategy had been moved into position. This was ensured by planned moves on the political, military and diplomatic fronts. On the home political front, a herculean effort was made to provide shelter and sustenance to some 10 million refugees. The inevitable tensions between refugees and host communities competing for living space and jobs were successfully contained, and most importantly, the central and state authorities had ensured maintenance of communal harmony, at a time when millions of Hindus were being driven across the border by the Pakistan army. On the military front, hand in hand with the Mujibnagar authorities, the Indian army had trained and equipped a vast army of freedom fighters, who were making their presence felt all over the East Bengal countryside. Indian troop movements to the eastern border had commenced in October. On the diplomatic front, India had taken prompt action to countervail an unforeseeable 'geo-political revolution' and an emerging quasi-alliance between Pakistan, the United States and China.

Post-war planning

On her return from the United States, Indira Gandhi met with the Bangladesh leaders Syed Nazrul Islam and Tajuddin Ahmed on 16

November to pick up the threads from their discussions on the eve of her tour to the western capitals. The Indian prime minister briefed the Bangladesh leaders on her talks in Europe and the United States. This was followed by a survey of developments on the liberation war front.[1]

Following up on these discussions, D.P. Dhar arrived in Kolkata on 19 November for detailed consultations with Tajuddin and senior Mujibnagar officials. These wide-ranging discussions covered not only questions of military cooperation to bring the liberation struggle to a speedy and successful conclusion, but also planning for the immediate post-liberation months. Dhar also addressed a question that is often overlooked by military planners – of bringing the Indian troops back home within a specific time frame. He emphasized that India wanted to withdraw its forces from Bangladesh as soon as possible after its liberation, lest it should lose the goodwill it had earned. He spelled out his question in clear terms: how soon, in the opinion of his interlocutors, would India be able to withdraw its forces from Bangladesh? The Mujibnagar authorities replied that the answer depended on several factors. If Pakistan resorted to a 'scorched earth' policy, or if it still retained a capacity to pose a continuing threat to an independent Bangladesh, Dhaka might require an Indian military presence on Bangladesh for a longer period. In the absence of these complications, it might be hoped that the Bangladesh government would be able to cope with the situation within three or four months. This period would be shortened if Sheikh Mujib was freed from his Pakistani prison and allowed to return to Bangladesh to lead his country.

Dhar's question also led to a discussion of other formidable problems that would confront post-liberation Bangladesh. Foremost of these was the restoration of law and order in a country where this had ceased to exist and which was awash with arms. A large number of freedom fighters would have to be disarmed after liberation and given opportunities for their absorption into nation-building tasks. Weapons would also have to be recovered from the criminal Razakar bands armed by the Pakistanis. Then there was the massive problem of speedily repatriating and rehabilitating some 10 million Bangladeshi refugees from India. The communications infrastructure – roads, bridges, railways and ports – damaged during the liberation war would have to be made functional as soon as possible. Distribution of foodstuff and other essential commodities would have to be ensured. The administrative system, disrupted by the war, would have to be restored.[2] The scope and scale of the required operations were nothing less than heroic. The speedy restoration of normalcy in post-liberation Bangladesh was a tribute to the foresight of the planners.

As the Mujibnagar government addressed these challenges in the latter half of November 1971, it sought New Delhi's assistance where necessary. Virtually every department of the Government of India – cabinet secretariat, PMO, defence ministry, home ministry, planning commission, railways, shipping, food and agriculture, and health, among others – closely cooperated with the Mujibnagar government in drawing up plans for a post-war Bangladesh. A flavour of these consultations emerges from the agenda of Mujibnagar Cabinet Secretary Imam's discussions on 19 November with D.K. Bhattacharya, joint secretary in the PMO, who had flown over to Kolkata for the meeting. The list of issues raised by Imam included restoration of law and order; provision of essential commodities; rehabilitation of displaced persons; provision of essential health services; and civil–military relations.[3]

Military moves

As we saw in Chapter 5, the rising tempo of Mukti Bahini operations brought about a major shift in Pakistan's military deployments in East Bengal. The Pakistan army decided in mid-September 1971 to adopt a forward posture of defence, with the aim of preventing the Mukti Bahini from carving out a liberated zone. This envisaged the defence of important border outposts – to prevent ingress by the Mukti Bahini and deny a secure territorial base to them. Troops were redeployed to the border from the 'Dhaka bowl'. Other interior strongholds and reserves were also depleted. This fell in with the Indian strategy of drawing Pakistani forces to the border, bypassing their fortified defensive positions, paralysing the opponent by destroying the Pakistani command and control network, and crossing the Padma and Meghna rivers as opportunity arose to advance on Dhaka in support of the main thrust from the north.[4] Thus the Mukti Bahini operations prepared the ground for a rapid advance by regular forces.

The intensification of coordinated actions by the Indian army and the Mukti Bahini necessitated an understanding regarding the line of command and control. Following informal discussions, the Mujibnagar cabinet decided towards the end of October to place Bangladesh forces under the command of Indian army formations. Col. Osmani, commander-in-chief of the Bangladesh forces, initially objected to this arrangement, but finally fell in with the views of the cabinet.[5] This decision was the precursor to the Joint Command formed after the outbreak of war.

With the intensification of Mukti Bahini cross-border operations in October, the scale and intensity of the Pakistani response registered a corresponding increase. Indian border outposts came under heavy shelling from Pakistani artillery. In response to this development, New Delhi decided in November to allow the Indian army to cross the border up to a distance of 10 miles in order to silence Pakistani guns. In carrying out these instructions, the army also took care to secure specific positions that would strengthen its offensive posture, with an eye on the impending war.[6]

This led to some major battles between Indian and Pakistani troops, involving significant casualties on both sides. On 20 November, Indian forces launched an operation in the Boyra area, in the course of which Pakistan lost fourteen tanks and three aircraft. On 23 November, a determined attack was launched against the Pakistani forces in Hilli on 23 November, on orders from Manekshaw. In the heavy fighting that ensued, Indian losses included sixty-seven killed and ninety wounded. Indian forces were able to register some advances, but Pakistan held onto Hilli itself till the outbreak of war. Maj. Gen. Jacob summed up his assessment of the net effect of the November operations:

> Pakistanis were thrown off balance and our strategy of drawing the Pakistanis to the border began to work. We secured suitable jumping off places, particularly where obstacles had to be crossed, and such operations also gave our troops realistic initiation into battle.[7]

A Pakistani military analyst offers a similar assessment:

> By November 20, we [Pakistanis] had lost most of the border outposts . . . Indian forces had established their forward bases inside our territory to facilitate offensive operations.[8]

Yahya Khan reacted to these developments by accusing India on 22 November of launching an 'all-out attack against East Pakistan'. He proclaimed a state of national emergency the following day.

India and the superpowers

The intensification of the crisis in November led to a further crystallizing of American and Soviet positions. Nixon's 'tilt' towards Pakistan became more pronounced while Moscow shed its reservations about a direct Indian role in the liberation war.

United States

As tensions mounted in South Asia, the State Department recommended a balanced approach. In a meeting chaired by Kissinger on 22 November, Deputy Secretary of State Irwin proposed two parallel initiatives: to persuade Yahya to open a dialogue with Mujib's designated representatives, and to bring up the issue in the UN. The first proposal was aimed at promoting an internal settlement of the crisis, while the other was designed to restrain India from carrying out operations across the international border. Kissinger immediately shot down the first proposal. 'Because Yahya has been attacked, you would bring pressure on Yahya?' he asked sarcastically. '[If] Yahya does not agree to talk to Mujib, we would be contributing to putting Yahya in the wrong.'[9] The proposal for approaching the UN was examined in detail and was dropped later, on the ground that while it might restrain India, it would probably also bring the internal situation in East Pakistan under the spotlight. It was decided to leave it to Pakistan to choose the timing of an appeal to the UN.[10]

In view of the differences between Kissinger and Irwin, Secretary of State Rogers and Kissinger met Nixon on 24 November to seek his instructions. Rogers proposed that the United States should urge restraint on both sides at the highest level 'so that everyone can look at the record and see that we have done everything we can diplomatically'.

'The leverage we have on India is very minimal. If we decide to take some action against them, which you might decide to do, it would be symbolic rather than substantive,' he added. Nixon did not contest this evaluation, but he remained steadfast in calling for a 'tilt' towards Pakistan. '[L]ooking at the balance there, the Indians are going to win . . . Pakistan eventually will disintegrate,' he acknowledged. '[Yet], apart from the fact that Yahya has been more decent to us than she [Indira Gandhi] has . . . I think our policy wherever we can should definitely be tilted toward Pakistan . . . she [Mrs Gandhi] knows that we did not shoot blanks when she was here.'[11]

Washington now launched a new initiative to check India–Bangladesh cross-border movements. India had earlier rejected a call for the stationing of UN personnel on both sides of the border with the ostensible purpose of facilitating refugee repatriation. The White House suggested to Yahya Khan that he request a UN presence on his side of the border, even if India refused to allow a similar presence on its side. The UN presence would have the effect of deterring Indian forces from crossing the border. Yahya at once accepted the suggestion and made a formal request to the UN secretary general on 28 November.[12]

On receiving confirmation of Yahya's acceptance of his suggestion, Nixon wrote to Mrs Gandhi expressing his distress at the 'ominous trend of events' and India's admission that its armed forces have been engaged in Pakistani territory. He reminded her of his warning that the American people would not understand it if Indian actions led to large-scale hostilities. This would 'inevitably affect our ability to be helpful in many other ways', he added, in a scarcely veiled threat of terminating economic aid and military sales to India. Nixon urged Mrs Gandhi to accept the proposal for a mutual pull-back of forces from the West Pakistan border. Nixon also endorsed the latest 'Pakistani' move for stationing UN observers on their side of the East Pakistan border.[13] Simultaneously, the US president wrote to Kosygin seeking his support for these proposals.[14]

Ambassador Keating handed over Nixon's letter to Mrs Gandhi on 29 November. After reading it quickly but carefully, she replied that India had great respect for the United States, but every country must first look at its national interests. The current situation was not of India's making. Yahya Khan's problems were self-created, and India was not in a position to make the situation easier for him. Yahya's latest proposal to hold farcical elections in East Bengal would have no impact whatsoever. 'We are not going to listen to advice that weakens us.' Mrs Gandhi stated that she did not know how to tell the Indian people that they must continue to wait. 'I can't hold it,' she said. Keating reported that Mrs Gandhi spoke with 'clarity and more grimness' than on any previous occasion. The ambassador drew the conclusion that 'in the absence of some major development toward a meaningful political accommodation, India will assure that the efforts of the Mukti Bahini to liberate East Pakistan do not fail'.[15]

On 1 December, the United States imposed an immediate cut-off of military sales to India.[16] This was largely a symbolic act, since India was not seriously dependent on US military supplies, but it was a clear signal of the US position on the war that was about to break out.

The Soviet Union

While providing strong support to India, the Soviet Union had also been urging New Delhi not to get directly involved in a Pakistani civil war. As we saw earlier, there was a partial but significant modification of the Soviet assessment of the crisis during Indira Gandhi's Moscow visit. The Soviet leaders accepted that 'in some respects' the Mukti Bahini's struggle was a 'war of national liberation'. After Yahya's rebuff to Podgorny at Persepolis, the Soviet Union was compelled to abandon its hopes for a peaceful resolution of the civil war. The escalation of the conflict in November brought home to Moscow the inevitability of a war. Before the end of the month, the Soviet Union came to accept that the conflict in East Pakistan involved the principle of self-determination. Finally, at the end of November, Moscow offered India unambiguous assurances of support in the diplomatic battles that lay ahead in the United Nations.

With the approach of war, the Soviet Union closely coordinated its positions with India. Ambassador Pegov met daily with Indian policymakers to keep abreast with developments. On the morning of 27 November, he met twice with D.P. Dhar. In the first meeting, Dhar informed the ambassador that the 'inexorable movement of events in East Bengal is proceeding towards a large-scale conflict. India is no longer in a position to prevent this'. Dhar added that he was confident that India could count on the 'help, understanding and friendship' of the Soviet Union. Pegov said that he fully understood India's position and assured Dhar that the Soviet Union would be a reliable friend and ally. He suggested, in his 'personal capacity', that if an escalation was imminent, it would be advisable for the Indian prime minister to inform the Soviet leaders in the greatest confidence; this would avoid any misunderstanding. Dhar and Pegov met for a second time the same morning. This time, Dhar asked for the envoy's views regarding the timing of India's recognition of Bangladesh. Not surprisingly, the Soviet ambassador expressed no clear opinion on the subject.[17]

On 29 November, Pegov met Foreign Secretary Kaul for a wide-ranging discussion, covering Nixon's letters to Mrs Gandhi and Kosygin, the likelihood of war, the timing of India's recognition of Bangladesh, and Soviet support for India at the UN. Pegov (who was to meet Prime Minister Gandhi the next day) said that the Soviet and Indian responses to Nixon should be on identical lines. When he observed that war seemed imminent, Kaul responded that it depended on Pakistan. India would have preferred a peaceful solution. However, if Pakistan continued to deny independence to Bangladesh, it could only result in intensification of the Mukti Bahini resistance. Pakistan might treat this as an excuse for launching a war against India, in the expectation that this would bring the UN Security Council into the picture. Kaul stressed that India did not want a war on the West Pakistan front. Pegov assured Kaul that the Soviet Union would fully support India in the UN Security Council.[18]

On 30 November, Ambassador Pegov met the Indian prime minister with a message from Moscow. Referring to Nixon's letter to Kosygin, he said, 'I am authorised to convey that our position on these matters is the same as yours, and in future also we shall proceed on the basis of mutual agreement with you . . . Our comrades have directed me to request you for your opinion before they reply to President Nixon.'

Mrs Gandhi's reply left no doubt about India's position. 'The Pakistani army is still killing people in Bangladesh, not only the Mukti Bahini but ordinary peasants also, in an attempt to annihilate as many of them as they can. If at this stage, without any other guarantee, we abandon these people to their fate, what will happen to them?' She said she was not going to reply to Nixon's letter immediately, but would do so later.[19] (With an exquisite sense of timing, Mrs Gandhi chose to reply to Nixon's letter on 15 December, on the eve of the Pakistani surrender in Dhaka!)

Kosygin's message conveyed an unambiguous offer of support to India in the diplomatic battles that lay ahead. On the same day that this message was delivered in New Delhi, the Soviet ambassador at the UN, Yakov Malik, called on the UN secretary general to inform him of the Soviet position. U Thant records in his memoirs:

> He [Malik] said that the basic problem in South Asia was the implementation of self-determination in East Pakistan and the transfer of power to the Awami League. He saw no other alternative. When I asked him what he thought of Security Council action, he replied that if the Security Council were to meet, the only 'sensible thing' for it to do would be to deal with the basic political issue of East Pakistan.[20]

The Cabinet Secretary's Report

It will be recalled that a Special Committee of Secretaries was set up in April to monitor and coordinate implementation of all policies related to the East Bengal crisis. The committee worked ceaselessly throughout November to ensure that no loose ends were left unattended. Finally, on 28 November, the chairman of the committee, Cabinet Secretary Swaminathan, reported to the prime minister: 'Time is running out and the Committee of Secretaries feels that the movement [sic, moment?] for decisive action has come . . . PM [Prime Minister] is aware that over the last several weeks we have made all the preparations necessary in case there are full-scale hostilities, in several fields, e.g. defence, civil supplies, security arrangements, etc. etc. and an international build-up explaining our position and our objectives.' The cabinet secretary attached to his report notes prepared by the different departments. The defence ministry confirmed: 'As soon as a decision is taken, the Defence Services are in a position to secure the defeat and surrender of the occupying forces in East Bengal in the shortest possible time.' The home ministry reported: 'All the States and particularly the border States have confirmed that necessary measures for maintenance of internal security have been taken . . . The need for utmost vigilance to maintain communal peace has been impressed upon the State Governments.' While calling for 'effective action' to liberate Bangladesh 'at the earliest date possible', the foreign ministry suggested, '. . . we should provoke Pakistan into starting a war against us by granting *de jure* recognition to Bangla Desh'. On economic preparations, the cabinet secretary announced: '. . . our foreign exchange reserves are in a fairly comfortable position and no serious situation is likely to emerge in the short term.'[21]

The question of recognition

India did not intend to fire the first shot in an all-out war. New Delhi planned to extend formal recognition to Bangladesh on 4 December, expecting Pakistan to respond by starting the war. In the event, Pakistan launched its offensive across India's western border on 3 December itself, thus providing legal justification for a declaration of war by India. New Delhi therefore decided to delay recognition of Bangladesh till 6 December, in order to de-link the declaration of war from the act of recognition of Bangladesh. Asoke Ray, head of the Indian liaison office in Kolkata, reported the reaction of the Bangladesh leaders when they were informed of the act of recognition on the morning of 6 December. Acting President Syed Nazrul Islam and Prime Minister Tajuddin Ahmed 'were so deeply moved when we informed them of "recognition" that they could hardly speak. The Prime Minister was almost in tears and after a long silence said that his conviction, which dates from his first meeting with our Prime Minister, had proved to be absolutely correct.'[22]

13

War and Diplomacy

On 29 November, Yahya Khan decided to launch an all-out attack on India on the western front. He had scant hope of success, but he felt that the reputation of the Pakistan army would suffer irreparable damage if it were to lose East Pakistan without a full-scale war. He later admitted that the army could not have lived down the ignominy of surrendering East Pakistan without fighting an all-out war with India. His chief of general staff, Lt Gen. Gul Hasan, is reported to have said: '... we had to take this action, otherwise we will not be able to wear our uniforms.'[1] The date of the attack was set for 2 December, but it was later postponed by a day. New Delhi was hoping for just such a decision. It hoped that Pakistan itself would initiate a full-fledged war, conceding to India the legal and political advantage. When Pakistan finally launched its attack on Indian forward airbases on the western front on the evening of 3 December 1971, the Indians were fully prepared. Early warning radars had been suitably positioned, and aircraft had been dispersed and camouflaged.[2] The attack turned out to be a fiasco. The air strikes were followed up with assaults on Indian ground positions in the Chhamb and Ferozepur areas.

With these attacks across India's western borders, Pakistan started the war that India had been preparing to fight since April 1971. By the end of November, India had completed its military and diplomatic preparations for a short and decisive military campaign leading to the liberation of Bangladesh. Its armed forces were in position. It had ensured that the Soviet Union would veto a hostile US or Chinese resolution in the Security Council, and signals had also been received from two other permanent members of the Security Council – France and the UK – indicating differences with their US ally.

The war launched by Pakistan gave India the justification it was seeking for according formal recognition to the People's Republic of Bangladesh. On 6 December, Indira Gandhi announced in parliament:

> Now that Pakistan is waging war against India, the normal hesitation on our part not to do anything which could come in the way of [a] peaceful solution, or which might be construed as intervention, has lost its significance. The people of Bangladesh battling for their very existence and the people of India fighting to defeat aggression, now find themselves partisans in the same cause.
>
> I am glad to inform the House that in the light of the existing situation and in response to the repeated requests of the Government of Bangla Desh the Government of India have after the most careful consideration, decided to grant recognition to the GANA PRAJATANTRI BANGLA DESH.[3]

The next day, India and Bangladesh entered into an agreement to create a Joint Command for the liberation war under Lt Gen. Jagjit Singh Aurora. The general was explicitly instructed to report to both the Indian and Bangladesh governments.

The military operations leading up to the Pakistani surrender at Dhaka have been studied in detail by several analysts, including many of the leading protagonists. It is not our intention to enter this well-trodden field. Our aim is to study the interplay between the military and diplomatic moves that enabled military operations to be pursued without interruption to a decisive conclusion; the attainment of the overall political aim of assisting the speedy emergence of the new state of Bangladesh and the return of the millions of Bangladeshi refugees to their homeland.

The 'tilt'

Nixon's 'tilt' towards Pakistan posed the most formidable challenge to the attainment of India's aims. On 1 December, even before the outbreak of war, Nixon suspended military sales to India. This, in itself, was a matter of little practical consequence, since India's arms imports from the US were negligible. Indeed, the State Department had earlier pointed out the futility of the move.[4] When Keating conveyed the presidential decision to Kaul, the Indian foreign secretary received it with equanimity, stating firmly that pressure tactics would not work with India.[5] Nor was suspension of foreign aid, announced shortly thereafter, of great importance – at least in the short run. India, in 1971, was no longer as critically dependent on foreign aid as it had been in the past two decades.

More serious were three other manifestations of the White House 'tilt'. First, immediately upon the outbreak of war, the United States raised the issue in the United Nations. It spared no effort to impose an immediate ceasefire and troop withdrawals through a Security Council resolution, before the liberation war could be brought to a successful conclusion. An early ceasefire imposed by the Security Council was precisely the contingency that India had feared and anticipated in drawing up its strategic plans. India relied on a Soviet veto to thwart such initiatives until military operations had reached a successful conclusion. Second, Nixon and Kissinger attempted to 'scare off' or intimidate India by sending a nuclear carrier task force into the Indian Ocean while also encouraging China to exert military pressure on India's borders. While New Delhi had anticipated the UN move, a menacing US naval presence in the Indian Ocean had previously been dismissed by Indian policymakers as inconceivable. Finally, the White House tried to undercut Soviet support for India by linking this issue with the prospects of detente. The Bangladesh crisis erupted at a time when the United States and the Soviet Union were engaged in exploring the possibility of detente. A major breakthrough was expected during Nixon's planned visit to Moscow in May 1972. The White House strongly hinted that continued Soviet support for India would prejudice the prospects of detente. A fundamental feature of Nixon's interpretation of detente was the concept of 'linkage'. This meant, in Nixon's own words, that '... crisis or confrontation in one place and real cooperation in another cannot long be sustained simultaneously'.[6]

The United Nations

On the outbreak of war, the United States took the lead in calling for an urgent meeting of the UN Security Council, marshalling eight other members as co-signatories. Pakistan itself had not requested a meeting, fearing that a Security Council debate might raise awkward questions about the origins of the crisis. Hence, China was not among the co-signatories of the US proposal.

Meanwhile, a Bangladesh delegation led by a renowned high court judge, Justice Abu Sayeed Chowdhury, had arrived in New York to present its views to the United Nations. When the Security Council met on 4 December, the first item on its agenda was a request from Justice Chowdhury for a hearing in the Council. '[T]he United Nations has not addressed itself so far to the basic problem, nor has it so far taken into account the party most concerned in this tragic and dangerous crisis, namely, the 75 million people of Bangladesh . . . [T]here can be no proper evaluation of the present situation, its causes, present state, and future solution, without Bangladesh being given a hearing,' wrote Justice Chowdhury in a letter to the president of the Security Council.[7]

The Bangladesh request was strongly supported by the USSR and Poland. It was opposed by Argentina (which alleged that acceptance would amount to interference in the internal affairs of Pakistan) and

– more venomously – by China, which denounced Justice Chowdhury as the 'representative of rebellious elements within East Pakistan'. The United States, supported by four other members, proposed postponing consideration of Justice Chowdhury's request. The president of the Council for the month of December, Sierra Leone, ruled in favour of postponement.

Pakistan and India then took the floor. Agha Shahi of Pakistan charged India with aggression and with 'openly demand[ing] that Pakistan dismember itself'. Invoking the principles of territorial integrity of States and non-interference in domestic affairs, he argued that '[the] nature of Pakistan's internal crisis is outside the Security Council's concern . . . The Security Council is concerned with international peace, not with the internal peace and political life of a member State.' He acknowledged that the presence of 'displaced persons' on Indian soil had an international character, but it was a humanitarian – not a political – problem.[8] Countering these arguments, India's Samar Sen stated that 'it is not India that is breaking up Pakistan; it is Pakistan that is breaking up Pakistan itself and, in the process, creating aggression against us'. By driving millions of refugees across the border, Pakistan had inflicted strain on India's social structure, ruined its finances, and compelled it to give up land for sheltering the refugees. This was aggression, just as much as the 'more classical type', argued Sen. Pakistan had followed up this 'refugee aggression' with 'military aggression' on 3 December.[9]

Shahi and Sen thus highlighted a basic question before the Security Council. Should the Council confine itself to merely calling for a ceasefire and withdrawal of Indian and Pakistani forces to their respective territories, or was it imperative also to address the underlying cause of the conflict, if peace was to be restored? The five permanent members of the Security Council – the US, the USSR, the UK, France and China – were divided on this question. The United States pressed for an immediate ceasefire and withdrawal of forces. It viewed the refugee problem as a purely humanitarian issue and was prepared only to call upon both Pakistan and India to create a 'climate' conducive to the voluntary return of the refugees to East Pakistan. The Soviet Union adopted the contrary position. It maintained that the basic cause of the conflict was the absence of a political settlement in East Pakistan and that a solution of this underlying problem would automatically lead to peace. Challenging the argument that the domestic affairs of a country lay outside the concerns of the Security Council, the Soviet representative argued that '. . . under the Charter, the Security Council unquestionably has the right to examine the causes of the emergence of dangerous situations that threaten international peace and security'. The refugee exodus had created serious tension in the social, economic and political life of India'. Restoration of peace required a 'political settlement in East Pakistan that would take into account the will and the inalienable rights and lawful interests of its population'.[10] France and the UK distanced themselves from the US by recognizing the dual nature of the issue. The French representative, Kosciusko-Morizet, made his point with Gallic clarity. The conflict had two dimensions: it concerned 'relations between the Government of Islamabad and the population of East Pakistan', as well as relations between Pakistan and India as a consequence of the refugee influx. 'A civil war has thus been transformed into a war between nations.'[11] Ambassador Crowe of the UK called for a 'comprehensive approach', hinting at the need to also address the underlying causes of the conflict.[12] China, yet to recover from the vitriolic diplomatic style of the Cultural Revolution, attacked the 'scheme of India and her behind-the-scenes boss, Soviet social imperialism, to invade and occupy Pakistan territory and to dismember the State of Pakistan'.[13] Such were the divergent positions of the five permanent members invested with the right of veto in the Council.

Ambassador George H.W. Bush of the United States was the first to table a resolution on 4 December, calling on the Security Council to oppose military intervention by a country in the affairs of another country. The US resolution called for an immediate ceasefire, withdrawal of armed personnel to their own side of the border, and – if requested by either Pakistan or India – stationing of UN observers along the borders to supervise the ceasefire and withdrawal. It also invited India and Pakistan to accept the good offices of the UN secretary general to secure and maintain peace on the continent. Regarding the refugees, it merely called upon Pakistan *and India* to 'exert their best efforts' to create a 'climate' conducive to the voluntary return of the refugees to East Pakistan.[14] This implied that India shared the responsibility for the resolution of the refugee problem. The proposal was totally silent on the situation that had led to the refugee exodus and which prevented their voluntary return to their homeland. In short, the resolution was designed to stop the war and secure withdrawal of Indian forces, without accommodating Bangladeshi political aspirations.

When the US resolution was put to the vote, only the USSR and Poland cast negative votes. Significantly, however, France and the UK abstained on the vote, taking into account domestic opinion and Indian diplomatic representations. The US resolution had majority support but was blocked by the Soviet veto.

The USSR tabled a counter-resolution the same day.[15] In sharp contrast to the US resolution, it addressed the root causes of war, calling for a 'political settlement in East Pakistan, which would inevitably result in a cessation of hostilities'. It also called on Pakistan to 'cease all acts of violence by Pakistani forces in East Pakistan'. When the resolution was put to the vote the next day, it was defeated, receiving only two votes in favour (the USSR and Poland), one against (China), with all other members abstaining. In view of the Chinese veto, it was unnecessary for the US to cast a negative vote.

The People's Republic of China tabled its own resolution, accusing India of launching 'large-scale attacks on Pakistan', strongly condemning India for 'creating a so-called "Bangla Desh"' and for 'subverting, dismembering and committing aggression against Pakistan'. It called on all other states to 'support the Pakistan people in their just struggle to resist Indian aggression'.[16] This extreme position found no support and China did not ask for a vote on its resolution.

Another draft resolution was co-sponsored by all the non-permanent members of the Security Council except two (Poland and Syria). This simply called for an immediate ceasefire and troop withdrawals, while vaguely recognizing the 'need to deal appropriately at a subsequent stage . . . with the issues which have given rise to the hostilities'.[17] The vote on this was identical to that on the US resolution: 11-2-2. The USSR and Poland cast the dissenting votes; France and the UK abstained; all others voted in favour. The resolution did not carry because of the Soviet veto.

On 6 December, India extended formal recognition to the People's Republic of Bangladesh. At the Security Council, Ambassador Samar Sen of India read out the full text of the prime minister's speech in parliament, underlining its legal, political and constitutional significance.[18] Though the Soviet Union had yet to recognize Bangladesh, it immediately took into account the Indian position. On 6 December, the USSR presented a new resolution. While the other resolutions had been addressed to the governments of India and Pakistan, the new Soviet draft called upon 'all parties' to observe an immediate ceasefire, linking this with a simultaneous 'political settlement in East Pakistan, giving immediate recognition to the will of the East Pakistan population as expressed in the elections of December 1970'.[19] The new resolution implicitly recognized that there was a third party in the conflict, even as it continued to speak of 'East Pakistan'.

Blocked by the Soviet veto, the eleven members of the Security Council that supported the US resolution moved to refer the matter to the General Assembly under a procedure known as 'Uniting for Peace'. (While the General Assembly has no enforcement powers, it may submit recommendations for such measures to the Security Council, if invited to do so, under the provisions of the 'Uniting for Peace' resolution adopted in 1950 during the Korean War.) Since this was a procedural resolution, it could not be vetoed. The resolution was carried by a majority of eleven votes in favour, none against, with four abstentions (France, Poland, the USSR and the UK).

The outcome of the General Assembly debate was a foregone conclusion. As Haksar had presciently noted right at the beginning of the crisis, the principles of territorial integrity and non-interference in domestic matters were at the time deeply entrenched in international law and practice. The newly independent countries of Asia and Africa were particularly attached to these principles. Indeed, many of them experienced tribal or ethnic conflicts in their own countries. Many Latin American countries, living under the shadow of the United States, placed a premium on such protection as was available under international law relating to state sovereignty and non-interference in internal matters.

Ambassador Sen battled on bravely in the General Assembly, resolutely supported by his Soviet colleague, but met with little success. Guided by the United States, no less than thirty-four countries – drawn mostly from Latin America and Africa – jointly sponsored a resolution calling upon India and Pakistan to observe an immediate ceasefire and withdraw their forces to their own side of the borders. As regards the underlying cause of the conflict, the resolution merely urged an intensification of efforts to create conditions for the speedy return of the East Pakistan refugees to their homes, without linking this to the ceasefire. The draft resolution also called upon the Security Council to take 'appropriate action in the light of the present resolution'.[20] The resolution bore an unmistakable similarity to the earlier US Security Council resolution. The Soviet Union presented its own counter-draft, on lines that were identical to the proposal it had presented in the Security Council the previous day.[21]

Fifty-eight countries took part in the debate that lasted for more than ten hours. Finally, late in the night on 7 December, the US-inspired resolution was put to the vote. It was adopted by a massive majority – 110 in favour, 11 against, with 10 abstentions. Bhutan joined India and the Soviet bloc (excluding Rumania) in opposing the resolution. Three West European countries (Denmark, France and the UK), four Asian countries (Afghanistan, Nepal, Oman and Singapore), and one each from Africa (Malawi) and Latin America (Chile) abstained on the vote. With just five exceptions, India was deserted by its non-aligned partners, including Yugoslavia and Egypt. (Yugoslavia partly redeemed itself by calling for a political settlement in East Pakistan 'in cooperation with the elected representatives there'.)[22] The Soviet Union prudently refrained from calling for a vote on its own draft resolution.

The resolution adopted by the General Assembly was a public relations setback for India, but it did not affect the situation on the ground. General Assembly resolutions are not backed by an enforcement provision. The resolution was only in the nature of a recommendation submitted to the Security Council, and it did nothing to break the deadlock there.

A ceasefire appeal and its repudiation

While the United Nations was locked in these debates, the ground realities were changing rapidly. The Indian army raced towards Dhaka from three directions – west, north and north-east. It received an enthusiastic welcome everywhere from the local population. The freedom fighters spread out all over the countryside. On 6 December, CIA Director Richard Helms reported that on a conservative estimate, it would take ten days for India to compel Pakistani forces to surrender on the eastern front.[23] On 8 December, the day after the adoption of the General Assembly resolution, Yahya Khan confided to the American ambassador that the situation in East Pakistan was 'beyond hope'.[24] Thus, within the first week of the war, the Pakistani collapse in the eastern theatre was clear to all informed observers.

On 9 December, Nixon despondently said to Kissinger: 'The partition of Pakistan is a fact . . . You see those people welcoming the Indian troops when they come in . . . Why then are we going through all this agony?' Kissinger, the agile geopolitical theorist, shored up the president's resolve by arguing that if a 'combination of the Soviet Union and the Soviet-armed client state [India]' were allowed to succeed, it would lead to a 'complete collapse of the world's psychological balance of power'![25]

That very day, 9 December, the governor of East Pakistan, Dr A.M. Malik, sent a signal to Yahya pointing out the futility of further resistance:

> Once again urge you to consider immediate cease-fire and political settlement(.) Otherwise once Indian troops are free from East Wing in a few days even West Wing will be in jeopardy(.) Understand local population has welcomed Indian army in captured areas and are providing maximum help to them(.) Our troops are finding it impossible to withdraw and manoeuvre due to rebel activity(.) With this clear alignment sacrifice of West Pakistan is meaningless(.)[26]

Yahya authorized the governor to take whatever decision he thought fit: '. . . take decisions on your proposals . . . I will approve of any decision you take and I am instructing Gen. Niazi simultaneously to accept your decision and arrange things accordingly.'[27] Thus, on 10 December, the governor's political adviser Maj. Gen. Rao Farman Ali handed over a message from the governor to the senior UN official in Dhaka, Paul Marc Henri. The message, prepared in consultation with Lt Gen. Niazi, stated that the governor had been authorized by President Yahya Khan to call upon the UN to arrange for a peaceful transfer of power to the elected representatives of East Pakistan.

> As the conflict arose as a result of political causes, it must end with a political solution. I therefore having been authorised by the President of Pakistan do hereby call upon the elected representatives of East Pakistan to arrange for the peaceful formation of the government in Dacca. In making this offer I feel duty bound to say the will of the people of East Pakistan would demand the immediate vacation of their land by the Indian forces as well. I therefore call upon the United Nations to arrange for a peaceful transfer of power and request:- ONE: An immediate ceasefire. TWO: Repatriation with honour of the Armed Forces of Pakistan to West Pakistan. THREE: Repatriation of all West Pakistan personnel desirous of returning to West Pakistan. FOUR: The safety of all persons settled in East Pakistan since 1947. FIVE: Guarantee of no reprisal against any person settled in East Pakistan since 1947. The question of surrender of Armed Forces will not be considered and does

> not arise and if this proposal is not accepted the Armed Forces will continue to fight to the last man.[28]

The message caused a flurry of excitement in New York – until it was repudiated by the Pakistani president. Yahya had been ready to accept a ceasefire, but not an agreed transfer of power on terms that seemed to imply acceptance of an independent Bangladesh. Moreover, the governor was expected to make the appeal on his own (delegated) authority, without saddling the president with the responsibility! The governor's message, Yahya complained to him, '... has gone much beyond what you suggested and I had approved. It gives the impression that you are talking on behalf of Pakistan when you have mentioned the subject of transfer of power, political solution and repatriation of troops from East to West Pakistan, etc. This virtually means the acceptance of an independent East Pakistan.' Yahya authorized the governor to make an alternative offer limited to a ceasefire in East Pakistan, guarantees of the safety of Pakistani armed forces and prevention of reprisals. 'The question of transfer of power and political solution will be tackled at National level.' Hours later, Yahya changed his mind and countermanded these instructions. He instructed the governor to take no action regarding even a ceasefire. 'Important diplomatic and military moves are taking place by our friends. It is essential that we hold out for another 36 hours at all costs,'[29] he advised the governor. Yahya was pinning his hopes on a rescue operation by the White House.

During this episode, India refrained from commenting on the governor's proposals, pending clarification of their status. The proposals handed over by Gen. Rao Farman Ali would have met India's primary objective by arranging for an early de facto transfer of power to the Bangladesh government and freeing the country of the presence of the Pakistani armed forces. Had they been authenticated by Yahya, the terms may well have been accepted by India. With the repudiation of the governor's initiative, Pakistan lost the opportunity for a negotiated ceasefire and paved the way for an unconditional surrender in the eastern front.

'Scaring off the Indians'

On 8 December, as Nixon and Kissinger pondered over ways to rescue Pakistan, Kissinger suggested that they should 'try to scare off the Indians'. Two days earlier, Nixon had mooted the idea of encouraging the Chinese to move troops to the Indian border. Kissinger reverted to this idea, linking it with the dispatch of a carrier force into the Bay of Bengal. He believed that deployment of the task force would provide the necessary encouragement to China to move against India. Moreover, it would send a signal to the Soviet Union. 'We have only one hope now … to convince the Indians the thing is going to escalate. And to convince the Russians that they are going to pay an enormous price.'[30] Nixon readily agreed.

A basic flaw in the plan soon came to light. John Connally, the influential secretary of the Treasury, pointed out that American public opinion would be strongly opposed to the deployment, interpreting it as a threat of military intervention in support of Pakistan. Shaken by Connally's warning, Kissinger came up with the idea of moving only a helicopter ship, instead of a carrier task force. 'From a Chinese angle,' he explained to the president, 'I would like to move the carrier. From the public opinion angle, what the press and television would do to us if an American carrier showed up there . . .' he said, leaving the sentence unfinished. A helicopter ship, he argued, would avoid these problems and would still be a token that something more would follow. Nixon remained unconvinced. 'Why are we doing it anyway? Aren't we going in for the purpose of [demonstrating] strength?' he asked. Sensing the president's mood, Kissinger deftly reverted to his earlier stand. 'I'd move the carrier so that we can tell the Chinese tomorrow to move their forces to the frontier.'[31]

Thus, on 10 December, a Presidential Order was issued creating Task Force 74, comprising the nuclear aircraft carrier *Enterprise*, with accompanying escorts and supply ships. Task Force 74 was ordered to sail from the Gulf of Tonkin to Singapore, in the first instance. The C-in-C of the Pacific Fleet, Admiral Elmo Zumwalt, Jr, voiced his concern over the fact that no specific mission had been assigned the task force. The admiral had already earned Kissinger's ire by pointing out that the 'tilt' in favour of Pakistan would serve only to strengthen the Soviet position in India.[32]

On the same day that Nixon created the naval task force, Kissinger secretly met with Ambassador Huang Hua, the Chinese permanent representative at the United Nations, in a CIA safe house in New York. He gave the Chinese envoy an account of the steps taken by the White House to support Pakistan, highlighting that many of the initiatives were taken without the knowledge of the State Department. Kissinger offered to share with China satellite intelligence concerning Soviet troop deployments near the Chinese border. After revealing the decision to move a carrier task force to the Indian Ocean, he came to the main point. In carefully chosen words, Kissinger informed the Chinese ambassador that '. . . the President wants you to know that . . . if the People's Republic were to consider the situation on the Indian subcontinent a threat to its security, and if it took measures to protect its security, the US would oppose efforts of others to interfere with the People's Republic'. Here was the implicit offer of support, which Kissinger believed would turn the scales in favour of a Chinese decision to intervene. He concluded by observing that '. . . if East Pakistan is to be preserved from destruction, two things are needed – maximum intimidation of the Indians and, to some extent, the Soviets. Secondly, maximum pressure for the ceasefire.'[33]

Two days later, Huang Hua requested an urgent meeting. This sent Kissinger into a tizzy of excitement. 'They're going to move. No question, they are going to move,' he told the president. His dreams were shattered when the message was delivered. Huang Hua had been instructed to convey China's support for the latest US-sponsored Security Council resolution calling for an immediate ceasefire and withdrawal of forces. This put at rest hopes in the White House of inducing China to make a military move against India.

Kissinger's strategy reflected a flawed understanding of Chinese policy. It was unrealistic to expect that the promise of an American security umbrella would induce China to embark on a risky military adventure. In January 1972, Kissinger's deputy, Alexander Haig, discussed the December war with Chinese Premier Zhou En-lai when he visited Beijing to prepare for the Nixon visit. Haig unwittingly offended his hosts when he said that the United States had a fundamental interest in the maintenance of 'China's viability' and that Nixon and Kissinger were concerned on this account during the recent South Asia crisis. When Zhou En-lai reported the conversation to Mao, the chairman commented: 'Why should our viability become America's concern . . . If China's independence and viability should be protected by the Americans, it is very dangerous [for us].' Zhou later told Haig that he was 'greatly surprised' by the US leaders' concern for 'protecting China's independence and viability'. China firmly believed that 'no country should depend upon a foreign power in maintaining its own independence and viability'. Otherwise, the dependent country would become a 'subordinate or colony'.[34]

By 12 December, when Huang Hua's message was received, the primary argument for deploying the nuclear carrier *Enterprise* in the Indian Ocean had been proved false. Kissinger's promise that the United States '. . . would oppose the efforts of others to interfere with the People's Republic' failed to induce Chinese military intervention. The *Enterprise*-led naval task force was scheduled to pass through the Straits of Malacca that day, but Nixon and Kissinger decided to hold up the movement for twenty-four hours. In his memoirs, Kissinger says that the delay was intended to give Moscow more time to respond to a hotline message concerning coordinated action in the Security Council. This may have been a factor, but the records show that the White House was once again assailed by fears concerning US public reaction. On 13

December, Kissinger cabled Haig from the Azores: 'As for the fleet, I am weighing [the] advantage of moving it against [the] risk of [it] being called off prematurely by public pressure . . . in any event, [the] fleet should go into [the] Indian Ocean, not [the] Bay of Bengal.'[35] Thus, the *Enterprise* headed towards Colombo, not Chittagong.

The appearance of Task Force 74 in the Indian Ocean failed to 'scare off' the Indians. New Delhi was well aware of the constraints imposed on the White House by Congressional and public opinion in the United States. Addressing a massive rally in New Delhi, Indira Gandhi delivered a message intended for both an Indian and American audience. Playing on the rift in Washington between the White House and its opponents in the Congress and media, she declared:

> A foreign power has threatened us. It has told us that it is bound by certain treaty alliances with Pakistan. We were aware of these alliances. There were many Pacts and as far as I am aware, they were intended to contain Communism. The object of these alliances was certainly not to fight democracy, or to suppress justice or the voice of the oppressed.

For the Indian public, she struck a note of defiance:

> However weak we may be [compared with that foreign power] . . . the Indian spirit is indomitable – indomitable because we follow the path of truth and justice. We shall show the world that despite the opposition of all those forces, there is no power on earth that can bend us.[36]

While the deployment of the *Enterprise* failed to deter India, it produced a last flicker of hope in Pakistan. On 13 December, Ambassador Raza conveyed an urgent appeal from his president. Yahya requested that the US Seventh Fleet be tasked to keep the Bay of Bengal and Arabian Sea open to Pakistani shipping and to prevent India from attacking Pakistani ports. This was followed up the next day by a personal message from Yahya to Nixon:

> The time has come for the United States to go beyond warnings and demarches if its determination to punish aggression across international borders is to have any effect on the Soviet Union and India. The Seventh Fleet does not only have to come to our shores but also to relieve certain pressures which we by ourselves are not in a position to cope with.[37]

The desperate appeal fell on deaf ears.

With the approach of the *Enterprise*, the Soviet navy too signalled its presence in the Indian Ocean. The USSR had quietly reinforced its modest presence in the Indian Ocean right at the beginning of the war. On 3 December, the Soviet presence consisted of a destroyer, a conventional F-Class submarine, a minesweeper and a tank landing ship. These ships were nearing completion of their six-month deployment period. A relief force consisting of a destroyer and a minesweeper arrived in the Indian Ocean through the Straits of Malacca on 5 December. Moscow decided to retain the original contingent; thus, the newly arrived ships became a reinforcement, instead of a replacement. A second Soviet task force was sighted by the Japanese as it passed through the Straits of Tsushima on 9 December. It must therefore have left Vladivostok on 6 December or 7 December, soon after the outbreak of the war – and before the US decision to send the *Enterprise*. These deployments reflect Soviet contingency planning in the context of the Indo-Soviet Treaty *before* the movement of the US task force. Yet another Soviet task force was dispatched *after* the US deployment of Task Force 74. It was first sighted by the Japanese when it passed through the Straits of Tsushima on 15 December. Though it arrived in the Indian Ocean only on 18 December, the Americans were aware that it was on the way. When the *USS Enterprise* arrived in the Indian Ocean, Soviet submarines in the area announced their presence by surfacing, as Soviet and American ships warily watched each other.[38]

The superpower naval minuet in the Indian Ocean was accompanied by an exchange of messages between Washington and Moscow and between Moscow and New Delhi, as the White House sought to impress upon the Kremlin the 'linkage' between detente and Soviet policy in the Indo-Pakistan war.

'Linkage': Detente and a regional war

In parallel with its moves in the United Nations, the White House invoked the doctrine of 'linkage' to bring pressure to bear on Moscow. Early in the crisis, on 6 December, Nixon complained to Brezhnev that the Soviet position in the South Asian crisis was inconsistent with progress towards detente:

> It had been my understanding . . . that we were entering a new period in our relations which would be marked by mutual restraint and in which neither you nor we would act in crises to seek unilateral advantages . . . [However,] what is happening now in South Asia, where you are supporting the Indian Government's open use of force against the independence and integrity of Pakistan . . . runs counter to the recent encouraging trends in international relations.

Nixon called upon Brezhnev to use his 'great Influence' in New Delhi to bring about a ceasefire and restore the territorial integrity of Pakistan. If India was allowed to achieve its objectives by military action, it would 'long complicate the international situation and undermine the confidence that we and you have worked hard to establish'. Nixon concluded pointedly that the spirit in which the two leaders had agreed to meet in Moscow in May required 'most urgent action to end the conflict and restore territorial integrity in the Subcontinent'.[39]

Brezhnev replied that he agreed with Nixon's understanding that neither party should seek unilateral advantages in a crisis. He also agreed on the need for an immediate ceasefire. However, the ceasefire would have to be 'connected with a simultaneous decision for a political settlement based on the recognition of the will of the East Pakistani population. Otherwise, it is impossible to ensure the respect for the lawful rights and interests of the people of East Pakistan and to create conditions for the return of the millions of refugees.' Without these conditions, a ceasefire would not be stable. Brezhnev proposed that negotiations between the Pakistan government and the leaders of East Pakistan should be resumed from the stage at which they had been broken off in March.[40]

Not satisfied with the response, the White House decided to turn on the pressure on Moscow. The Soviet minister of agriculture, Vladimir Matskevich, happened to be visiting Washington. He was summoned to the White House on 9 December to receive a tough message from Nixon himself. Matskevich was totally at sea about a question unconnected with his official responsibilities. The bemused agriculture minister was informed that if the Soviets continued with their policy in East Pakistan, it would 'poison the whole new relationship between the United States and the Soviet Union'. Moscow, he was warned, should consider whether its gains in India were 'worth jeopardising the relationship with the United States'. Nixon drew the Soviet minister's attention to US treaty obligations to Pakistan.[41] He followed up the next day with a message to Brezhnev, urging him 'in the strongest terms to restrain India with which, by virtue of your treaty, you have great influence and for whose actions you must share responsibility'. He specifically sought an assurance that India would accept a ceasefire in the west immediately after a ceasefire had been agreed in the eastern theatre.[42]

Though the Soviet leaders rejected the contention that progress towards detente required them to align their South Asia policy with that of the United States, they could not afford to simply brush aside American concerns. Kissinger had repeatedly expressed concern over India's designs regarding West Pakistan. Moscow knew these were unfounded and was prepared to serve as a channel for communicating an official Indian denial to Washington. Partly for this reason and, more generally, because of the need for timely coordination with India in a rapidly evolving situation, the Soviet leaders sent Vasily Kuznetsov, the senior-most deputy foreign minister, to New Delhi for consultations under the Indo-Soviet Treaty. India reciprocally sent D.P. Dhar to Moscow.

Kuznetsov arrived in New Delhi on 12 December and immediately called on Mrs Gandhi, who readily confirmed that India had no territorial designs on West Pakistan – an assurance that New Delhi had already communicated directly to Washington on more than one occasion. Indian leaders confirmed that India was fighting a defensive war on the western front and had no intention of going on a strategic offensive in the west. India was ready to accept a general ceasefire if Pakistan agreed to withdraw its forces from Bangladesh and transfer power to the Awami League.

India, in turn, raised its concerns about the arrival of the *Enterprise* in the Indian Ocean. Kuznetsov was told that far from fraying Indian nerves, the threatening posture adopted by the United States had the effect of strengthening its determination. Notwithstanding this, India requested the Soviet Union to make a public announcement at the highest level that interference by other countries in the affairs of the subcontinent would only aggravate the existing situation. A TASS statement to this effect had, indeed, been issued early in the war, but in India's view this did not suffice. India requested an official statement at the highest level, pointing out the consequences of third-party intervention.[43]

In light of these consultations, Brezhnev sent a reply to Nixon's message of 10 December. Brezhnev rejected Nixon's allegation that there was a lack of clarity concerning India's intentions. India had no plans for seizing West Pakistan territory. India was ready to accept a general ceasefire if Pakistan withdrew its forces from the eastern theatre and transferred power to the lawful representatives of the people, thereby creating conditions for the refugees in India to return to their homes. Regarding the *Enterprise*, Brezhnev said that it was 'difficult for us to understand how it is possible to combine striving for a peaceful settlement of the problem by collective efforts of our countries with such unilateral actions like demonstrative movements of naval forces and so on. Suppose the other side will also embark on the path of taking similar measures – what then will be the net result?'[44]

Kissinger claims in his memoirs that India's intention was to 'smash'

West Pakistan after achieving its aims in the eastern theatre. He claims that his aim was only to prevent the destruction of West Pakistan. The facts contradict these claims. The Soviet resolution of 6 December would have brought about a ceasefire on both fronts had it not been rejected by the United States and its allies. When Nixon raised the question with Brezhnev, the latter formally confirmed that the Indian government would readily accept a general ceasefire after Bangladesh had been liberated. Kissinger dwells on the fact that Indian officials declined to clarify their objectives in Kashmir. He fails to mention that when the question was put to the Indian ambassador in Washington, L.K. Jha, the latter asked whether a similar assurance had been obtained from Pakistan – a question to which the State Department had no answer.[45] Despite this reservation, India did, in fact, give the US a broad hint of its intentions. On 12 December, Foreign Secretary T.N. Kaul informed the US ambassador to the UN, George H.W. Bush, that India had no major ambitions regarding Pakistan-Occupied Kashmir, adding that India and Pakistan had discussed minor rectifications even in peacetime.[46] The significance of this comment was not lost on the Americans. Kissinger incorporated it in his Situation Report to Nixon the same day.[47] He, however, fails to mention these facts in his voluminous memoirs.

Kissinger's real intentions were reflected in the draft UN Security Council resolution tabled by the United States on 12 December.[48] This called on India and Pakistan to observe an immediate ceasefire and withdraw their forces to their own sides of the India–Pakistan borders. In other words, India was required to withdraw troops from liberated Bangladesh territory, while Pakistani armed forces remained in that territory. The question of a 'political solution' was left for the future. The clear intention was to prolong Pakistani rule in Bangladesh.

End game

The US resolution ignored ground realities. Pakistani forces were collapsing everywhere in the eastern front. On 11 December, Indian paratroopers had been airdropped in the Tangail area, inside the Dhaka bowl, where they linked up with Bangladeshi freedom fighters under Kader 'Tiger' Siddiqui. The strategically important town of Jamalpur was liberated the same day. Indian and Bangladeshi forces were positioning themselves for the final march to Dhaka.

Speaking on the US resolution, Swaran Singh urged the Security Council to accept the reality of Bangladesh. He argued that 'International law requires that where a mother State has irrevocably lost the allegiance of such a large section of its people . . . and cannot bring them under its sway, conditions for the separate existence of such a State come into being'. The Council should recognize the right of the people of Bangladesh to be heard in the debate and to be a party to any ceasefire arrangement. Moreover, a political solution had to be found in accordance with the wishes of the people of Bangladesh, as already declared by their elected representatives. If these three 'essential ingredients' were accepted, an immediate ceasefire could be adopted, together with withdrawals of Indian and Pakistani forces from Bangladesh, as well as mutual Indian and Pakistani withdrawals from each other's territory 'through appropriate consultations'.[49]

Swaran Singh's suggestions were brushed aside, even though they addressed the stated US concern about an immediate ceasefire on both fronts. The vote on the resolution was identical to that on the earlier US resolution of 4 December – eleven in favour, two opposing (Poland and the USSR) and two abstaining (France and the UK). The resolution was blocked by the Soviet veto – the third in nine days.

US allies Italy and Japan immediately followed up with a proposal similar to the vetoed US resolution. Their proposal called for a ceasefire and appointment of a Security Council committee to assist India and Pakistan in achieving reconciliation on the basis of the General Assembly resolution of 7 December. Like the US draft, the proposal tabled by Italy and Japan aimed to restore Pakistani control over Bangladesh, leaving for the future the 'issues which have given rise to these hostilities'[50] – namely, the slaughter of hundreds of thousands of unarmed civilians and the flight of some 10 million refugees.

In New Delhi, Kuznetsov and Haksar worked out a counter-move, using the Farman Ali proposals as a starting point.[51] They agreed that a third party might be encouraged to present a resolution in the Security Council based on the following elements: peaceful transfer of power in Bangladesh/East Pakistan to the elected representatives of the people headed by Sheikh Mujibur Rahman; a temporary ceasefire for seventy-two hours; withdrawal of Pakistani armed forces to designated places in Bangladesh/East Pakistan for the purpose of their evacuation from the eastern theatre; evacuation under UN supervision of West Pakistan civil personnel and other persons wishing to return to West Pakistan, and similar evacuation of Bangladesh personnel from West Pakistan; ceasefire to become permanent on commencement of preceding steps; and, recognizing the principle that territorial gains acquired through application of force may not be retained, India and Pakistan to commence negotiations to apply this principle to the western sector.

In presenting this proposal to the Political Affairs Committee of the cabinet, Haksar explained the political and tactical advantages of the move: '. . . [w]e shall gain time. We would not appear negative and intransigent and . . . we would be able to say that we are ready to respond to anything which is reasonable.' India would be free to seek elucidation and propose amendments.[52] A draft resolution on these lines was tabled by Poland on 14 December.[53]

By the time Poland presented its resolution in the Security Council, the Pakistani position in the eastern theatre was on the verge of total collapse. On the evening of 13 December, Lt Gen. Niazi reported to Rawalpindi:

> All fortresses under heavy pressure. No replenishment even of ammunition. Rebels have already surrounded the city. Indians also advancing. Situation serious. Promised [Chinese] assistance must take practical shape by December 14. Will be effective in Siliguri not NEFA and by engaging enemy air bases.[54]

On 14 December, the civil administration in 'East Pakistan' ceased to exist. Acting on the basis of an intercepted signal, the Indian Air Force launched a rocket attack on the Governor's House in Dhaka while a cabinet meeting was in progress. The panic-stricken governor wrote out his resignation and fled for shelter to the Intercontinental Hotel, which was under a UN umbrella. West Pakistani civil servants in Dhaka had already sought shelter there earlier in the day.[55] The same afternoon, Lt Gen. Niazi received a reply from Yahya:

> You have now reached a stage where further resistance is no longer humanly possible...You should now take all necessary measures to stop the fighting and preserve the lives of all armed forces personnel, all those from West Pakistan and all loyal elements . . .[56]

Niazi met Spivack, the US consul-general, and asked him to transmit a message to Manekshaw requesting a ceasefire. He also requested the UN representative in Dhaka to arrange a ceasefire on terms similar to those in the earlier appeal of 11 December (which was subsequently withdrawn). It took Washington twenty hours to relay Niazi's appeal to Manekshaw. The Indian army chief received the message at 1430 hours Indian Standard Time (IST) on 15 December. Manekshaw sent his reply to Niazi within two hours, calling on the latter to 'issue orders to all forces under your command in Bangladesh to cease fire immediately and surrender to my advancing forces wherever they are located'.[57]

Meanwhile, the Security Council remained occupied in a surreal debate. On 15 December – the eve of the Pakistani surrender in Dhaka – three new draft resolutions were tabled: an Anglo-French, a Syrian and a new Soviet proposal. Also, Poland tabled an amendment to the resolution it had presented the previous day. No less than five draft resolutions contended for attention. None of the sponsors sought a vote. The intention was only to signal the preferred outcome. The Anglo-French proposal called for an immediate ceasefire and for the 'urgent conclusion of a comprehensive political settlement in accordance with the wishes of the people concerned as declared through their elected and acknowledged representatives and in conformity with the purposes and principles the United Nations Charter'.[58] India pointed out to the sponsors that the proposed political negotiations remained only a 'pie in the sky'![59] The Syrian resolution sought an immediate ceasefire, withdrawal of troops to their own side of the border and the ceasefire line in Kashmir, and appointment of a UN special representative to assist a comprehensive settlement between Pakistan and the 'elected representatives of East Pakistan'.[60] The Soviet proposal introduced an element of reality, calling for an immediate ceasefire on both fronts, and the 'simultaneous conclusion of a political settlement in accordance with the wishes of the people of East Pakistan as declared through their already elected representatives'.[61] In the midst of the Security Council debate on 15 December, Bhutto staged a theatrical walkout, positioning himself advantageously in the domestic power struggle that lay ahead!

The next day, Maj. Gen. Jacob flew to Dhaka in the morning to present the terms of surrender to Niazi. Advance elements of the Indian army and the Mukti Bahini were already present in the city. After an initial show of reluctance, Niazi accepted the terms of the instrument of surrender. At 4.31 p.m. IST on 16 December, in the presence of a vast crowd of jubilant Bangladeshis, Lt Gen. Niazi formally surrendered to Lt Gen. Aurora, General Officer Commanding-in-Chief of the Indian and Bangladesh forces in the Eastern Theatre. Announcing the surrender in parliament, Prime Minister Indira Gandhi declared, to thunderous applause, that 'Dhaka is now the free capital of a free country'.[62] It was the proudest moment in the annals of the Indian armed forces.

India's aims having been achieved, Prime Minister Gandhi ordered a unilateral ceasefire in the western front, effective from 17 December. Pakistan followed suit, ending the fourteen-day war.

14

Victory

The iconic photograph of the Pakistani surrender at Dhaka fails to do full justice to the historic grandeur of the event. The photograph shows Lt Gen. Niazi signing the instrument of surrender in the presence of Lt Gen. Aurora, witnessed by senior officers of the Indian armed forces. A picture from a different angle brings in Group Capt. Khondaker, who was standing next to Vice Admiral Krishnan. (Khondaker represented the Bangladesh armed forces in the absence of Col. Osmani, who was unable to be present for logistical reasons.) A wide-angle lens would have covered at least a part of the huge crowd of jubilant Bangladeshis who had gathered at the scene to celebrate the liberation of their country from Pakistani rule. The iconic photograph depicts an Indian military victory over Pakistan; the other pictures capture also the success of a multidimensional grand strategy for the liberation of a new nation-state through the joint action of the Indian army and the Mukti Bahini.

On 21 December – five days after the Pakistani surrender – the UN Security Council finally accepted the new ground reality. It adopted Resolution 307 (1971), which noted that a ceasefire and cessation of hostilities prevailed in the subcontinent and demanded that this be strictly observed until troops were withdrawn to 'their respective territories and to positions which fully respect the ceasefire line in

Jammu and Kashmir supervised by the United Nations Military Observer Group in India and Pakistan'.[1]

India's response was a qualified acceptance. Addressing the Security Council, Foreign Minister Swaran Singh stated that India would give 'due consideration' to the resolution. He observed that Pakistan had violated the ceasefire line in Jammu & Kashmir in 1965 and again in 1971, and pointed to the 'need to avoid the repetition of such incidents by making some adjustments in the ceasefire line in order to make it more stable, rational and viable'.[2]

Adjustment of the 1949 ceasefire line was an add-on to the war aims decided earlier in the year. It evolved during the course of the December war. As we noted earlier, an indication of the aim was given to the United States during Swaran Singh's meeting with Bush on 12 December. It was not India's intention to *impose* the adjustment on Pakistan but rather to arrive at a *negotiated* change.

This limited escalation in the political objective was, in a sense, a replay of 1965. At the outset of the 1965 war, India's aim was simply to repulse the Pakistani assault on Kashmir, but during the course of the war, New Delhi came to appreciate the importance of holding on to some of the strategically significant Pakistani posts it had occupied across the ceasefire line in the Haji Pir, Tithwal and Kargil areas, and India declared its intention to retain these areas. At Tashkent, however, Kosygin was able to gently persuade Lal Bahadur Shastri to give up the demand for a readjustment of the ceasefire line, just as he had persuaded Ayub Khan to drop the Pakistani demand for reopening of the Kashmir issue.[3] This broke the deadlock in the talks and cleared the path for the Tashkent Declaration.

There was a certain similarity in India's post-war aims in 1965 and 1971, in the sense that both involved minor territorial adjustments. However, there was also a basic difference. In 1965, India only sought an adjustment of the 1949 ceasefire line originating from a UN Security Council resolution. In 1971, India aimed at replacement of the UN-ordained ceasefire line by a *bilaterally* negotiated Line of Control. This involved not merely minor territorial adjustments, but a more basic shift to managing or resolving differences through *bilateral* negotiations, rather than negotiations at a multilateral forum.

The Security Council resolution of 21 December implicitly recognized the irreversibility of the outcome of the liberation war. It was only a matter of time before the international community extended formal *diplomatic recognition* to Bangladesh. Bhutan had joined India in recognizing the infant state on 6 December. In early January 1972, the German Democratic Republic extended formal recognition, followed by other members of the Soviet bloc. In February 1972, the major West European countries, including the UK, France, and the Federal Republic of Germany, followed suit. The United States formally recognized Bangladesh on 8 April. Thus, by early April 1972, most of the major powers, including all the permanent members of the UN Security Council, with the solitary exception of China, had accorded diplomatic recognition to the newly independent People's Republic of Bangladesh.

Plans for restoration of the civil administration in post-war Bangladesh had already been drawn up by the Mujibnagar authorities in November. These plans were speedily implemented after liberation. The very next day after the Pakistani surrender, appointments of senior district officials (deputy commissioners and superintendents of police) were announced over the radio. On 18 December, an advance team of senior Mujibnagar officials, led by Chief Secretary Ruhul Quddus, arrived in Dhaka to take over the reins of administration. Acting President Syed Nazrul Islam, Prime Minister Tajuddin Ahmed and other cabinet ministers followed on 22 December. Thus, within a week after liberation, all the organs of the new state had begun to function across the length and breadth of Bangladesh.

Pakistan came under increasing international pressure to release Sheikh Mujibur Rahman. In early January 1972, Zulfikar Ali Bhutto, who had replaced the disgraced Yahya Khan as president and chief martial law administrator, decided to release the Bangabandhu from prison. Mujib was flown out to London, from where he returned to

Dhaka, after a brief halt in New Delhi on 10 January. 'I decided to stop over in the historic capital of your great country on my way to Bangladesh, for this is the least I could do to pay a personal tribute to the best friend of my people, the people of India and to your Government under the leadership of your magnificent Prime Minister, Mrs. Indira Gandhi,' Mujib declared on his arrival at Delhi's Palam airport.[4]

Mujib returned to Dhaka on 10 January 1972 to a deliriously joyful welcome. His triumphal return invested the government of the new state with an authority it had not possessed earlier. The task of disarming ex-freedom fighters and channelling their energies into nation-building tasks could now be taken up more effectively. Reconstruction of the war-devastated economy posed an immense challenge. Bridges and railway lines had to be repaired on a massive scale; power generation and distribution had to be restored; the major port of Chittagong had to be cleared of mines; scarcities of essential goods had to be addressed. On 17 January, India agreed to supply Bangladesh a list of essential commodities, including consumer items such as sugar, salt and baby food; medicines and drugs; oilseeds and cotton yarn for rural industries; cement, steel and steel products; power generation and transmission equipment; and transport vehicles.[5] Chittagong port was cleared with Indian assistance. India helped to rehabilitate the railway network in Bangladesh. In the immediate post-liberation period, the burden of foreign aid was mainly shouldered by India. This changed only after the major traditional donor countries extended diplomatic recognition to Bangladesh.

With their country freed from Pakistani occupation, the millions of refugees returned speedily to their homes. Nearly 7 million refugees were repatriated within six weeks of the liberation of Bangladesh.[6] By 25 March 1972, all but a handful of the nearly 10 million refugees had returned to their homeland. The massive task of providing transportation to the refugees and resettling them in their homes could not have been accomplished in so short a time but for detailed advance planning by the Indian and Mujibnagar authorities.

Less than a month after his return to Bangladesh, Mujib visited

Kolkata to express his gratitude to the 'Government and people of India, especially to the neighbouring States of West Bengal, Tripura, Meghalaya and Assam, for the assistance and hospitality given to millions of Bangladesh citizens and for the moral and material support given by the Government and people of India to the struggle for liberation'.[7] The visit afforded an opportunity for extensive discussions between Mujib and Indira Gandhi on the potential for cooperation in diverse fields – industry, agriculture, communications, development and utilization of water and power resources, as well as cooperation in the fields of culture, science and technology. An important decision was that the withdrawal of Indian armed forces from Bangladesh would be completed by 25 March 1972.[8]

Indian planners had not failed to address a question that is all too frequently overlooked when troops are sent abroad – bringing the troops home within a specific time frame. D.P. Dhar had driven home this point in his discussions with the Mujibnagar authorities in November. When Mujib passed through New Delhi in January, Mrs Gandhi took the opportunity to emphasize that she wanted the Indian troops in Bangladesh to return home as soon as Mujib felt they could do so. The two prime ministers discussed this question in greater detail during Mujib's Kolkata visit, and, as we noted, it was mutually agreed that the withdrawal would be completed by 25 March 1972. Later, when it was agreed to schedule Mrs Gandhi's return visit to Dhaka for 17 March, she requested that the withdrawal be completed before her arrival. Accordingly, it was agreed to bring forward the date of withdrawal to 15 March. On 12 March, Bangabandhu Sheikh Mujibur Rahman took the salute at the Indian army's spectacular farewell parade at a packed Dhaka stadium.

Indira Gandhi received a rapturous welcome when she visited Dhaka in March 1972. Posters bearing her portrait were plastered on city walls throughout the capital. A massive crowd assembled to hear her public address. When she went on a cruise down the Buriganga with Mujib and other Bangladesh leaders, tens of thousands of people cheered her from the riverbank throughout the journey. Few statesmen have been privileged to receive such an emotional welcome on foreign soil. It was during this river cruise that Mujib and Mrs Gandhi decided to enter into a Treaty of Peace and Friendship, signalling the close ties between the two neighbouring countries.

Thus, by the end of March 1972, the aims of India's grand strategy had been fully achieved. The Bangladesh liberation war had been brought to a speedy and successful conclusion, averting the prospect of an extended guerrilla war, in which power might have passed into the hands of pro-Naxalite and pro-Chinese extremists. A new state, the People's Republic of Bangladesh, had gained wide diplomatic recognition. Millions of refugees, whose continued presence in India would have imposed unbearable stresses on the economy and social stability of West Bengal and the north-eastern states, had been enabled to return to their homeland. A looming threat to the security of India had been decisively repulsed, despite the combined opposition of a superpower and a major regional power. Last but not least, having achieved these objectives, India had brought back its troops from Bangladesh.

It remained only to achieve the add-on objective adopted in December 1971 – to persuade Pakistan to accept a negotiated modification in the delineation and status of the 1949 ceasefire line. This objective was achieved in the Indo-Pakistan summit held in Simla at the end of June 1972.

Road to Simla

Indira Gandhi's twin objectives at Simla were to replace the 1949 UN-mandated ceasefire line in Kashmir with a new bilaterally agreed Line of Control based on the ground situation at the time of the 17 December ceasefire; and to secure agreement on the principle of resolving all differences with Pakistan peacefully through bilateral negotiations. These arrangements would result in a basic shift of focus from a multilateral to a bilateral approach in settling issues of discord with Pakistan. An agreement abjuring the threat or use of force to change the new Line of Control would also endow it with the characteristics of a de facto – but not de jure – boundary.

Contrary to widespread belief, India did not seek a final settlement of the Kashmir issue in Simla. In Indira Gandhi's view, the time was not ripe for a final solution on these lines. Quite apart from the question of its acceptability to Pakistan, relinquishing or 'surrendering' India's claims to Pakistan-Occupied Kashmir would trigger strong public protests in India fanned by opposition parties. P.N. Dhar, secretary to the prime minister, recalls that 'Mrs. Gandhi was worried that a formal withdrawal of the Indian claim on Pak-occupied Kashmir could create trouble for her'.[9] Indira Gandhi hoped that the bilaterally agreed Line of Control would *eventually* evolve into a mutually accepted international boundary, but the *final settlement* was to be left for a future date, when public opinion in both India and Pakistan was better prepared to accept a realistic solution. The *immediate* objective was to persuade Pakistan to accept a new, bilaterally agreed Line of Control in replacement of the UN-determined 1949 ceasefire line and, more generally, to resolve all differences with Pakistan peacefully through bilateral negotiations, without involving outside powers.

D.P. Dhar met with Aziz Ahmed, secretary general in Pakistan's foreign ministry, in Murree in the last week of April 1972, to prepare the ground for a summit between Mrs Gandhi and Bhutto. Aziz Ahmed was a highly respected civil servant and diplomat who had served under Bhutto as foreign secretary in 1965 and was known as a hardliner on questions relating to India. Aziz Ahmed flatly rejected Dhar's proposal for replacing the ceasefire line with a new Line of Control. An impasse appeared to have been reached on the very first day. Dhar threatened to return home the next day. The situation was saved in a one-to-one meeting between Dhar and Bhutto, in which the Pakistani president indicated that he was prepared in principle to accept a new Line of Control in Jammu & Kashmir, provided other issues were resolved. Looking into the future, he said that with normalization of relations, increasing exchanges across the border and the ceasefire line or Line of Control, the latter would become irrelevant with the passage of time.[10]

This was not the first time that Bhutto had touched on this long-term prospect. In an interview to Kuldip Nayar in March, he had declared:

> We can make the Ceasefire Line as the basis of initial peace. Let the people of Kashmir move between the two countries freely. One thing can lead to another. Why should it be ordained on me and Mrs. Gandhi to resolve everything today? We should set things in motion in the right direction. Others can pick up from it. We cannot clear the decks in one sweep.[11]

On the basis of the confidential understanding with Bhutto concerning the Line of Control, Dhar reached an agreement with Aziz Ahmed on the summit agenda. This took the form of a compilation of the items suggested by each party. Dhar's contribution accorded pride of place to the elements of 'durable peace', including 'inviolability of the frontier/boundary between India and Pakistan'. Dhar left his Pakistani interlocutors in no doubt that the elements of 'durable peace' included a new Line of Control in Kashmir. Aziz Ahmed, on his part, placed repatriation of POWs and withdrawal of forces at the top of his list of priorities.

Just when the road to the Simla summit seemed to have been cleared, Bhutto made a serious faux pas. Playing on his vanity, the Italian journalist Oriana Fallaci drew him into making some unflattering comments on Mrs Gandhi. Bhutto described her as a 'diligent drudge . . . devoid of initiative and imagination' and as a 'mediocre woman with a mediocre mind'[12]. This provoked an angry reaction in India, jeopardizing the prospects of the summit. Bhutto wriggled out of this awkward situation by issuing a categorical denial of the reported remarks.

At this point, we may pause briefly to take note of Mrs Gandhi's own perception of Bhutto. One of the hardy perennials in popular accounts of the Simla summit is that a gullible Indira Gandhi was fooled by a wily Bhutto. The actual record shows that she deeply distrusted Bhutto, not only because of his history of adopting virulently anti-India postures but also because she had information about the steps he had begun to take in 1972 to build up Pakistan's military strength. Mrs Gandhi felt it was important for India to retain a certain margin of military superiority in order to deter a new Pakistani military adventure. The Soviet Union was duly approached for the required arms, but Moscow, which had responded to earlier requests with exemplary promptitude, chose to maintain silence on this occasion. Swaran Singh pressed the case with Soviet leaders in April 1972 during his Moscow visit, but failed to elicit a positive response. Mrs Gandhi herself wrote to Brezhnev on 26 April to explain her misgivings about Bhutto and the justification for the requested weapons. About Bhutto, she wrote:

> . . . he is a leader whose career so far . . . casts doubt on his goodwill towards India and his devotion to peace. It may be that recent events have infused in him a genuine desire to turn his back on the past and make a new start; but at the moment, we cannot regard this as more than a possibility . . . He should also be made to feel that such recourse to arms in future is bound to fail. It is in order to restrain him and his foreign friends from yielding to the temptation of choosing an adventurist course in preference to a peaceful settlement that we should exert ourselves to build up our military strength.[13]

These are hardly the words of a naive and gullible woman! Despite her pleas, Moscow remained unconvinced; it withheld a positive response to India's new requests for arms till after the Simla summit.

Simla Summit

So many myths have sprung up around the Simla conference (28 June to 2 July 1972) that, even at the risk of the tedium it may bring, a brief day-by-day account of the proceedings is necessary. The negotiating history that follows is based on the Indian records of the daily meetings, supplemented by accounts left by three of the participants – the Pakistani delegates Rafi Raza and Abdul Sattar, and P.N. Dhar.[14] As secretary in Mrs Gandhi's PMO and as a member of her delegation in Simla, P.N. Dhar provides some invaluable insights about the conference. The Pakistani archives remain closed.

Day 1

After a brief, formal opening session, the two leaders, assisted by their principal advisers, met behind closed doors to review the Murree discussions and spell out their main concerns. Bhutto emphasized the need for a step-by-step approach and pressed the case for respecting the 1949 ceasefire line. Mrs Gandhi readily agreed that the numerous outstanding issues between the two countries could not be resolved immediately in a single package. She was unyielding, however, in her insistence on reaching an agreement on the new Line of Control.[15] *Thus, the one point on which the two leaders were agreed was that 'all outstanding issues' – meaning, principally, the Kashmir question – could not be settled at Simla.*

The officials met later in the day. Aziz Ahmed led off with a skilful presentation of the Pakistani case for immediate repatriation of all POWs and withdrawal of troops from occupied territories. Complaining about India's insistence that Mujib must be a party to any decision regarding repatriation of POWs who had surrendered in the eastern front, he posed a direct question to D.P. Dhar. If agreement could be reached on the 'elements of durable peace', would India be in a position to make a declaration about repatriation of POWs without reference to Mujib? Dhar replied that the POWs who had surrendered on the western front could be released. Aziz Ahmed had already dismissed this as insignificant, since it involved only some 600 men, against the 93,000 Pakistanis who had surrendered on the eastern front. He emphasized that Bhutto could not possibly return with only a peace settlement, without POW repatriation and troop withdrawals. There would be little merit in continuing a discussion that showed no visible progress on Pakistani concerns.[16] In short, at the outset of the conference, Aziz Ahmed explored the possibility of driving a wedge between India and Bangladesh by hinting at accommodating Indian concerns in return for India's agreeing to repatriate all POWs without reference to Bangladesh. Dhar made it clear that this was a non-starter.

Day 2

On 29 June, the two delegations exchanged initial drafts on the outcome document of the summit. The Pakistani draft took the form of a short 'Joint Statement on Basic Principles of Relations between India and Pakistan'.[17] This called for settlement of disputes between the two countries through 'bilateral negotiations or mediation and, should these methods fail, by arbitration or judicial settlement'. An arbitral or judicial tribunal would be set up if requested by *either* party, and its award would be binding on both countries. The draft joint statement was a mere recapitulation of the traditional Pakistani position on a 'self-executing mechanism' for resolving the Kashmir issue.

D.P. Dhar spelled out his objections to departing from a bilateral approach to resolving outstanding issues. If bilateral talks did not yield results, he pointed out, the two sides could always decide, by *mutual* agreement, to approach a judicial tribunal.[18] His presented a counter-proposal in the form of a 'Treaty for Reconciliation, Good Neighbourliness and Durable Peace'.[19] This ruled out the threat or use of force and committed the two countries to settle all issues 'bilaterally and exclusively by peaceful means'. It also called for cessation of hostile propaganda; promotion of economic and cultural ties; and facilitation of travel between the two countries.

The Indian and Pakistani drafts both dealt with the *modalities* of a final settlement of the Kashmir issue. The final settlement itself was reserved for future discussions. This was specifically reflected in a note appended to the Indian draft, which stated that the 'question of Jammu and Kashmir will be discussed separately . . . [and] the Agreement reached at such discussion shall be incorporated' in the treaty. Aziz Ahmed, predictably, rejected the Indian draft. The Indian draft failed to provide for a 'self-executing machinery' for dispute settlement, which, he said, was an essential prerequisite for any agreement on non-use of force.[20]

Day 3

Pakistan presented its second draft, bearing the title 'Agreement on Bilateral Relations'.[21] This incorporated some steps for progressive normalization of relations (such as cessation of hostile propaganda, opening of border posts, and even resumption of trade 'as far as possible'), but made no concession on the basic principle of resolving outstanding issues on an exclusively bilateral basis. Moreover, it called for implementation of the UN Security Council resolution of 21 December 1971 (concerning troop withdrawals to the 1949 ceasefire line and repatriation of POWs) and expressly stipulated that Pakistan would ratify the agreement only after this clause had been implemented. The draft thus reflected the Pakistani position that reaffirmation of the 1949 ceasefire line, troop withdrawals to that line, as well as repatriation of all POWs in accordance with the UN Security Council resolution of 21 December 1971 were *prerequisites* for any agreement on durable peace.

D.P. Dhar was in hospital, following a minor heart attack the previous day. P.N. Haksar, who took over as leader of the Indian delegation, drew attention to India's expressed reservations concerning the UN Security Council resolution of December 1971. Haksar said that in order to remove the 'endless curse of conflicts on the question of Kashmir', it was important to know the 'parameters within which Pakistan envisaged a solution to the question . . . even if we do not come to any agreement'. Aziz Ahmed refused to be drawn into discussion on this point and would only say that Kashmir could be discussed between the two leaders, Mrs Gandhi and Bhutto.[22]

Day 4

On the penultimate day of the conference, India presented its second draft, offering some modest concessions.[23] In the title, 'Treaty' was replaced by 'Agreement'. While continuing to exclude any mention of UN resolutions, a new clause referred generally to the 'principles and purposes' of the UN Charter. Finally, while reiterating that all differences must be resolved peacefully through bilateral negotiations, the draft added 'or any other peaceful means mutually agreed between them'. This took into account the Pakistani insistence on including the options of arbitration or judicial settlement, but qualified it by requiring consent of *both* parties, thus bringing the option into the ambit of a bilateral accord. (It will be recalled that Dhar had already made this offer on 29 July.)

Pakistan tabled some radical amendments in what amounted to a counter-draft.[24] This required both parties to withdraw troops to their respective territories and to positions which fully respect the ceasefire line in Jammu & Kashmir, and to repatriate all POWs and civilian internees. Another clause introduced a loophole in the Indian proposal for bilateral resolution of all outstanding issues. The Pakistani amendment proposed that the 'basic issues and cause of conflict which have bedeviled the relations between the two countries for the last 25 years [code words for Kashmir] shall be resolved bilaterally and by peaceful means'. The wording was open to the interpretation that, in addition to bilateral negotiations, recourse might also be had to *other* peaceful means, such as UN resolutions or international arbitration or adjudication.

Indira Gandhi and Bhutto met in the afternoon, together with leading members of their delegations, to explore possibilities of breaking the deadlock. Nothing substantial emerged from the meeting. Mrs Gandhi's contribution to the discussions consisted of a few short but pointed comments. The 'ceasefire line has no validity; it did not keep the peace';

the latest Pakistani draft 'weakens the bilateral approach'; and she also reiterated the Indian position on repatriation of POWs. In response, Bhutto pleaded that, for historical reasons, anything resembling a 'No War' Pact conjured up in Pakistan a sense of capitulation. If the agreement failed to provide for troop withdrawals and repatriation of POWs, the pact would be seen as the product of negotiations under duress. The Pakistani President said it would be a 'great tragedy' if agreement on repatriation of POWs were to 'flounder on Sheikh Mujib's caprice'. As regards Kashmir, Bhutto said that 'in the foreseeable future an agreement will emerge. It will evolve into a settlement. Let there be a line of peace, let people come and go. Let us not fight over it.' 'My back is to the wall,' he pleaded. 'I cannot make any more concessions.' At this point, T.N. Kaul intervened to highlight India's principal requirement. 'If in Jammu & Kashmir the Line of Actual Control could be made into a line of peace, other steps could follow,' he stated.[25]

Thus, the Simla conference remained deadlocked till the very last day. Almost the only positive result of the discussions at the level of officials was convergence on the title of a possible accord – that it should be called an 'agreement', rather than a 'treaty' (as India had proposed) or a mere 'joint communique' (as suggested by Pakistan)! India had presented two drafts in an attempt to reach an agreement on the 'elements of durable peace' – focusing on peaceful settlement of all outstanding issues on a bilateral basis – as a step towards an agreement to replace the UN-mandated 1949 ceasefire line by a new bilaterally agreed Line of Control in Jammu & Kashmir. This had run into a wall of uncompromising opposition. *The only substantive point of agreement between the two parties was that a final settlement of the Kashmir issue could not be found at Simla and had to be left to a later date.* Discussions revolved around the *modalities* for arriving at a final settlement. On the penultimate day, Bhutto repeated his hint that the 1949 ceasefire line should become a 'line of peace' which would evolve into a boundary in course of time. Kaul suggested that the new Line of Control should be treated as a line of peace.

Final day

On the last day of the conference, the Indian delegation decided to force the issue. It handed over a new draft (see Annexure 3) which, for the first time, comprehensively covered India's goals. Previous Indian drafts had dwelt on the requirements of durable peace, reserving for future talks not only a final settlement of the Kashmir issue but also questions of immediate concern for Pakistan – troop withdrawals and repatriation of POWs. India's core objective – replacement of the ceasefire line in Kashmir with a new Line of Control – had not figured in specific terms in previous drafts. The new draft filled this gap. Paragraph 4 of the final Indian draft said: 'In Jammu & Kashmir, the line of control resulting from the cease-fire of December 17, 1971, shall henceforth be respected by both sides as a line of peace. Neither side shall seek to alter it unilaterally, irrespective of mutual differences and legal interpretations. Both sides further undertake to refrain from the threat or the use of force in violation of this line.' The paragraph also provided for minor adjustments to this line 'or the rest of the 'international border' by mutual agreement, and for a joint body of supervision for the effective observance of peace along the Line of Control 'or the rest of the international border'. These tangential references to the Line of Control as part of the 'international border' gave the line the character of a de facto boundary. Paragraph 6 called for future meetings to discuss the question of a 'final settlement of Jammu & Kashmir', thus making it clear that the Line of Control was not a de jure boundary.

As we noted earlier, Mrs Gandhi was not ready to immediately convert the Line of Control in Jammu & Kashmir into a full-fledged international boundary, lest she should be accused of 'surrendering' territory across the line. She envisaged this as the long-term solution, and wished to move in this direction. Indian negotiators groped for a formulation to capture this complex position. Thus, in Murree and in the early stages of the Simla conference, D.P. Dhar had spoken of a 'frontier' in Jammu & Kashmir. In a similar vein, the Indian draft of 2

July included a couple of tangential references to the Line of Control as a 'border' (as distinguished from a de jure 'boundary'). The clauses providing for minor adjustments to the Line of Control and for the creation of a supervisory body in the final Indian draft also applied to the 'rest of the border' between the two countries. The draft thus drew a fine distinction between a de jure international 'boundary' in Jammu & Kashmir (which was left for future settlement) and the wider concept of a 'border' that included both the de jure and de facto boundaries.

The officials, led by Haksar and Aziz Ahmed, met in the afternoon to consider the draft. It was a brief meeting. Aziz Ahmed straight away announced that the draft was unacceptable. Pakistan could not accept that the ceasefire line had ceased to exist; moreover, repatriation of POWs would remain a pending question. Haksar said that he was troubled not by Pakistan's rejection of the draft but by its reason for the rejection. 'We are not asking Pakistan to give up her position on Jammu & Kashmir,' he emphasized. The Indian side had anticipated the rejection and had come prepared with an appropriately worded draft communique covering up the failure of the summit. Playing for time, the Pakistani delegation said it would submit its own draft later in the evening. 'We did not prolong the argument because we knew that Aziz Ahmed could not dare say "yes" and only his boss Bhutto could,' T.N. Kaul explains.[26]

On the afternoon of 2 July, the conference seemed to have ended in failure. Yet an agreement emerged by the late hours of the night. Amidst high drama, Bhutto called on Mrs Gandhi; meetings were held between the principal negotiators and, finally, around midnight, agreement was reached on an amended version of the final Indian draft.

The meeting between Mrs Gandhi and Bhutto has found a place in Indian political mythology. According to this myth, Bhutto succeeded in this meeting in persuading Mrs Gandhi to drop the demand for a final settlement of the Kashmir question. This ignores the fact that each of the three Indian drafts presented in Simla, including the final draft presented on the last day of the conference, specifically stipulated that a final settlement would be left for a future date. Bhutto's own impressions of his encounter with Mrs Gandhi have been recorded by Rafi Raza, his special assistant and confidant. Raza, who spoke to Bhutto immediately after the meeting, writes: '. . . despite all his [Bhutto's] assurances of improving relations and settling disputes between the two countries, she [Indira Gandhi] remained adamant on the text of the agreement prepared by her officials. Clearly she did not trust him; at least this was what he [Bhutto] told me.'[27]

What did Bhutto actually say to Mrs Gandhi? Swaran Singh briefed the Soviet ambassador on his return from Simla. The Indian record of the meeting says:

> F.M. [Foreign Minister] said that the Indo-Pakistan summit had gone off very well and we were happy over the outcome. If Bhutto carries out his obligation to settle the differences between India and Pakistan peacefully and bilaterally, a good basis for durable peace would be laid. He had conceded that the line of actual control in Jammu & Kashmir would not be altered by Pakistan. In fact, he had virtually accepted that this would be the line of a final settlement. He went on to say that public opinion in Pakistan was, at this moment, not fully prepared for a settlement of Kashmir on the basis of the line of actual control . . . [H]e would continue to make statements that he stands for the self-determination of the people of Kashmir but he would not raise this matter in the United Nations, would not internationalise it, would not use force to upset the line of control and would not give any encouragement to secessionist elements in Kashmir. He would continue to say that he stands for the principle of self-determination but would take no action to back the statement in any manner.[28]

A comparison of the Simla Agreement (Annexure 4) with the text of the final Indian draft (Annexure 3) reveals the give and take in the negotiations on the last night. The only significant amendments are to be found in subparas (ii), (iii) and (iv) of Article 4.

Subpara (ii) of the Indian draft set out India's core position. It read:

> In Jammu & Kashmir, the line of control resulting from the cease-fire of December 17, 1971, shall henceforth be respected by both sides, as a line of peace. Neither side shall seek to alter it unilaterally, irrespective of mutual differences and legal interpretations. Both sides further undertake to refrain from the threat or the use of force in violation of this line.

The phrase 'without prejudice to the recognised position of either side' was inserted at the end of the first sentence, on Pakistan's request. The author of the amendment was the lawyer, Rafi Raza, who advised Bhutto that Pakistan could accept the Indian draft with the insertion of this phrase. This presented no problem to the Indian side, since it also applied to India's claim to the entire territory of Jammu & Kashmir. The phrase 'line of peace' – originally a Pakistani formulation – was also dropped from the sentence.

Subparas (iii) and (iv) relating to minor adjustments to the Line of Control by mutual agreement, and to a joint supervisory body, were also deleted. The deletion of the provision concerning minor territorial modifications by mutual agreement was not, in itself, of much consequence. In a sense, it was superfluous. Despite deletion of the clause, India and Pakistan did, in fact, negotiate minor adjustments to the Line of Control in the wake of the Simla Agreement. By contrast, deletion of the provision for a supervisory body had material consequences. As Abdul Sattar points out, by persuading the Indian side to drop this clause, Pakistan 'checkmated India's move' to withdraw the UN Military Observers Group in India and Pakistan (UNMOGIP).[29] Agreement to set up a bilateral supervisory body would have implied acknowledgement of the fact that the UNMOGIP had become redundant. After the Simla Agreement, India declared that the UNMOGIP no longer had a role to play, since the 1949 ceasefire line had ceased to exist, having been replaced by the new Line of Control. Pakistan, however, welcomed a UNMOGIP role in Jammu & Kashmir.

It is noteworthy that neither the legal expert Raza nor the accomplished diplomat Sattar chose to dwell on the secondary feature of the dropped clauses. The provisions for minor adjustments and joint supervision applied to the Line of Control and the 'rest of the international border'. The fact that major Pakistani accounts do not focus on this feature suggests that the references to the Line of Control as a 'border' was not a bone of contention in the final negotiations. The Pakistani delegation knew that India was not seeking a final resolution of the Kashmir question at Simla. Indeed, this was specifically spelled out in Article 6 of India's final draft. The intention behind the formulation was to signal to the Pakistani side that the Line of Control should be treated as a de facto boundary. On the other hand, had the original wording been retained in the final agreement, it would have been next to impossible to explain to the Indian public the arcane and tenuous legal distinction between a 'border' and a 'boundary', or to defend the government against the charge of 'surrendering' the territory across the Line of Control.

In the final analysis, therefore, India succeeded in achieving its principal objective of replacing the UN-determined ceasefire line in Jammu & Kashmir with a bilaterally agreed Line of Control and in securing a Pakistani commitment to settle all differences by 'peaceful means through bilateral negotiations or by any other peaceful means mutually agreed upon'. However, by agreeing to drop the provision concerning a joint body to supervise the Line of Control, India allowed Pakistan to create a loophole in the bilateral approach, enabling Islamabad to retain a UNMOGIP presence on its side of the line.

15

Conclusion

In 1971, two celebrated geopolitical theorists operated from the White House, but the more successful practitioners of geopolitics were to be found in New Delhi's Central Secretariat. Nixon and Kissinger produced elaborate, if unconvincing, geopolitical justifications for their South Asia policy. Mrs Gandhi and her principal aide, Haksar, could not match the theoretical sophistication of their American counterparts. Yet, they had a clear vision of the challenges that confronted India and the available options; and it was they who, in the final reckoning, achieved success.

The Awami League's victory in the Pakistani general elections in December 1970 gave rise to hope as well as apprehension in New Delhi. Indian policymakers hoped that the Awami League, which had won an absolute majority of parliamentary seats in the Pakistan parliament, would be allowed to form the federal government. They believed this offered the only hope of a breakthrough in India–Pakistan relations. A transfer of power from the army and its allies in the West Pakistani political establishment to a democratic, East Bengal–based political party would open the doors to mutually beneficial trade and cultural exchanges, together with constructive engagement on the difficult Kashmir issue. On the other hand, they were apprehensive that a prolonged civil war would break out if the Pakistan army decided to thwart the transition to democracy by crushing the East Bengal 'rebels'. New Delhi feared that a long-drawn-out guerrilla war would pass under the control of extremist elements linked to China and India's own Naxalites. West Bengal had been devastated by Naxalite violence in the 1960s, and the insurrectionary movement had only recently been brought under control. Anarchy in East Bengal could not for long be confined within its borders; it posed a potential threat to peace and security in eastern India.

Yahya's decision to crush Bengali aspirations by unleashing a reign of terror in East Bengal delivered the final death blow to Pakistan's unity. As had long been anticipated in New Delhi, the crackdown precipitated an armed uprising and popular resistance on a massive scale. It also triggered a massive refugee exodus, which New Delhi feared would expand to a magnitude exceeding India's coping capacity and pose a threat to its security. Apprehensive about the consequences of an extended guerrilla war and an unending refugee exodus on an unprecedented scale, India decided to assist the freedom fighters to bring their struggle to a successful conclusion before the end of the year. An immediate march on Dhaka was ruled out, not only because the army had no contingency plans for such an operation, but more importantly because a government installed by the Indian army would not be accepted by the international community. Bangladesh could be liberated only by her own sons and daughters. India could only play a supporting role.

Indian policymakers drew up a multidimensional grand strategy to achieve this aim. On the military side, this included a massive programme to train and equip Bangladesh freedom fighters, and parallel preparations for direct intervention before the year end in order to bring the liberation war to an early conclusion. These military preparations were interlinked with diplomatic initiatives aimed at mobilizing international support for the liberation struggle, and ensuring that military operations would not be thwarted either by Chinese intervention or a premature UN-imposed ceasefire. India's grand strategy was sufficiently flexible to cope with unforeseeable diplomatic or military developments. When the risks associated with the strategy registered a sharp and unexpected increase as a result of a dramatic reordering of Sino-US relations, India was able to rise to the challenge by harnessing the countervailing power of the Soviet Union.

Together with defence and foreign policy, home affairs and economic management were integral elements of India's grand strategy. While India generously provided shelter to the millions of refugees fleeing from the Pakistan army, it was determined to enable all the refugees to return to their homes. To facilitate this, the refugees were accommodated in camps situated along the border, even though their dispersal to different parts of India would have reduced the stress on the host communities. (In some cases – most notably, in Tripura – the refugees actually outnumbered the host community.) The host communities everywhere extended a warm welcome to arriving refugees. Local authorities helped to defuse the occasional tensions over access to jobs and scarce commodities. After the first few weeks of the Pakistani crackdown in East Bengal, a large majority of the arriving refugees consisted of Hindus fleeing from the Pakistan army's pogrom against the minority community. State governments were given strict instructions to ensure communal harmony, and these instructions were scrupulously implemented. One of India's great successes in 1971 was the uninterrupted maintenance of communal harmony in the country, despite severe Pakistani provocation. On the economic side, apart from finding resources for defence preparations and refugee relief, Indian policymakers anticipated a possible oil embargo, shortages of certain critical non-ferrous metals required by defence production units, and the need for ensuring adequate foreign exchange reserves during and immediately after the impending war. As we saw earlier, New Delhi factored in a possible oil embargo imposed by Iran and other allies of Pakistan. Immediately after signing the Indo-Soviet Treaty, India requested the USSR to divert Soviet oil purchases from Iraq to Indian ports, in the event of an oil embargo against India. Soviet assistance was also sought in respect of non-ferrous metals. We also noted that, on the eve of the war, specific confirmation was received from the finance ministry that foreign exchange reserves were adequate. India was prepared for the suspension of US aid.

Thus, India marshalled all available instruments of state power in a coordinated grand strategy to achieve its political aim of speeding up the liberation of Bangladesh. The achievement was all the more remarkable in the absence of supporting institutional structures. India had no equivalent of the US National Security Council, nor even an integrated structure for the three defence services. These severe institutional limitations were compensated to some extent by ad hoc patchwork arrangements. We have noted the measures adopted by the defence services to facilitate joint operations, drawing upon the lessons of the 1965 war. The Special Committee of Secretaries, chaired by the cabinet secretary, made a crucial contribution by coordinating the actions of all the relevant government departments.

The credit for formulating the grand strategy and overseeing its implementation goes to a small circle of officials who enjoyed the trust and confidence of Prime Minister Indira Gandhi. The leading figure in this group was P.N. Haksar;[1] other members included D.P. Dhar, Foreign Secretary T.N. Kaul and the RAW chief, R.N. Kao. Haksar derived his authority from the prime minister, and his leading role was never questioned even though, until his elevation to the rank of principal secretary in December 1971, he was outranked in the official hierarchy by both Dhar and Kaul. The core group met frequently, often in the presence of the army chief, General Manekshaw, who, in turn, kept the other service chiefs in the picture regarding government policy. Fortuitously, the members of this quintet were on easy and informal terms with one another and were able to work together in harmony. Mrs Gandhi generally went by Haksar's advice, but there were important exceptions. In the case of the Indo-Soviet Treaty, the prime minister's closest advisers – Haksar, Dhar and Kaul – were all in favour of concluding the treaty even before Kissinger dropped his July bombshell after his pathbreaking visit to China. Indira Gandhi withheld her approval of the treaty and finally cleared the proposal only after the United States signalled the implications of its new ties with China.

Though these ad hoc arrangements stood the test in 1971, their limitations were obvious. Lt Gen. Jacob points out that the 'absence of a National Security Council to formulate and coordinate political, economic and foreign policy and military strategy was felt greatly'.[2] In the absence of continuous, institutionalized interaction with their civilian counterparts, it is not surprising that even very senior military officers were left unclear about the interplay between diplomatic and military developments. Jacob was the most articulate in questioning the clarity of India's political aims, and his doubts were shared by others. Even the air force chief, Air Chief Marshal P.C. Lal, later confessed as much.

> . . . a doubt which had existed in my mind, and also in the minds of others, as to what the objectives of the 1971 war were . . . It was clear from the beginning that that our government did not intend, at any time, to destroy the power of Pakistan in the West . . . We did intend, however, that the people of East Pakistan should determine their own future to the extent possible. The possibility that the Pakistani forces in East Pakistan would collapse altogether, as they did, that Dhaka would fall and that the whole country would be available to the freedom movement in East Pakistan, was not considered something that was likely to happen.[3]

Jacob questions whether there was a clear political aim. 'The concept of total victory was only evolved by Army Headquarters just prior to hostilities,' he wrote to Manekshaw after the war. 'What was the political aim? If the political aim was the independence of Bangladesh, that meant the occupation of the whole country including Dacca.'[4]

'Total victory', for Jacob, meant total military occupation. He remained unconvinced by Manekshaw's explanation that liberation of the greater part of Bangladesh, occupation of the entry ports and isolation of the Pakistani forces in Dhaka and a few other garrisons that were cut off from supplies and reinforcement, would inevitably lead to the liberation of the entire territory of Bangladesh. Jacob was not informed about the unqualified assurance of support in the

Security Council offered by Moscow on the eve of the war, or that this was a factor that prompted issue of the new instructions to free the whole of Bangladesh from Pakistani occupation. In Jacob's view, the Polish resolution of 14 December would have been 'disastrous' had it been adopted, since it called for withdrawal of Indian forces from Bangladesh.[5] He was unaware of the fact that the resolution was drafted in close consultation with India; he was also unable to parse the complex diplomatic document which did indeed call for an Indian withdrawal, but only *after* transfer of power to the Awami League and withdrawal of Pakistani troops from Bangladesh. Such were the limitations of a system that allowed for little interaction between soldiers and diplomats.

~

Henry Kissinger is unquestionably one of the most brilliant and profound contemporary analysts of international affairs. He was not at his best, however, in the 1971 crisis. Brushing aside all evidence to the contrary, he maintained that India's aim was to 'smash' West Pakistan. In his memoirs, he misquotes a CIA report to justify this assessment. He claims that the report indicated that India intended to continue fighting on the western front after liberating Bangladesh, in order to destroy the Pakistani army and air force, thus rendering Pakistan defenceless.[6] Views differed concerning the accuracy of the report, and in any case the report only claimed that India intended to destroy Pakistani 'armoured forces', not its army! The CIA cable stated explicitly that the aim was to 'destroy Pakistani military striking power', in other words, its *offensive* – not defensive – capacity.[7] Raymond Garthoff, historian of detente, points out that if Kissinger's aim was only to halt hostilities in the western front. 'India and the Soviet Union undoubtedly would have accepted this outcome at *any* time in the crisis, without the acrobatics of triangular diplomacy waged by a master geopolitician'.[8] Indeed, the Soviet resolution of 6 December called for a ceasefire on both fronts, along with 'effective action towards a political settlement in East Pakistan'.

'We are standing alone against our public opinion, against our whole bureaucracy at the very edge of legality,' Kissinger informed Bhutto on 11 December.[9] By pursuing a policy that found little support in the US Congress or public opinion, Nixon and Kissinger deprived themselves of the most effective instruments of intervention in Third World conflicts. Direct arms transfers to Pakistan were ruled out by Congressional opinion. Economic assistance was subject to tight controls. The threat of direct military intervention lacked credibility, in view of US public opinion, as was evidenced in the voyage of the *USS Enterprise*. Suspension of military sales and economic aid to India had no more than a marginal impact, as had been pointed out in advance by the State Department. What remained was an unequalled US diplomatic influence in the United Nations. This was demonstrated in the Security Council debates in December, during which the United States was always able to rally the support of the majority of the non-permanent members.

Kissinger's geopolitical model suffered from a basic flaw. By viewing India as a mere 'client state' or even a 'proxy' subject to Soviet control,[10] Kissinger converted a regional conflict into a global contest between the superpowers, brushing aside the contrary views of the State Department. Kissinger's wild exaggeration of the degree of Soviet influence in India led him to correspondingly overestimate the potential for 'linkage' between the South Asian conflict and progress towards detente between the superpowers. His apocalyptic predictions of the geopolitical consequences of an Indian victory proved to be baseless. Likewise, his expectation that deployment of the *Enterprise* in the Indian Ocean would induce Chinese military intervention turned out to be totally erroneous. His geopolitical model was a caricature of international realities.

~

With the minor exception of the 1965 clashes in the Rann of Kutch, the 1971 conflict was the only Indo-Pakistan war in which India's primary objective was not focused on Kashmir. The strategic aim of the war was to speed up the liberation of Bangladesh, not to resolve the Kashmir question. This fact is lost on critics, who allege that India 'won the war but lost the peace' in 1971 because a permanent solution was not found for the Kashmir issue.

During the course of the war, once attainment of the basic strategic aim was in sight, India adopted a secondary, add-on objective – replacement of the UN-authorized 1949 ceasefire line in Jammu & Kashmir by a bilaterally agreed Line of Control. The minor territorial modification was less important than the underlying principle of bilateralism. The aim was to make a permanent transition from multilateral to bilateral forums for resolution of disagreements between India and Pakistan. The Simla Agreement was a giant step towards this goal. It shifted the focus from outdated UN resolutions to bilaterally negotiated agreements for settlement of differences between India and Pakistan. Five decades later, this contribution continues to be relevant.

The myth that Indira Gandhi was persuaded by a cunning Bhutto to give up her original aim of reaching a final agreement on Kashmir at the Simla conference is belied by the facts. Every Indian draft presented in the conference, including the final draft presented on the last day, reserved a final settlement on Kashmir for a future date. Mrs Gandhi did, indeed, hope for a final settlement on the basis of converting the Line of Control to a formal international boundary over a period of time, but she feared that her political opponents would condemn her for 'surrendering' Indian territory if she were to do so at Simla. Public opinion was not ready to accept an accord on these terms – either in Pakistan or India. Indira Gandhi aimed to initiate a move in the desired direction at Simla, while leaving a final settlement to a future date.

Critics have argued that India held powerful bargaining counters in Simla in the form of the 93,000 Pakistani POWs and the Pakistan territory occupied by Indian forces; that these levers could have been used to compel Pakistan to accept conversion of the Line of Control in Jammu & Kashmir into a permanent international boundary; and that Mrs Gandhi allowed herself to be persuaded by Bhutto to desist from pressing for a final settlement of the Kashmir issue at Simla. Their arguments show little understanding of international realities or of Mrs Gandhi's objectives.

International law categorically prohibits the use of POWs as a bargaining counter. Article 118 of the 1949 Geneva Convention Relative to the Treatment of Prisoners of War says: 'Prisoners of War shall be released and repatriated *without delay* after the cessation of active hostilities [emphasis added].' Violation or rejection of the Geneva Convention would not only have invited condemnation by the international community but would also have deprived India of the protection of the convention in any future conflict with Pakistan or other powers. In calling for the surrender of Pakistani forces, Gen. Manekshaw had repeatedly promised to respect the Geneva Convention. These promises would have been dishonoured had India chosen to flout international law. India had also repeatedly assured the international community that it had no territorial designs against Pakistan. Specific assurances in this regard had been given to the two superpowers, the USSR and the US. The consensus UN Security Council of 21 December 1971 'demanded' that 'withdrawals take place, as soon as practicable, of all armed forces to their respective territories'. While entering a caveat in regard to the 1949 ceasefire line, India had committed itself to an early withdrawal from occupied territory in West Pakistan.

Indira Gandhi did not seek a final resolution of the Kashmir issue at Simla. In the absence of a consensus on the matter in her own country, she feared that she would be accused of 'surrendering' Pakistan-occupied Jammu & Kashmir, if she were to press for immediate conversion of the Line of Control into an international boundary. Her aim at Simla was to shift the focus from a multilateral to a bilateral approach towards the Kashmir issue, and on this basis to gradually transform the Line of Control into an international boundary. She succeeded in large measure in achieving the first objective. A final settlement of the Kashmir question will follow when a sober and pragmatic calculation of the national interest triumphs over ideological rigidity and hypernationalism in both Pakistan and India.

~

Henry Kissinger famously described the infant state of Bangladesh in 1972 as an 'international basket case'. History has proved him wrong. The former East Pakistan had lagged behind West Pakistan in economic development. But five decades later, Bangladesh has a *higher* per capita GDP (PPP) than Pakistan. It is also ahead of Pakistan in terms of important social indicators, such as life expectancy at birth, years of schooling, and the Gender Gap Index. Yesterday's 'basket case' holds out promise of emerging as an Asian success story.

Acknowledgements

Much of the archival research for this book was conducted in the Nehru Memorial Museum and Library, which houses two particularly important collections – the P.N. Haksar and the T.N. Kaul Papers. The Ministry of External Affairs (MEA) files available in the National Archives of India were also important sources of information. My thanks are due to the ever-helpful staff of these fine institutions for facilitating my work.

When I began working on this book, some years after my retirement from the Indian Foreign Service, I requested the MEA for permission to consult the relevant records. I am grateful to the ministry for giving me access to its archives. The archives threw further light on some important questions, in particular, India's assessment of developments in East Pakistan prior to 1971 and policy debates before and after the 25 March crackdown on East Bengal by Pakistan. My findings were set out in 'The Decision to Intervene: First Steps in India's Grand Strategy in the 1971 War', *Strategic Analysis,* IDSA, 40:4, 321–33.

I am grateful to the Jawaharlal Nehru Memorial Trust for awarding me a Nehru Fellowship (2018 and 2019) for researching this book. This encouraged me to complete my archival research at the Nehru Memorial Museum and Library (NMML) and the National Archives of India (NAI).

Nandini Mehta has been a constant source of encouragement ever since I embarked on this project. I have derived much benefit also from her judicious editorial advice.

Last but not least, I am inexpressibly grateful to my wife, Devika, and our children, Sanjoy and Chitralekha. Mostly unknowingly, they provided invaluable help in undertaking this task. By shielding me from the mundane distractions of daily life, my guardian angel, Devika, enabled me to remain pleasantly absorbed in the contemplation of historical events. Large sections of this book were drafted in the conducive peace and tranquillity of my children's homes in California. I am grateful to them for their silent encouragement.

Annexure 1

Treaty of Peace, Friendship and Cooperation between the Government of India and the Government of the Union of Soviet Socialist Republics

New Delhi

DESIROUS of expanding and consolidating the existing relations of sincere friendship between them,

BELIEVING that the further development of friendship and cooperation meets the basic national interests of both the States as well as the interests of lasting peace in Asia and the world,

DETERMINED to promote the consolidation of universal peace and security and to make steadfast efforts for the relaxation of international tensions and the final elimination of the remnants of colonialism,

UPHOLDING their firm faith in the principles of peaceful coexistence and cooperation between States with different political and social systems,

CONVINCED that in the world today international problems can only be solved by cooperation and not by conflict, REAFFIRMING their determination to abide by the purposes and principles of the United Nations Charter,

The Republic of India on one side, and The Union of Soviet Socialist Republics on the other side,

HAVE decided to conclude the present Treaty, for which purposes the following Plenipotentiaries have been appointed:

On behalf of the Republic of India:
SARDAR SWARAN SINGH,
Minister of External Affairs.

On behalf of the Union of Soviet Socialist Republics:
Mr. A.A. GROMYKO,
Minister of Foreign Affairs.

WHO, having each presented their Credentials, which are found to be in proper form and due order,

HAVE AGREED AS FOLLOW:

Article I

The High Contracting Parties solemnly declare that enduring peace and friendship shall prevail between the two countries and their peoples. Each Party shall respect the independence, sovereignty and territorial integrity of the other party and refrain form interfering in the other's internal affairs. The High Contracting Parties shall continue to develop and consolidate the relations of sincere friendship, good neighbourliness and comprehensive cooperation existing between them on the basis of the aforesaid principles as well as those of equality and mutual benefit.

Article II

Guided by the desire to contribute in every possible way to ensure enduring peace and security of their people, the High Contracting Parties declare their determination to continue their efforts to preserve and to strengthen peace in Asia and throughout the world, to halt the arms race and to achieve general and complete disarmament, including both nuclear and conventional, under effective international control.

Article III

Guided by their loyalty to the lofty ideal of equality of all Peoples and Nations, irrespective of race or creed, the High Contracting Parties condemn colonialism and reclaims in all forms and manifestations, and reaffirm their determination to strive for their final and complete elimination.

The High Contracting Parties shall cooperate with other States to achieve these aims and to support the just aspirations of the peoples in their struggle against colonialism and racial domination.

Article IV

The Republic of India respects the peace loving policy of the Union of Soviet Socialist Republics aimed at strengthening friendship and co-operation with all nations.

The Union of Soviet Socialist Republics respects India's policy of non-alignment and reaffirms that this policy constitutes an important factor in the maintenance of universal peace and international security and in the lessening of tensions in the world.

Article V

Deeply interested in ensuring universal peace and security attaching great importance to their mutual cooperation in the international field for achieving those aims, the High Contracting Parties will maintain regular contacts with each other on major international problems affecting the interests of both of States by means of meetings and exchanges of views between their leading statesmen, visits by official delegations and special envoys of the two Governments, and through diplomatic channels.

Article VI

Attaching great importance to economic, scientific and technological co-operation between them, the High Contracting Parties will continue to consolidate and expand mutually advantageous and comprehensive co-operation in these fields as will as expand trade, transport and communications between them on the basis of the principles of equality, mutual benefit and most-favoured-nation treatment, subject to the existing agreements and the special arrangements with contiguous countries as specified in the Indo-Soviet Trade Agreement of December 26, 1970.

Article VII

The High Contracting Parties shall promote further development of ties and contacts between them in the fields of science, art, literature, education, public health, press, radio, television, cinema, tourism and sports.

Article VIII

In accordance with the traditional friendship established between the two countries each of the High Contracting Parties solemnly declares that it shall not enter into or participate in any military alliance directed against the other party.

Each High Contracting Party undertakes to abstain from any aggression against the other Party and to prevent the use of its territory for the commission of any act which might inflict military damage on the other High Contracting Party.

Article IX

Each High Contracting Party undertakes to abstain from providing any assistance to any third party that engages in armed conflict with the other Party. In the event of either Party being subjected to and attach or a threat thereof, the High Contracting Parties shall immediately enter into mutual consultations in order to remove such threat and to take appropriate effective measures to ensure peace and the security of their countries.

Article X

Each High Contracting Party solemnly declares that it shall not enter into any obligations, secret or public, with one or more states, which is incompatible with this Treaty. Each High Contracting Party further declares that no obligation exists, nor shall any obligation be entered into, between itself and any other State or States, which might cause military damage to the other Party.

Article XI

This treaty is concluded for the duration of twenty years and will be automatically extended for each successive period of five years unless either High Contracting Party declares its desire to terminate it by giving notice to the other High Contracting Party twelve months prior to the expiration of the Treaty. The Treaty will be subject to ratification and will come into force on the date of the exchange of Instruments of Ratification which will take place in Moscow within one month of the signing of this Treaty.

Article XII

Any difference of interpretation of any Article or Articles of this Treaty that may arise between the High Contracting Parties will be settled bilaterally by peaceful means in a spirit of mutual respect and understanding.

The said Plenipotentiaries have signed the present Treaty in Hindi,

Russian and English, all texts being equally authentic and have affixed thereto their seals.

DONE in New Delhi on the ninth day of August in the year one thousand nine hundred and seventy one.

On behalf of the Republic of India:
Sd/-
SARDAR SWARAN SINGH,
Minister of External Affairs.

On behalf of the Union of Soviet Socialist Republics:
Sd/-
Mr. A..A. GROMYKO,
Minister of Foreign Affairs.

Annexure 2

Instrument of Surrender, 16 December 1971

The Pakistan Eastern Command agree to surrender all Pakistan Armed Forces in Bangla Desh to Lieutenant-General Jagjit Singh Aurora, General Officer Commanding in Chief of the Indian and Bangladesh forces in the Eastern Theatre. This surrender includes all Pakistan land, air and naval forces as also all paramilitary forces and civil armed forces. The forces will lay down their arms and surrender at the places where they are currently located to the nearest regular troops under the command of Lieutenant-General Jagjit Singh Aurora.

The Pakistan Eastern Command shall come under the orders of Lieutenant-General Jagjit Singh Aurora as soon as this instrument has been signed. Disobedience of orders will be regarded as a breach of the surrender terms and will be dealt with in accordance with the accepted laws and usages of war. The decision of Lieutenant-General Jagjit Singh Aurora will be final, should any doubt arise as to the meaning or interpretation of the surrender terms.

Lieutenant-General Jagjit Singh Aurora gives a solemn assurance that personnel who surrender shall be treated with dignity and respect that soldiers are entitled to in accordance with the provision of the Geneva Convention and guarantees the safety and well-being of all Pakistan military and paramilitary forces who surrender. Protection will be provided to foreign nationals, ethnic minorities and personnel of West Pakistan origin by the forces under the command of Lieutenant-General Jagjit Singh Aurora.

(Jagjit Singh Aurora)	(Amin Abdullah Khan Niazi)
Lieutenant-General	Lieutenant-General
General Officer Commanding in Chief	Martial Law Administrator Zone B and Commander Eastern Command (Pakistan)
Indian and Bangla Desh Forces in the Eastern Theatre	
16 December 1971	16 December 1971

Annexure 3

Final Indian Draft, Simla, 2 July 1971

Agreement on Bilateral Relations between the Government of India and the Government of Pakistan

1. The Government of India and the Government of Pakistan are resolved that the two countries put an end to the conflict and confrontation that have hitherto marred their relations and work for the promotion of a friendly and harmonious relationship and the establishment of durable peace in the subcontinent, so that both countries may henceforth devote their resources and energies to the pressing task of advancing the welfare of their peoples.

In order to achieve this objective, the Government of India and the Government of Pakistan have agreed as follows:

(i) That the principles and purposes of the Charter of United Nations shall govern the relations between the two countries;

(ii) That the two countries are resolved to settle their differences by peaceful means through bilateral negotiations or by any other peaceful means mutually agreed upon between them. Pending the final settlement of any of the problems between the two countries, neither side shall unilaterally alter the situation and both shall prevent the organization, assistance or encouragement of any acts detrimental to the maintenance of peaceful and harmonious relations;

(iii) That the pre-requisite for reconciliation, good neighbourliness and durable peace between them is a commitment by both the countries to peaceful coexistence, respect for each other's territorial integrity and sovereignty and non-interference in each other's internal affairs, on the basis of equality and mutual benefit;

(iv) That the basic issues and causes of conflicts which have bedeviled the relations between the two countries for the last 25 years shall be resolved by peaceful means;

(v) That they shall always respect each other's national unity, territorial integrity, political independence and sovereign equality;

(vi) That they will refrain from the threat or use of forces against the territorial integrity or political independence of each other.

2. Both Governments will take steps within their power to stop hostile propaganda directed against each other. Both countries will encourage the dissemination of such information as would promote the development of friendly relations between them.

3. In order progressively to restore and normalize relations between the two countries step by step, it was agreed that:

(i) Steps shall be taken to resume communications, postal, telegraphic, sea, land including border posts, and air links including over-flights;

(ii) Appropriate steps shall be taken to promote travel facilities to the nationals of the other country;

(iii) Trade and co-operation in economic and other agreed fields will be resumed as far as possible;

(iv) Exchange in the fields of science and culture will be promoted.

In this connection delegations from the two countries will meet from time to time to work out the necessary details.

4. In order to initiate the process of the establishment of durable peace, both the Governments agree that:

(i) Indian and Pakistan forces shall be withdrawn to their side of the international border.

(ii) In Jammu & Kashmir, the line of control resulting from the cease-fire of December 17, 1971, shall henceforth be respected by both sides, as a line of peace. Neither side shall seek to alter it unilaterally, irrespective of mutual differences and legal interpretations. Both sides further undertake to refrain from the threat or the use of force in violation of this line.

(iii) Minor adjustments of the Line of Peace in Jammu & Kashmir or the rest of the international border considered necessary by both sides to make the border more rational and viable may be made by mutual agreement.

(iv) A joint body composed of an equal number of representatives, nominated by each Government, shall be appointed to establish ground rules and to supervise the effective observance of the Line of Peace and the rest of the border between the two countries. The withdrawals shall commence upon entry into force of this Agreement in accordance with the ground rules evolved by the above-mentioned joint body and shall be completed within a period of 30 days thereof.

5. This Agreement will be subject to ratification by both countries in accordance with their respective constitutional procedures, and will come into force with effect from the date on which the Instruments of Ratification are exchanged.

6. Both Governments agree that their respective Heads will meet again at a mutually convenient time in the future and that, in the meanwhile, the representatives of the two sides will meet to discuss further the modalities and arrangements for the establishment of durable peace and normalization of relations, including question of repatriation of

prisoners of war and civilian internees, a final settlement of Jammu & Kashmir and the resumption of diplomatic relations.

(Indira Gandhi)	(Zulfikar Ali Butto)
Prime Minister	President
Republic of India	Islamic Republic of Pakistan

Simla, the _____ July, 1972

Annexure 4

Agreement between the Government of India and the Government of the Islamic Republic of Pakistan on Bilateral Relations (Simla Agreement)

Simla, July 2, 1972

1. The Government of India and the Government of Pakistan are resolved that the two countries put an end to the conflict and confrontation that have hitherto marred their relations and work for the promotion of friendly and harmonious relationship and the establishment of durable peace in the sub-continent, so that both countries may henceforth devote their resources and energies of the pressing task of advancing the welfare of their people.

In order to achieve this objective, the Government of India and the Government of Pakistan.

Have agreed as follows:

(i) That the principles and purposes of the Charter of the United Nations shall govern the relations between the two countries;

(ii) That the two countries are resolved to settle their differences by peaceful means through bilateral negotiations or by any other peaceful means mutually agreed upon between them. Pending the final settlement of any of the problems between the two countries, neither side shall unilaterally alter the situation and both shall prevent the organization, assistance or encouragement of any acts detrimental to the maintenance of peaceful and harmonious relations;

(iii) That the pre-requisite for reconciliation, good neighbourliness and durable peace between them is a commitment by both the countries to peaceful co-existence, respect for each other's internal affairs, on the basis of equality and mutual benefit;

(iv) That the basic issues and causes of conflict which have bedeviled the relations between the two countries for the last 25 years shall be resolved by peaceful means;

(v) That they shall always respect each other's national unity, territorial integrity, political independence and sovereign equality;

(vi) That in accordance with the Charter of the United Nations they will refrain from the threat or use of force against the territorial integrity or political independence of each other.

2. Both Governments will take all steps within their power to prevent hostile propaganda directed against each other. Both countries will encourage the dissemination of such information as would promote the development of friendly relations between them.

3. In order progressively to restore and normalize relations between the two countries step by step, it was agreed that:

(i) Steps shall be taken to resume communications, postal, telegraphic, sea, land including border posts, and air links including overflights;

(ii) Appropriate steps shall be taken to promote travel facilities for the national of the other country;

(iii) Trade and co-operation in economic and other agreed fields will be resumed as far as possible;

(iv) Exchange in the fields of science and culture will be promoted.

In this connection delegations from the two countries will meet from time to time to work out the necessary details.

4. In order to initiate the process of the establishment of durable peace, both the Governments agree that:

(i) Indian and Pakistani forces shall be withdrawn to their side of the international border;
(ii) In Jammu and Kashmir, the line of control resulting from the cease-fire on December 17, 1971 shall be respected by both sides without prejudice to the recognized position of either side. Neither side shall seek to alter it unilaterally, irrespective of mutual differences and legal interpretations. Both sides further undertake to refrain from the threat or the use of force in violation of this Line;
(iii) The withdrawals shall commence upon entry into force of this Agreement and shall be completed within a period of 30 days thereof.

5. This Agreement will be subject to ratification by both countries in accordance with their respective constitutional procedures, and will come into force with effect from the date on which the Instruments of Ratification are exchanged.

6. Both Governments agree that the respective Heads will meet again at a mutually convenient time in the future and that, in the meantime, the representatives of the two sides will meet to discuss further the modalities and arrangements for the establishment of durable peace and normalization of relations, including the questions of repatriation of prisoners of war and civilian internees, a final settlement of Jammu and Kashmir and the resumption of diplomatic relations.

Sd/-
Indira Gandhi
Prime Minister
Republic of India

Sd/-
Zulfikar Ali Butto
President
Islamic Republic of Pakistan

Simla, The 2nd July, 1972

Notes

1. Prelude: The Alienation of East Bengal

1. Cited in Richard Sisson and Leo E. Rose, *War and Secession* (Berkeley: University of California Press, 1990), 15–16. For Abul Mansur Ahmad's own account, see his memoirs, *Aamaar Dekha Rajniti Panchas Bachhar* (Fifty Years of Politics as I Saw It) (Dhaka: Navroz Publishers, 1970), 2nd edn, 385–91.
2. Sisson and Rose, *War and Secession*, 10.
3. Ibid.
4. Mohammad Ayub Khan, *Friends Not Masters* (London: Oxford Universities Press, 1967), 26.
5. For a detailed account of Jinnah's visit to East Pakistan, see Badruddin Umar, *Purba Banglar Bhasa Andolan o Tatkalin Rajniti* (The Language Movement of East Bengal and Contemporary Politics) (Dhaka: Mowla Brothers, 1970), Vol. 1, 104–26.
6. Talukder Maniruzzaman, *The Bangladesh Revolution and Its Aftermath* (Dhaka: Bangladesh Books International, 1980), 57.
7. Ayesha Jalal, *The Struggle for Pakistan* (Cambridge, Mass.: Harvard University Press, 2014), 86.
8. Ibid., 90.
9. Ayesha Jalal, *The State of Martial Rule: The Origins of Pakistan's Political Economy of Defence* (New Delhi: Cambridge University Press, Indian edition, 1992), 254.
10. Ahmed, *Aamaar Dekha Rajniti Panchas Bachhar*, 364–78.
11. Jalal, *The State of Martial Law*, 253.
12. Khan, *Friends Not Masters*, 54.
13. For the full text, see Ibid., 186–91.
14. Ibid., 221.

15. Ibid., 217.
16. Rounaq Jahan, *Pakistan: Failure in National Integration* (Bangladesh: OUP, 1973), 159.
17. Syed Badrul Ahsan, *Sheikh Mujibur Rahman* (New Delhi: Niyogi Books, 2014), 63; Maj. Gen. A.T.M. Abdul Wahab, *Mukti Bahini Wins Victory* (Dhaka: Columbia Prakashani, 2004), 65.
18. Mohammad H.R. Talukdar, ed., *Memoirs of Huseyn Shaheed Suhrawardy* (Karachi: OUP, 2009), 207, 214.
19. Jahan, *Pakistan: Failure in National Integration,* 166.
20. Chandrashekhar Dasgupta, 'The Decision to Intervene: First Steps in India's Grand Strategy in the 1971 War', *Strategic Analysis*, vol. 40, no. 4. (2016), 322. For Ray's recollections, see Salam Azad, *Contribution of India in the Liberation of Bangladesh* (New Delhi: Bookwell, 2006), 283.
21. Jalal, *The Struggle for Pakistan*, 130.
22. *Daily Star*, Dhaka, 12 June 2010.
23. Syed Badrul Ahsan, *Sheikh Mujibur Rahman* (New Delhi: Niyogi Books, 2014), 128.
24. Jahan, *Pakistan: Failure in National Integration*, 175.
25. Oehlert to State Department, 25 April 1969, FRUS 1969–1976, E-7, doc. 18.
26. Hughes to Rogers, 20 February 1969, FRUS 1969–1976, E-7, doc. 9.
27. See Dasgupta, 'The Decision to Intervene', 322.

2. Birth of a Nation

1. Shuja Nawaz, *Crossed Swords* (Karachi: OUP, 2017), 2nd edn., 260.
2. Nawaz, *Crossed Swords*, 264–65.
3. Sisson and Rose, *War and Secession*, 60.
4. On Bhutto's collusion with the army, see Rafi Raza, *Zulfiqar Ali Bhutto and Pakistan 1967–1977* (Karachi: OUP, 1997), 82–85.
5. Kamal Hossain, *Bangladesh: Quest for Freedom and Justice* (Karachi: OUP, 2013), 66.
6. Deputy High Commissioner of India, Dhaka, Fortnightly Political Report for 1–15 January, 1971, F. no. HI/1012(32)/71, National Archives of India.
7. Jairam Ramesh, *Intertwined Lives: P.N. Haksar and Indira Gandhi* (New Delhi: Simon & Schuster, 2018), 496. Haksar was a civil servant of exceptional ability and integrity – a combination that explained both his rise and fall from grace under Indira Gandhi. Ramesh offers an excellent survey of the complex relationship between the two.

8. Haksar to Prime Minister, 5 January 1971, P.N. Haksar Papers III, F. no. 163, Nehru Memorial Museum and Library.
9. Haksar to Prime Minister, 9 March 1971, P.N. Haksar Papers III, F. no. 164, NMML.
10. Dasgupta, 'The Decision to Intervene', 321–33.
11. Hossain, *Bangladesh: Quest for Freedom and Justice*, 67–8.
12. Sisson and Rose, *War and Secession*, 66–68.
13. Ibid., 69–70.
14. Raza, *Zulfiqar Ali Bhutto and Pakistan 1967–1977*, 84–85.
15. Farland to State Department, 1 February 1971, FRUS 1969–1976, E-7, doc. 109.
16. Dasgupta, 'The Decision to Intervene', 325.
17. Hossain, *Bangladesh: Quest for Freedom and Justice*, 72.
18. *Pakistan Observer*, 6 February 1971, reproduced in *Bangladesh Documents*, I, 148–49.
19. Sisson and Rose, *War and Secession*, 81.
20. Raza, *Zulfiqar Ali Bhutto and Pakistan 1967–1977*, 62; Sisson and Rose, *War and Secession*, 85.
21. Sisson and Rose, *War and Secession*, 90.
22. Hossain, *Bangladesh: Quest for Freedom and Justice*, 80.
23. Cited in Blood, *The Cruel Birth of Bangladesh*, (Dhaka: University Press, 2002), 28.
24. Raja, *A Stranger in My Own Country: East Pakistan 1969–1971* (Karachi: OUP, 2012), 51.
25. Ibid., 52.
26. Ibid., 63, fn; also see Nawaz, *Crossed Swords*, 266.
27. Raja, *A Stranger in My Own Country*, 65.
28. Hossain, *Bangladesh: Quest for Freedom and Justice*, 86.
29. Raja, *A Stranger in my Own Country*, 61–2.
30. *Dawn*, Karachi, 8 March 1971, reproduced in *Bangladesh Documents*, I, 216–18.
31. Raza, *Zulfiqar Ali Bhutto and Pakistan*, 71; Nawaz, *Crossed Swords*, 264.
32. Note (unsigned) on 'PM's Instructions about Assessment of East Pakistan Affairs', P.N. Haksar Papers, III, F. no. 220. The unsigned note was probably Kao's draft.
33. Mayeedul Hasan, *Muldhara Ekattar* (Main Currents of 1971), Dhaka: University Press, 1986, 9–11.
34. Foreign Secretary from Sen Gupta, 14 March 1971, P.N. Haksar Papers, III, F. 90 (a), NMML.

35. Hasan, *Muldhara Ekattar*, 9–11.
36. Ibid.
37. Kissinger's memorandum to Nixon, 22 February 1971, FRUS 1969–1976, E-7, doc. 118.
38. Ibid.
39. Farland to Secretary of State, 25 February 1971, FRUS 1969–1976, E-7, doc. 119.
40. Farland (from Dhaka) to Secretary of State, 28 February 1971, 1969–1976, E-7, doc. 121.
41. Memorandum from Saunders and Hoskinson to Kissinger, 1 March 1971, FRUS 1969–1976, E-7, doc. 2.
42. Memorandum from the NSC Staff Secretary, 3 March 1971, FRUS 1969–1976, E-7, doc. 123.
43. Minutes of Senior Review Group Meeting, 6 March 1971, FRUS 1969–1976, vol. XI, doc. 6. Christopher Van Hollen, 'The Tilt Policy Revisited: Nixon–Kissinger Geopolitics and South Asia', *Asian Survey*, vol. 20, no. 4 (April 1980), 340–41.
44. Blood to Secretary of State, 10 March 1971, FRUS 1969–1976, E-7, doc. 124.
45. Raja, *A Stranger in My Own Country*, 70–71.
46. There are differing accounts of the talks between Yahya and Mujib. The narrative here is drawn largely from the first-hand account of Kamal Hossain, Mujib's constitutional adviser, and the well-researched study of Pakistani sources by Hasan Zaheer. See Hossain, *Bangladesh: Quest for Freedom and Justice*, 92–103, and Zaheer, *The Separation of East Pakistan*, 149–59.
47. Blood, *The Cruel Birth of Bangladesh*, 193–94.
48. Dennis Kux, *The United States and Pakistan 1947–2000: Disenchanted Allies* (Washington, D.C.: Woodrow Wilson Centre Press, 2001), 186.
49. *The New York Times*, 28 March 1971, cited in *Bangladesh Documents*, I, 380–81.
50. Blood's Telegram to State Department, 28 March, 1971, FRUS 1969–76, E-7, doc. 125.

3. Towards a Grand Strategy

1. P.N. Dhar, *Indira Gandhi, the 'Emergency', and Indian Democracy* (New Delhi: OUP, 2000), 151.
2. Keating to State Department, 27 March 1971, FRUS, 1969–76, vol. XI, doc. 12.

3. For texts of the speeches of the prime minister and external affairs minister on 27 March, see *Bangladesh Documents,* I, 669–71. See also G.K. Reddy's front-page report on the proceedings in *The Hindu*, 28 March 1971.
4. *Bangladesh Documents*, I, 669–71.
5. Mayeedul Hasan, *Muldhara Ekattar*, 13–14. For Tajuddin's meetings with BSF officials, see also Anirudh Deshpande, ed., *The First Line of Defence: Glorious 50 Years of the Border Security Force* (New Delhi: Shipra Publications, 2015), 30–31. For the Teliapara meeting, see Maj. Gen K.M. Shafiullah, *Bangladesh at War,* 2nd edn. (Dhaka: Academic Publishers, 1995).
6. Cited in D.P. Dhar's note to Prime Minister, 13 November 1971, MEA Archives.
7. Dhar, *Indira Gandhi, the 'Emergency', and Indian Democracy'*, 157.
8. Maj. Gen. Sukhwant Singh, *India's Wars Since Independence, Vol. I: The Liberation of Bangladesh* (New Delhi: Lancer Publishers, 1980), 20.
9. Haksar's note on 'Points which P.M. may like to make at the meeting with the Opposition Leaders, to be held on Friday, May 7'. P.N. Haksar Papers, III, F. no. 277, NMML.
10. 'Final Review of Operation Jackpot', appended in Manekshaw to Lall (Defence Secretary), 4 May 1972. MEA Archives.
11. Lt Gen. J.F.R. Jacob, *An Odyssey in War and Peace: An Autobiography* (New Delhi: Roli Books, 2011), 78.
12. Dhar, '*Indira Gandhi, the 'Emergency,' and Indian Democracy,*' 156.
13. Blood to Rogers, 19 April 1971, cited in Gary J. Bass, *The Blood Telegram: India's Secret War in East Pakistan* (Noida: Random House India, 2013), 84.
14. Bass, *The Blood Telegram*, 84.
15. Ibid.
16. Haksar's note, 17 April 1971, P.N. Haksar Papers III, F. no.165, NMML.
17. Cabinet Secretary's note to Prime Minister, 28 November 1971, MEA Archives.

4. Mujibnagar

1. *Bangladesh Documents,* I, 282–86.
2. Hasan, *Muldhara Ekattar*, 17–18; also see reports in *Times of India*, 13 April 1971, and in *Bangladesh Documents,* I, 286–87.
3. *Bangladesh Documents,* I, 289–91; Maj. Gen. A.T.M. Abdul Wahab, *Mukti Bahini Wins Victory* (Dhaka, Columbia Prakashani, 2004), 143–50.
4. H.T. Imam, *Bangladesh Sarkar 1971* (Dhaka: Agami Prakashani, 2004), 173–78, 206–07.

5. The P.N. Haksar Papers in NMML include copies of several classified Pakistani documents.
6. Mizanur Rahman Chowdhury's report to Acting President, Bangladesh (undated), P.N. Haksar Papers III, F. no. 229, NMML.
7. Hasan, *Muldhara Ekattar*, 31–2.
8. Imam, *Bangladesh Sarkar 1971*, 77–79, 171.
9. Dhar, *Indira Gandhi, the 'Emergency', and Indian Democracy,* 167–68.
10. Hasan, *Muldhara Ekattar,* 8, 77–78.
11. Ibid., 152; Imam, *Bangladesh Sarkar 1971*, 79.
12. Hasan, *Muldhara Ekattar,* 50–51.
13. Ibid., 51–52.
14. *Bangladesh Documents,* I, 298–303, 307–17.
15. Text of address in *Bangladesh Documents,* I, 282–86.
16. Hasan, *Muldhara Ekattar*, 39–40. Haksar's note to Prime Minister, 6 May 1971, PNH III, F. no. 166.
17. Haksar to Dhar, 22 May 1971, P.N. Haksar Papers III, F. no. 166; Haksar's notes to PM dated 13, 14 and 26 July 1971, P.N. Haksar Papers III, F. no.169. NMML.
18. Hasan, *Muldhara Ekattar*, 75–77.
19. Ibid., 84-93; Imam, *Bangladesh Sarkar 1971*, 241–44, 304, 538–41.
20. Hasan, *Muldhara Ekattar*, 105–08.
21. Imam, *Bangladesh Sarkar 1971*, 167, 169–70, 388.
22. Hasan, *Muldhara Ekattar*, 151–52; Imam, *Bangladesh Sarkar 1971*, 313.
23. FRUS 1969–1976, Vol XI, documents No. 115, 133, 136, 149, 150, 164.
24. FRUS, 1969–1976, Vol XI, doc. 164.
25. J.N. Dixit, *India–Pakistan: War and Peace* (New Delhi: Books Today, 2002), 195–96.
26. Dhar, *Indira Gandhi, the 'Emergency', and Indian Democracy*, 171; J.N. Dixit, *India–Pakistan*, 195–96; Hasan, *Muldhara Ekattar,* 173–74; Imam, *Bangladesh Sarkar 1971*, 316.
27. Hasan, *Muldhara Ekattar.*

5. Mukti Bahini

1. Mayeedul Hasan, *Muldhara Ekattar*, 15; Talukder Maniruzzaman, *The Bangladesh Revolution and its Aftermath* (Dhaka: Bangladesh Books International, 1980), 112; Maj. Gen. K.M. Safiullah, *Bangladesh at War,* (Dhaka: Academic Publishers, 1995), 2nd edn., 71.

2. Text of minutes of cabinet meeting on 18 April 1971 in H.T. Imam, *Bangladesh Sarkar 1971* (Dhaka: Agami Prakashani, 2004), 379–80.
3. Anirudh Deshpande, ed., *The First Line of Defence: Glorious 50 Years of the Border Security Force* (New Delhi: Shipra Publications, 2015), 33.
4. Manekshaw to Lall (Defence Secretary), 4 May 1972, forwarding 'Final Review of Operation Jackpot', MEA Archives.
5. Lt Gen. J.F.R. Jacob, *Surrender at Dacca*, 90–91.
6. Manekshaw to Lall, 4 May 1972, 'Final Review of Operation Jackpot', MEA Archives.
7. S.N. Prasad and U.P. Thapliyal (eds.), *The India-Pakistan War of 1971* (Dehra Dun: Nataraj Publishers, 2014, an official publication of the Ministry of Defence, New Delhi), 51, 69.
8. Manekshaw to Lall, 4 May 1972, 'Final Review of Operation Jackpot', MEA Archives.
9. Mayeedul Hasan, *Muldhara Ekattar*, 105–08.
10. Jacob, *Surrender at Dacca*, 91–92; Maj. Gen. A.T.M. Abdul Wahab, *Mukti Bahini Wins Victory*, 203–05; Prasad and Thapliyal (eds.), *The India-Pakistan War of 1971, 57.*
11. Prasad and Thapliyal, *The India-Pakistan War of 1971*, 49.
12. For an account of the Kolkata conference, see Maj. Gen. K.M. Shafiullah, *Bangladesh at War* (Dhaka: Academic Publishers, 1995), (Revised Edition), 142–45; Rafiqul Islam, *A Tale of Millions: Bangladesh Liberation War – 1971* (Dhaka: Ananna, 1986), 234–43.; Hasan, *Muldhara Ekattar*, 48–49.
13. Report from Joint Director, RAW, Calcutta, 3 July 1971, P.N. Haksar III, F. no. 227. P.N. Banerji was a brilliant intelligence officer whose achievements still remain largely in the shadows. When RAW was carved out of the Intelligence Bureau (IB) in 1969 as an independent external intelligence agency, Banerji was assigned to the internal as well as the newly formed external intelligence agency, being regarded as indispensable by both. Banerji was responsible for handling Bangladesh affairs in the crucial pre- and post-war periods. He played a pivotal role in the integration of Sikkim in the Indian Union.
14. Maj. Gen. Sukhwant Singh, *India's Wars Since Independence*, 34.
15. Prasad and Thapliyal, *The India–Pakistan War of 1971*, 56.
16. Hasan, *Muldhara Ekattar*, 47. Hasan cites Lt Gen. B.N. Sarkar as the source of the figure for destroyed Pakistani border outposts.
17. Hasan, *Muldhara Ekattar*, 122. Hasan cites Maj. Gen. Sarkar as the source of this information.

18. Fazal Muqeem Khan, *Pakistan's Crisis in Leadership* (Islamabad: National Book Foundation, 1973), 109.
19. Jacob, *Surrender at Dacca*, 87. Manekshaw's review of Operation Jackpot for September 1971, MEA Archives.
20. For the full text of Osmani's new Ops Plan, see Hasan, *Muldhara Ekattar*, 269–75.
21. Jacob, *Surrender at Dacca*, 43.
22. See note. 13 above.
23. Fazal Muqeem Khan, *Pakistan's Crisis in Leadership*, 108–09.
24. Ibid., 119.
25. Manekshaw's review of Operation Jackpot for October 1971, MEA Archives.
26. Jacob, *Surrender at Dacca*, 87.
27. Ibid., 71.
28. Ibid., 73.

6. Military Plans

1. Maj. Gen. Sukhwant Singh, *India's Wars Since Independence: The Liberation of Bangladesh* (New Delhi: Lancer, 1980), Vol. 1, 18.
2. Lt Gen. J.F.R. Jacob, *Surrender at Dacca: Birth of a Nation* (New Delhi: Manohar, 2006), 46.
3. Jacob, *Surrender at Dacca*, 60.
4. Ibid., 61–62.
5. Lt Gen. K.P. Candeth, *The Western Front: Indo-Pakistan War 1971* (Dehradun: The English Book Depot, 1997), 17.
6. Maj. Gen. Sukhwant Singh, *India's Wars Since Independence*, 72–73, 90–91.
7. Jacob, *Surrender at Dacca*, 65–67.
8. Adm. S.N. Kohli, *We Dared – Maritime Operations in the 1971 Indo-Pakistani War* (New Delhi: Lancer International, 1989), 32.
9. Prasad and Thapliyal, *The Indo-Pakistan War of 1971: A History* (New Delhi: Nataraj Publishers, 2014), 105–07.
10. Prasad and Thapliyal, *The Indo-Pakistan War of 1971*, 106–08.
11. Maj. Gen. Lachhman Singh, *Victory in Bangladesh* (Dehra Dun: Nataraj Publishers, 1981), 46.
12. Maj. Gen. Sukhwant Singh, *India's Wars Since Independence*, 151.
13. Jacob, *Surrender at Dacca*, 77.
14. Jacob, *Surrender at Dacca*, 88–89; Maj. Gen. Shubhi Sood, *Leadership: Field Marshal Sam Manekshaw* (Noida: SDS Publishers, 2006), 205; Maj. Gen.

Ashok Krishna, *India's Armed Forces: Fifty Years of War and Peace* (New Delhi: Lancer, 1998), 98–99.

15. Sood, *Field Marshal Sam Manekshaw*, 205; Singh, *Victory in Bangladesh*, 285; Jacob, *Surrender at Dacca*, 171.
16. ACM P.C. Lal, *My Years with the IAF* (New Delhi: Lancer International, 1986), 167, 327.
17. Ministry of Defence (Government of India), *Annual Report 1971–72,* 13–14.
18. Ibid., 15–16.
19. Lal, *My Years with the IAF*, 175.
20. Kohli, *We Dared*, 38.
21. Lal, *My Years with the IAF*, 162–67.
22. Ibid., 171.

7. Mobilizing World Opinion

1. *Bangladesh Documents*, I, 672.
2. Cited in Thomas M. Franck and Nigel S. Rodley, 'After Bangladesh: The Law of Humanitarian Intervention by Military Force', *The American Journal of International Law,* vol. 67, no. 2 (April 1972), 297.
3. Srinath Raghavan, *1971: A Global History of the Creation of Bangladesh* (Ranikhet: Permanent Black, 2013), 133.
4. Cited in Ibid., 139.
5. Cited in Raghavan, 164.
6. Statement by the Acting Prime Minister of New Zealand, 14 April 1971, *Bangladesh Documents,* I, 505–06.
7. Statement by the Prime Minister of Australia, 22 April 1971, *Bangladesh Documents*, I, 502.
8. Podgorny to Yahya Khan, 2 April 1971, *Bangladesh Documents*, I, 510–11.
9. Statement by Abba Eban in the Knesset, 23 June 1971, *Bangladesh Documents,* II, 154–55.
10. Raghavan, *1971: A Global History of the Creation of Bangladesh*, 182–83.
11. Ibid., 147–48.
12. UNHCR's press conference, Paris, 9 July 1971, *Bangladesh Documents*, I, 612–14.
13. Statement by Ambassador S. Sen at the Social Committee of ECOSOC, 12 and 17 May 1971. *Bangladesh Documents*, Vol. I, 69–75.
14. Gandhi to Nixon, 13 May 1971, FRUS 1969–1976, XI, doc. 46.
15. Statement in Lok Sabha, 24 May, *Bangladesh Documents*, I, 672–75.

16. *Foreign Affairs Record*, November 1971. Ministry of External Affairs, New Delhi.
17. Swaran Singh's address to Indian diplomats, London, 20 June 1971, T.N. Kaul Papers (Parts I–III), F. no. 19, NMML.
18. Zaheer, *The Separation of East Pakistan*, 201.
19. Raghavan, *1971: A Global History of the Creation of Bangladesh*, 98.
20. Cited in Ibid., 166.
21. Heath to Yahya Khan, 11 June 1971, cited in Raghavan, *1971: A Global History of the Creation of Bangladesh*, 165.
22. Cited in Raghavan, ibid., 166.
23. Ibid., 166–67.
24. Swaran Singh address to Indian diplomats in London, 20 June 1971, T.N. Kaul Papers (Parts I–III), F. no. 19, NMML; Statement of the spokesman of the French Foreign Ministry, 12 June 1971, *Bangladesh Documents*, I, 505.
25. Swaran Singh's statement in Lok Sabha, 6 July 1971, *Bangladesh Documents*, I, 698.
26. Raghavan, *1971: A Global History of the Creation of Bangladesh*, 159.
27. Cited in ibid., 173.
28. Ibid., 173.
29. Cited in Henry Kissinger, WHY (Boston: Little, Brown and Co., 1979), 714.
30. Christopher Van Hollen, 'The Tilt Policy Revisited: Nixon–Kissinger Geopolitics and South Asia', *Asian Survey*, vol. 20, no. 4 (April 1980), 339–61.
31. FRUS, E-7, doc. 132; FRUS, SAC, doc. 32; *WHY*, 854.
32. FRUS 1969–1976, XI, doc. 36.
33. State Department to US Embassy in India, 17 June 1971, FRUS 1969–1976, XI, doc. 74.
34 State Department to Embassy in India, 17 June, 1971, FRUS, 1969–76, XI, doc. 74.
35. FRUS, XI, doc. 73 (Editorial Note).
36. Conversation among Nixon, Kissinger, Singh and Sisco, 16 June 1971, FRUS, E-7, doc. 138; editorial note, FRUS, 1969–1976, XI, doc. 73.
37. Swaran Singh's address to Indian diplomats, London, 20 June 1971, T.N. Kaul Papers (Parts I–III), F. no. 16, NMML.
38. Van Hollen, The Tilt Policy Revisited, 341, 343.
39. State Department to Embassy in India, 26 June 1971, FRUS, 1969–1976, XI, doc. 79.
40. India's reply to UNSG, 2 August 1971, *Bangladesh Documents*, I, 660–63.
41. UNSG's memorandum, 20 July 1971, *Bangladesh Documents*, I, 658–59.

42. India's reply to UNSG's aide memoire, 2 August 1971, *Bangladesh Documents*, I, 661.
43. UNGA General Debate – References to Bangladesh, *Bangladesh Documents*, II, 374–75.

8. A 'Geopolitical Revolution'

1. Kissinger, WHY, 171.
2. Chen Jian, *Mao's China and the Cold War,* Chapel Hill: University of North Carolina Press, 2001), chap. 9, 249.
3. Margaret MacMillan, *Nixon and Mao: The Week that Changed the World* (New York: Random House, 2008), xx.
4. Jian, *Mao's China and the Cold War*, 251.
5. Kissinger, WHY, 691.
6. Ibid., 698–704
7. Haksar to Dhar, 7 April 1971, P.N. Haksar Papers III, F. no. 165., NMML.
8. Haksar to Dhar, 15 April 1971, P.N. Haksar Papers III, F. no. 165, NMML.
9. Keating to State Department, 27 March 1971, FRUS 1969–1976, XI, doc. 12.
10. FRUS 1969–1976, XI, doc. 24.
11. FRUS 1969–1976, XI, docs 37 and 38.
12. FRUS 1969–1976, XI, doc. 39.
13. FRUS 1969–1976, XI, doc. 46.
14. FRUS 1969–1976, XI, doc. 62.
15. FRUS 1969–1976, doc. 73, Editorial Note.
16. Haksar's record of his discussions with Kissinger, 6 July 1971; record of discussions between Minister of External Affairs and Kissinger, P.N. Haksar Papers III, F. no. 229, NMML; FRUS 1969–1976, XI, docs 90–4; FRUS 1969–1976, E-7, doc. 139..
17. Haksar's record of his discussions with Kissinger, 6 July 1971, P.N. Haksar Papers III, F. no. 229.
18. Record of Kissinger's meeting with Defence Minister, 7 July 1971, P.N. Haksar Papers III, F. no. 229.
19. Memorandum, NSC Meeting, 16 July 1971, FRUS 1969–1976, XI, doc.103.
20. Jha to Kaul, 17 July 1971, MEA Archives.
21. Kissinger, *WHY*, 866.

9. The Indo-Soviet Treaty

1. The group comprised Ceylon (Sri Lanka), the United Arab Republic, Cambodia, Ghana, Indonesia and Burma.
2. Dhar to Kaul, 26 March 1969, MEA Archives.
3. Bhandari to Dhar, 27 March 1969, P.N. Haksar Papers, P.N. Haksar Papers, III, F. no. 203. NMML.
4. Haksar's marginal note on letter from Dhar to Kewal Singh, 31 March 1969, P.N. Haksar Papers, III, F. no. 203, NMML.
5. Kaul's note on discussions between Dhar and Dinesh Singh, 7 April 1969, P.N. Haksar Papers, III, F. no. 203, NMML. Dinesh Singh's marginal comments on Kaul's note are found in the MEA Archives.
6. Gandhi to Kosygin, n.d., circa 18 April 1969, P.N. Haksar Papers, II, F. no. 41., NMML.
7. Dhar to Kaul, 30 April 1969, MEA Archives.
8. Dinesh Singh's minute, 4 May 1969, MEA Archives.
9. Dhar to Kewal Singh, 29 May 1969, MEA Archives; Kaul to Dhar, 31 May 1969, MEA Archives.
10. Record of Soviet Ambassador's discussions with Foreign Minister on 21 April 1969, MEA Archives.
11. Record of conversation between Gandhi and Kosygin on 6 May 1969, P.N. Haksar Papers, III, F. no. 140, NMML.
12. Haksar to Gandhi, 3 June 1969, P.N. Haksar Papers, III, F. no. 140. NMML.
13. Kaul's note to Dinesh Singh, 25 August 1969, and linked draft treaty, MEA Archives.
14. Dhar to Kaul, 21 September 1969, MEA Archives.
15. Kaul to Dhar, 11 October 1969, MEA Archives.
16. Dennis Kux, *The United States and Pakistan 1947 –2000: Disenchanted Allies* (Washington, D.C.: Woodrow Wilson Centre Press, 2001), 180; Sultan Mohammed Khan, *Memories and Reflections of a Pakistani Diplomat*, 233–34.
17. Sultan Mohammed Khan, *Memories and Reflections of a Pakistani Diplomat*, 234.
18. Bhandari to Dinesh Singh, 2 November 1969, MEA Archives. See also Dhar to Kewal Singh, 31 March 1971, and enclosed letter from Bhandari, P.N. Haksar Papers, III, F. no. 203, NMML.
19. Lt. Gen. J.F.R. Jacob, *An Odyssey in War and Peace: An Autobiography* (New Delhi: Roli Books, 2011), 78.

20. Kaul's note to Haksar and Prime Minister, 15 June 1971, P.N. Haksar Papers, III, F. no. 89. NMML.
21. Ibid.
22. Ibid.
23. Kaul's note to Foreign Minister and Prime Minister, 17 July 1971, MEA Archives.
24. Ibid.
25. Jha to Kaul, 17 July 1971, MEA Archives.
26. Kaul's memorandum for Foreign Minister and Prime Minister, 3 August 1971, P.N. Haksar Papers, II, F. no. 49, NMML.
27. Jaipal (Ambassador in Belgrade) to Kaul, 9 August 1971, MEA Archives.

10. Working the Treaty

1. Record of Meeting, Swaran Singh–Gromyko, 9 August 1971 (afternoon), MEA Archives.
2. Records of Meetings, EAM–Gromyko, 10 August 1971 (morning and evening respectively), MEA Archives.
3. Record of Meeting, EAM–Gromyko, 11 August 1971, MEA Archives.
4. Jamsheed Marker, *Quiet Diplomacy: Memoirs of an Ambassador of Pakistan* (Karachi: OUP, 2010), 132.
5. Sultan M. Khan, *Memoirs and Reflections of a Pakistani Diplomat,* 320–22.
6. Marker, *Quiet Diplomacy*, 133.
7. Record of Dhar–Firyubin talks, 23 September 1971, MEA Archives.
8. Record of Dhar–Firyubin talks, 24 September 1971, MEA Archives.
9. Record of Prime Minister's meeting with Soviet leaders, 28 September 1971 (morning), MEA Archives.
10. Record of Prime Minister's meeting with Soviet leaders, 28 September 1971 (4–6 p.m.), MEA Archives.
11. D.P. Dhar's note to Haksar regarding his meeting with Sheikh Mujib, 29 January 1972, P.N. Haksar Papers, III, F. no. 233 (Supplement).
12. Indo-Soviet Joint Statement, September 29, 1971, *Bangladesh Documents,* II, 161–64.
13. Keating to Secretary of State, 9 October 1971, in F.S. Aijazuddin, ed., *The White House and Pakistan: Secret Declassified Documents, 1969–74* (Karachi: OUP, 2002), 305.
14. Marker, *Quiet Diplomacy*, 133.
15. Khan, *Memoirs and Reflections of a Pakistani Diplomat,* 341.

16. Venkateswaran's note to Foreign Secretary, 21 September 1971, MEA Archives.
17. S.K. Banerji's note on discussions between Foreign Minister and Firyubin, 25 October 1971, MEA Archives.
18. Note recorded by Counsellor Purushottam (Counsellor, Indian embassy, Moscow), 3 November 1971, MEA Archives.

11. Indira Gandhi Visits Western Capitals

1. Record of discussions between Foreign Minister and US ambassador, 12 October 1971, MEA Archives; Keating to State Department, 12 October 1971, FRUS 1969–1976, XI, doc. 167.
2. Indira Gandhi's broadcast to the nation, 23 October 1971, *Bangladesh Documents,* II, 251–52.
3. H.Y. Sharda Prasad, 'Vision and Warm Heart', in Bidyut Sarkar, ed., *P.N. Haksar: Our Times and the Man* (New Delhi: Allied Publishers, 1989); Raghavan, *1971: A Global History of the Creation of Bangladesh*, 226.
4. Raghavan, *1971: A Global History of the Creation of Bangladesh*, 229.
5. Record of Prime Minister's talks with UK Foreign Secretary, 1 November 1971, MEA Archives.
6. Summary of discussions between Kaul and Greenhill, 2 November 1971, MEA records.
7. Raghavan, *1971: A Global History of the Creation of Bangladesh*, 230.
8. Kaul's circular telegram to Indian missions on Prime Minister's tour, 18 November 1971, MEA Archives.
9. Raghavan, *1971: A Global History of the Creation of Bangladesh*, 229.
10. Kaul's circular telegram, 18 November 1971, MEA Archives.
11. Raghavan, *1971: A Global History of the Creation of Bangladesh*, 231.
12. Kaul's circular telegram, 18 November 1970, MEA Archives.
13. PM's discussions with Prime Minister Eyskens, 25 October 1971, MEA Archives.
14. Jha to Kaul, 12 August 1971, MEA Archives.
15. Jha to Kaul, 16 October 1971, MEA Archives.
16. Conversation between Nixon, Kissinger, British Foreign Secretary Douglas-Home and British Ambassador Cromer, 30 September 1971, FRUS 1969–1976, E-7, doc. 146.
17. FRUS 1969–1976, E-7, doc. 146, fn 3.
18. Memorandum for the President's File. Meeting Between President Nixon

and Prime Minister Indira Gandhi, 4 November 1971, FRUS 1969–1976, XI, doc. 179.

19. Farland to Kissinger, 19 November 1971, FRUS 1969–1976, XI, doc. 192.
20. Kaul–Irwin discussions, 5 November 1971, MEA Archives.
21. Kissinger, *WHY*, 873, 876, 881.
22. Memorandum from the Deputy Administrator of the Agency for International Development, 5 November 1971, FRUS 1969–1976, E-7, doc. 152.
23. FRUS 1969–1976, XI, doc. 188.
24. *Newsweek*, 15 November 1971 (reproduced in *Bangladesh Documents*, II, 295).
25. Prime Minister's statement in Parliament, 15 November 1971, *Bangladesh Documents*, II, 292–94.

12. Prelude to War

1. Imam, *Bangladesh Sarkar 1971* (Dhaka: Agami Prakashani, 2004), 315. Mayeedul Hasan, *Muldhara Ekattar*, 177.
2. Imam, *Bangladesh Sarkar 1971*, 316–17; Hasan, *Muldhara Ekattar*, 182.
3. Imam, *Bangladesh Sarkar 1971*, 319–20.
4. Jacob, *Surrender at Dacca*, 87; Maj. Gen. Sukhwant Singh, *India's Wars Since Independence*, 92.
5. Hasan, *Muldhara Ekattar*, 170.
6. Jacob, *Surrender at Dacca*, 71.
7. Ibid., 73.
8. Maj. Gen. Shaukat Riza, cited in Nawaz, *Crossed Swords: Pakistan, its Army, and the Wars Within* (Karachi: OUP, 2017), 2nd edn, 292.
9. Minutes of Washington Special Actions Group (WSAG) meeting, 22 November 1971, FRUS 1969–1976, XI, doc. 194.
10. Minutes of WSAG Meeting, 29 November 1971, FRUS 1969–1976, XI, doc. 209.
11. Conversation between Nixon, Kissinger and Rogers, 24 November 1971, FRUS 1969–1976, E-7, doc. 156.
12. Farland to Kissinger, 26 November 1971, FRUS 1969–1976, XI, doc. 204.
13. Irwin to Keating, 27 November 1971, FRUS 1969–1976, XI, doc. 206.
14. Irwin to Beam, 27 November 1971, FRUS 1969–1976, XI, doc. 207.
15. Kissinger's memorandum to Nixon, 1 December 1971, FRUS 1969–1976, doc. 211.
16. Rogers to Keating, 1 December 1971, FRUS 1969–1976, XI, doc. 212.

17. Dhar to Prime Minister, 28 November 1971 (10.30 a.m. and 12.30 p.m., respectively), MEA Archives.
18. Kaul to Swaran Singh, 30 November 1971, MEA Archives.
19. Record of Prime Minister's conversation with Ambassador Pegov, 30 November 1971, MEA Archives.
20. U Thant, *View from the UN* (Newton Abbot (UK: David & Charles, 1978), 427–28.
21. Cabinet Secretary's Note to Prime Minister, 28 November 1971, MEA Archives.
22. Dhar to Ray, 4 December 1971; Ray to Kaul, 6 December 1971, MEA Archives.

13. War and Diplomacy

1. Zaheer, *The Separation of East Pakistan*, 360.
2. Arjun Subramaniam, *India's Wars: A Military History, 1947–1971* (New Delhi: HarperCollins, 2016), 394.
3. *Bangladesh Documents*, II, 588.
4. Kissinger, *WHY*, 888.
5. Memorandum from Kissinger to Nixon, 2 December 1970, FRUS, XI, doc. 214.
6. Cited in Kissinger, *WHY*, 136.
7. Cited in K.P. Misra, *The Role of the United Nations in the Indo-Pakistan Conflict, 1971* (New Delhi: Vikas Publishing House, 1973), 63.
8. Statement by Agha Shahi, 4 December 1971. *Bangladesh Documents,* II, 417, 419–20.
9. Statement by Samar Sen, 4 December 1971, ibid., 427, 429.
10. Statement by Jacov Malik, 4 December 1971, ibid., 439–41.
11. Statement by Kosciusko-Morizet, 4 December 1971, ibid., 434.
12. Statement by Colin Crowe, 4 December 1971, ibid., 442.
13. Statement by Huang Hua, 5 December 1971, ibid., 443.
14. UN doc. S/10416, 4 December 1971.
15. UN doc. S/10418, 4 December 1971.
16. UN doc. S/10421, 5 December 1971.
17. UN doc. S/10423, 5 December 1971.
18. *Bangladesh Documents,* II, 462–67.
19. UN doc. S/10428, 6 December 1971.

20. UN doc. A/L 647/Rev. 1, 7 December 1971.
21. UN doc. A/L 648, 7 December 1971.
22. See Misra, *The Role of the United Nations in the Indo-Pakistani Conflict, 1971*, 90.
23. Minutes of NSC meeting, 6 December 1971, FRUS, SAC, doc. 237.
24. FRUS 1969–1976, XI, doc. 243, fn 4.
25. Nixon–Kissinger conversation, 9 December 1971, FRUS 1969–1976, E-7, doc. 168.
26. Zaheer, *The Separation of East Pakistan*, 381–82.
27. Ibid.
28. Ibid., 383–84.
29. Ibid., 388.
30. FRUS 1969–1976, XI, doc. 251 (editorial note).
31. Ibid., XI, doc. 256 (editorial note).
32. Elmo R. Zumwalt, Jr, *On Watch: A Memoir* (New York: Quadrangle/The New York Times Book Co., 1976), 360, 367.
33. Kissinger–Huang Hua conversation, 10 December 1971, FRUS 1969–1976, XI, doc. 274.
34. Chen Jian, *Mao's China and the Cold War* (Chapel Hill: The University of North Carolina Press, 2000), 273.
35. Kissinger to Haig, 13 December 1971, FRUS 1969–1976, E-7, doc. 294.
36. Indira Gandhi, *Years of Endeavour: Selected Speeches, August 1969 to August 1972*, New Delhi: Publications Division, Government of India.
37. Yahya Khan to Nixon, 14 December 1971, FRUS 1969–1976, XI, doc. 298.
38. Zumwalt, *On Watch*, 368; James M. McConnell and Anne M. Kelly, 'Superpower Naval Diplomacy: Lessons of the Indo-Pakistan Crisis 1971', *Survival* (November–December 1973), 15:6.
39. Nixon to Brezhnev, 6 December 1971, FRUS 1969–1976, XI, doc. 236.
40. Brezhnev to Nixon, 8 December 1971, FRUS 1969–1976, XI, doc. 253.
41. Conversation between Nixon and Soviet Minister of Agriculture, 9 December 1971, FRUS 1969–1976, E-7, doc. 169.
42. Nixon to Brezhnev, 10 December 1971, FRUS 1969–1976, XI, doc. 269.
43. Haksar to Dhar, 14 December 1971, P.N. Haksar Papers III, F. no. 174; Record of Dhar–Kosygin meeting, 14 December 1971, MEA Archives.
44. Message from the Soviet Leadership to President Nixon, 14 December 1971, FRUS 1969–1976, XI, doc. 295.
45. Jha–Irwin conversation, 12 December 1971, FRUS 1969–1976, E-7, doc. 181; Van Hollen, The Tilt Policy Revisited, 352; L.K. Jha, 'Kissinger and I', *India Today*, 1–15 November 1979, 55.

46. Bush to State Department, 12 December 1971, FRUS 1969–1976, XI, doc. 289.
47. Memorandum from Kissinger to Nixon, 12 December 1971, FRUS 1969–1976, XI, doc. 282.
48. UN doc. S/10446, 12 December 1971. On 13 December, the United States submitted a revised draft with a small amendment (UN doc. S/10446/Rev 1). The amended resolution was put to vote the same day.
49. Swaran Singh's speech, 13 December 1971, *Bangladesh Documents,* II, 532, 545.
50. UN doc. S/10451, 13 December 1971.
51. Haksar's note to Prime Minister, 13 December 1971, P.N. Haksar Papers III, F. no. 174.
52. Note for PAC (prepared by Haksar), 13 December 1971, P.N. Haksar Papers III, F. no. 174.
53. UN doc. S/10453, 14 December 1971.
54. Zaheer, *The Separation of East Pakistan,* 401.
55. Prasad and Thapliyal, *The India-Pakistan War of 1971*, 410; Zaheer, *The Separation of East Pakistan*, 405.
56. Prasad and Thapliyal, *The India–Pakistan War of 1971*, p. 402; See also Zaheer, *The Separation of East Pakistan*, 405.
57. Prasad and Thapliyal, *The India-Pakistan War of 1971*, 411.
58. UN doc. S/10455, 15 December 1971.
59. Haksar to Kaul, 15 December 1971, P.N. Haksar Papers III, F. no. 173.
60. UN doc. S/10456, 15 December 1971.
61. UN doc. S/10457, 15 December 1971.
62. Prime Minister's statement in parliament, 16 December 1971, *Bangladesh Documents,* II, 550.

14. Victory

1. For the full text, see *Bangladesh Documents,* II, 360.
2. Speech by Foreign Minister of India, Sardar Swaran Singh, 21 December 1971, *Bangladesh Documents,* II, 546–48.
3. Kewal Singh, *Partition and Aftermath: Memoirs of an Ambassador* (New Delhi: Vikas Publishing House, 1991), 211–13.
4. *Foreign Affairs Record,* Vol. XVIII, 1972.
5. Exchange of letters between Foreign Secretary Kaul and Bangladesh High Commissioner H.R. Choudhury, 17 January 1972. *Foreign Affairs Record,* Vol XVIII, 1972.

6. Indo-Bangladesh Joint Statement, 8 February 1972, *Bangladesh Documents*, II, 636–67.
7. Ibid.
8. Ibid.
9. Dhar, *Indira Gandhi, the 'Emergency,' and Indian Democracy* (New Delhi: OUP, 2000), 194.
10. Raza, *Zulfikar Ali Bhutto and Pakistan 1967–1977*, 200–02.
11. *The Statesman*, Kolkata, 27 March 1972.
12. For the text of the interview, see Oriana Fallaci, *Interview with History* (Boston: Houghton Mifflin, 1976), 182–209.
13. Indira Gandhi to Brezhnev, 26 April 1972, P.N. Haksar Papers III, F. no. 180.
14. The Indian records are compiled in Avtar Singh Bhasin, ed., *India-Pakistan Relations 1947–2007 – A Documentary Study*, vol. III, (New Delhi: Geetika Publishers, 2012), vol. III, 1710–54; Rafi Raza, *Zulfikar Ali Bhutto and Pakistan 1967–1977* (Karachi: OUP, 1997), 200–15; Abdul Sattar, *Pakistan's Foreign Policy 1947–2012* (Karachi: OUP, 2013), 3rd edn. chap. 11, 139–59; Dhar, *Indira Gandhi, the 'Emergency' and Indian Democracy* (New Delhi: OUP, 2000), chap. 9, 187–222; Dhar, 'Kashmir: The Simla Solution', *Journal of Peace Studies*, vol. 2, issues 9–10 (March–June 1995) (reprinted from *The Times of India*, 4 April 1995).
15. Raza, *Zulfikar Ali Bhutto and Pakistan 1967–1977*, 207–08.
16. Summary Record, 28 June 1972; Bhasin, 1711–18.
17. For the text, see Bhasin, 1732–33.
18. Summary Record, 29 June 1972 (10 a.m.); Bhasin, 1720–22.
19. For the text, see Bhasin, 1727–29.
20. Summary Record, 29 June 1972 (5.30 p.m.); Bhasin, 1723–26.
21. For the text, see Bhasin, 1730–31.
22. Summary Record, 30 June 1972 (3 p.m.); Bhasin, 1733–37.
23. For the text, see Bhasin, 1745–46.
24. For the text, see Bhasin, 1747–48.
25. Record of meeting between the Prime Minister and the Indian Delegation and President of Pakistan and the Pakistan Delegation held at 3.45 p.m. on 1 July 1972, Bhasin, 1738–44.
26. T.N. Kaul, *Diplomacy in Peace and War* (New Delhi: Vikas, 1979), 191.
27. Raza, *Zulfikar Ali Bhutto and Pakistan 1967–1977*, 209.
28. Record of discussions between Foreign Minister and Pegov, 5 July 1972, MEA Archives.
29. Sattar, *Pakistan's Foreign Policy 1947–2016*, 149–50.

15. Conclusion

1. For a fascinating account of the complex relationship between Haksar and the Prime Minister, see Jairam Ramesh, *Intertwined Lives: P.N. Haksar and Indira Gandhi* (New Delhi: Simon & Schuster, 2018).
2. Jacob, *Surrender at Dacca*, 160.
3. ACM P.C. Lal, *My Years with the IAF* (New Delhi: Lancers International, 1986), 171.
4. Jacob, *Surrender at Dacca*, 171.
5. Ibid., 163.
6. Kissinger, *WHY*, 901.
7. For the text of the CIA cable, see FRUS, XI, doc. 246. See also Bass, *The Blood Telegram*, 290.
8. Cited in Walter Isaacson, *Kissinger: A Biography*, 378.
9. Telephone conversation between Kissinger and Bhutto, December 11, 1971, FRUS, XI, doc. 280.
10. Kissinger regularly described India as a Soviet 'client state'. He describes the 1971 war as a 'proxy war' in *WHY* (1255).

Select Bibliography

Archives

P.N. Haksar Papers. Parts II and III. New Delhi: National Memorial Museum and Library.
T.N. Kaul Papers. Parts I–III. New Delhi: National Memorial Museum and Library.
Ministry of External Affairs Files, 1970–71. New Delhi: National Archives of India.
Records of the Ministry of External Affairs, Government of India (MEA Archives).

Publications

Ahmad, Abul Mansur. *Amar Dekha Rajnitir Panchas Bachhar* [Fifty Years of Politics as I Saw It]. 2nd edn. Dhaka: Nowroz Kitabistan, 1970.

Ahmad, Kamruddin. *A Social History of Bengal*. 3rd edn. Dhaka: Progoti Publishers, October 1970.

Ahsan, Syed Badrul. *Sheikh Mujibur Rahman*. New Delhi: Niyogi Books, 2014.

Aijazuddin, F.S. *From a Head, through a Head, to a Head: The Secret Channel between the US and China through Pakistan*. Karachi: OUP, 2000.

———. ed. *The White House and Pakistan: Secret Declassified Documents, 1969–1974*. Karachi: OUP, 2002.

Anderson, Jack. *The Anderson Papers*. New York: Random House, 1973.

Anisuzzaman. *Identity, Religion and Recent History*. Calcutta: Naya Udyog (for Maulana Abul Kalam Azad Institute of Asian Studies), 1995.

Arif, Gen. K.M. *Khaki Shadows: Pakistan 1947–1997*. Karachi: OUP, 2001.

Ayoob, Mohammad, and K. Subrahmanyam. *The Liberation War*. New Delhi: S. Chand & Co., 1972.

Azad, Salam. *Contribution of India in the War of Liberation of Bangladesh*. New Delhi: Bookwell, 2006.

Bass, Gary J. *The Blood Telegram*. Noida: Random House India, 2013.

Bhasin, Avtar Singh, ed. *India–Pakistan Relations, 1947–2007: A Documentary Study*. Vol. 3. New Delhi: Geetika Publishers, 2012.

Bhuiyan, Md. Abdul Wadud. *Emergence of Bangladesh and the Role of the Awami League*. New Delhi: Vikas Publishing House, 1982.

Bhutto, Zulfikar Ali. 'The Simla Accord', *Pakistan Horizon*, vol. 25, no. 3 (1972).

———. *The Great Tragedy*. Karachi: Pakistan People Party Publication, 1971.

Blood, Archer K. *The Cruel Birth of Bangladesh*. Dhaka: The University Press Ltd, 2002.

Burke, S.M. 'The Postwar Diplomacy of the Indo-Pakistan War of 1971'. *Asian Survey*, vol. 13, no. 11 (November 1973).

Candeth, Lt Gen. K.P. *The Western Front: Indo-Pakistan War 1971*. Dehra Dun: The English Book Depot, 1997.

Chaudhuri, Rudra. *Forged in Crisis: India and the United States since 1947*. New Delhi: HarperCollins India, 2014.

Choudhury, G.W. *Last Days of United Pakistan*. London: Hurst, 1974.

———. *India, Pakistan, Bangladesh, and the Major Powers*. New York: The Free Press, 1975.

Chen, Jian. *Mao's China and the Cold War*. Chapel Hill: University of North Carolina Press, 2001.

Dasgupta, Chandrashekhar. 'The Decision to Intervene: First Steps in India's Grand Strategy in the 1971 War'. *Strategic Analysis*, vol. 40, no. 4 (2016).

Daulet Singh, Zorawar. 'The Puzzle of the Shimla Summit, Or Why India Did Not Impose Its Will'. *The Wire*, 22 November 2017.

Deshpande, Anirudh, ed. *The First Line of Defence: Glorious 50 Years of the Border Security Force*. New Delhi: Shipra Publications, 2015.

Dhar, P.N. *Indira Gandhi, the 'Emergency', and Indian Democracy*. New Delhi: OUP, 2000.

———. 'The Kashmir Solution'. *Journal of Peace Studies*, vol. 2, issue 9–10 (March–June 1995).

Dixit, J.N. *Liberation and Beyond: Indo-Bangladesh Relations*. New Delhi: Konark, 1999.

———. *India–Pakistan: War & Peace*. New Delhi: Books Today, 2002.

Dobrynin, Anatoly. *In Confidence*. New York: Times Books, 1995.

Donaldson, Robert H., *The Soviet–Indian Alignment: Quest for Influence*. Monograph Series in World Affairs, Graduate Institute of International Studies. Denver: University of Denver, 1979.

Dutta, Lt Gen. H.C. *India's Military Power*. New Delhi: Manas Publications, 2016.

Fallaci, Oriana. *Interview with History*. Boston: Houghton Mifflin, 1976.

Feldman, Herbert. *Revolution in Pakistan: A Study of the Martial Law Administration*. Karachi: OUP, 1967.

———. *The End and the Beginning: Pakistan 1969–1971*. Karachi: OUP, 1975.

Franck, Thomas M., and S. Nigel Rodley. 'After Bangladesh: The Law of Humanitarian Intervention by Military Force'. *The American Journal of International Law*, vol. 67, no. 2 (April 1973).

Gandhi, Indira. *Years of Endeavour: Selected Speeches, August 1969–August 1972*. New Delhi: Publications Division, Government of India, 1975.

Ganguly, Sumit. *Conflict Unending: India–Pakistan Tensions Since 1947*. New Delhi: OUP, 2002.

Garthoff, Raymond L. *Détente and Confrontation: American Soviet Relations from Nixon to Reagan*. Washington D.C.: The Brookings Institute, 1985.

Garver, John. *China's Decision for Rapprochement with the United States, 1968–1971*. Boulder, Colorado: Westview Press (Replica Edition), 1982.

Gates, Robert M. *From the Shadows*. New York: Simon & Schuster, 1996.

Gauhar, Altaf. *Ayub Khan: Pakistan's First Military Ruler*. Karachi: OUP, 1996.

Gokhale, Nitin. *R.N. Kao: Gentleman Spymaster*. New Delhi: Bloomsbury, 2019.

Government of India. *Bangladesh Documents, Vols. I and II*. New Delhi, n.d.

Guha, Ramachandra. *India after Gandhi: The History of the World's Largest Democracy*. New Delhi: Picador India, 2008.

Haksar, P.N. *Premonitions*. Bombay: Interpress, 1979.

Haig, Alexander M., Jr. *Inner Circles*. New York: Warner Books, 1992.

Hanhimaki, Jussi M. 'An Elusive Grand Design'. In *Nixon in the World: American Foreign Relations 1969–1977*, edited by Frederick Logevall and Andrew Preston. New York: OUP, 2008.

Hasan, Mayeedul. *Muldhara Ekattar* (Bengali) [Main Currents of '71]. Dhaka: University Press, 1986.

Holdridge, John H. *Crossing the Divide: An Insider's Account of Normalisation of U.S.–China Relations*. Lanham, Maryland: Rowman & Littlefield, 1997.

Hossain, Kamal. *Bangladesh: Quest for Freedom and Justice*. Karachi: OUP, 2013.

Huque, Mahmudul. *From Autonomy to Independence: The United States, Pakistan and the Emergence of Bangladesh*. New Delhi: Wide Canvas, Times Group Books, 2014.

Imam, H.T. *Bangladesh Sarkar 1971* [Bangladesh Government 1971]. Dhaka: Agami Prakashani, 2004.

Isaacson, Walter. *Kissinger – A Biography*. New York: Simon & Schuster, 1992.

Islam, Rafiqul. *A Tale of Millions: Bangladesh Liberation War – 1971*. Dhaka: Annana, 1995.

Jackson, Robert. *South Asian Crisis: India–Pakistan–Bangladesh*. London: Chatto & Windus, 1975.

Jacob, Lt Gen. J.F.R. *Surrender at Dacca: Birth of a Nation*. New Delhi: Manohar, 1997.

———. *An Odyssey in War and Peace: An Autobiography*. New Delhi: Roli Books, 2011.

Jahan, Rounaq. *Pakistan: Failure in National Integration*. Bangladesh: OUP, 1973.

———. *Bangladesh Politics: Problems and Issues*. Dhaka: University Press, 1980.

Jalal, Ayesha. *The State of Martial Law: The Origins of Pakistan's Political Economy of Defence*. New Delhi: Cambridge University Press, Indian edition, 1992.

———. *The Struggle for Pakistan: A Muslim Homeland and Global Politics*. Harvard University Press, 2014.

Jha, L.K. 'Kissinger and I'. *India Today*, 1–15 November 1979.

Kaul, T.N. *Diplomacy in Peace and War*. New Delhi: Vikas, 1979.

Khan, Mohammad Asghar. *Generals in Politics: Pakistan 1958–1982*. New Delhi: Vikas, 1983.

Khan, Mohammad Ayub. *Friends Not Masters: A Political Autobiography*. London: OUP, 1967.

Khan, Maj. Gen. Fazal Muqeem. *Pakistan's Crisis in Leadership*. Islamabad: National Book Foundation, 1973.

Khan, Roedad, ed. *The American Papers: Secret and Confidential India–Pakistan–Bangladesh Papers 1965–1973*. Karachi: OUP, 1999.

Khan, Sultan M. *Memoirs and Reflections of a Pakistani Diplomat*. London: London Centre for Pakistan Studies, 1997.

Kissinger, Henry. *White House Years*. Boston: Little, Brown and Co., 1979.

———. *Diplomacy*. New York: Simon & Schuster, 1994.

Kohli, Adm. S.N. *We Dared – Maritime Operations in the 1971 Indo-Pakistani War*. New Delhi: Lancer International, 1989.

Krishna, Maj. Gen. Ashok. *India's Armed Forces: Fifty Years of War and Peace*. (New Delhi: Lancer, 1998).

Krishnan, Adm. N. *No Way but Surrender*. New Delhi: Vikas, 1980.

Kux, Dennis. *The United States and Pakistan, 1947–2000: Disenchanted Allies*. Washington, D.C.: Woodrow Wilson Center Press, 2001.

———. *Estranged Democracies: India and the United States, 1941–1991*. New Delhi: Sage Publications, 1993.

Lal, ACM P.C. *My Years with the IAF.* New Delhi: Lancer International, 1986.

Li, Gong. 'Chinese Decision Making and the Thawing of U.S.–China Relations'. In *Re-examining the Cold War: U.S.-China Diplomacy, 1954–1973,* edited by Robert R. Ross and Jiang Changbin. Cambridge, Mass.: Harvard University Asia Center, 2001.

MacMillan, Margaret. *Nixon and Mao: The Week that Changed the World.* New York: Random House, 2007.

———. 'Nixon, Kissinger and the Opening to China'. In *Nixon in the World: American Foreign Relations 1969–1977,* edited by Frederick Logevall and Andrew Preston. New York: OUP, 2008.

Majumdar, Ramendu, ed. *Bangladesh, My Bangladesh: Selected Speeches and Statements of Sheikh Mujibur Rahman.* New Delhi: Orient Longman, 1972.

Maniruzzaman, Talukder. *The Bangladesh Revolution and its Aftermath.* Dhaka: Bangladesh Books International, 1980.

Marker, Jamsheed. *Quiet Diplomacy: Memoirs of an Ambassador of Pakistan.* Karachi: OUP, 2010.

McConnell, James M., and M. Anne Kelly. 'Superpower Naval Diplomacy: Lessons of the Indo-Pakistan Crisis 1971'. *Survival,* 15:6 (November–December 1973).

McMahon, Robert J., 'The Danger of Geopolitical Fantasies'. In *Nixon in the World: American Foreign Relations 1969–1977,* edited by Frederick Logevall and Andrew Preston. New York: OUP, 2008.

Ministry of Defence, Government of India. *Annual Report, 1971–72.*

Misra, K.P., *The Role of the United Nations in the Indo-Pakistani Conflict, 1971.* New Delhi: Vikas Publishing House, 1973.

Nair, Sankaran. *Inside IB and RAW.* New Delhi: Manas Publications, 2008.

Nawaz, Shuja. *Crossed Swords: Pakistan, its Army and the Wars Within.* 2nd edn. Karachi: OUP, 2017.

Niazi, Lt Gen. A.A.K. *The Betrayal of East Pakistan.* New Delhi: Nataraj Publishers, 2014.

Nixon, Richard. *RN: The Memoirs of Richard Nixon.* New York: Grosset & Dunlap, 1978.

Porter, Bruce D. *The USSR in Third World Conflicts: Soviet Arms and Diplomacy in Local Wars 1945–1980.* Cambridge University Press, 1984.

Prasad, S.N., and U.P. Thapliyal, eds. *The India–Pakistan War of 1971: A History.* Dehra Dun: Nataraj Publishers, 2014.

Raghavan Srinath. *1971: A Global History of the Creation of Bangladesh.* Ranikhet: Permanent Black, 2013.

Raja, Maj. Gen. Khadim Hussain. *A Stranger in My Own Country: East Pakistan 1969–1971*. Karachi: OUP, 2012.

Rajgopal, P.V., ed. *The British, the Bandits and the Bordermen: From the Diaries and Articles of K.F. Rustamji*. New Delhi: Wisdom Tree, 2009.

Raman, B. *The Kaoboys of R&AW*. New Delhi: Lancer, 2007.

Ramesh, Jairam. *Intertwined Lives: P.N. Haksar and Indira Gandhi*. New Delhi: Simon & Schuster, 2018.

Ray, Jayanta Kumar. *Democracy and Nationalism on Trial: a Study of East Pakistan*. Simla: Indian Institute of Advanced Studies, 1968.

Raza, Rafi. *Zulfikar Ali Bhutto and Pakistan 1967–1977*. Karachi: OUP, 1997.

Roy, Vice Adm. M.K. *War in the Indian Ocean*. New Delhi: Lancer Publishers, 1995.

Roy Chowdhury, Subrata. *The Genesis and Publications, Dhaka, of Bangladesh: A Study in International Legal Norms and Permissive Conscience*. New Delhi: Asia Publishing House, 1972.

Safiullah, Maj. Gen. K.M. *Bangladesh at War*. 2nd edn. Dhaka: Academic Publishers, 1995.

Salik, Siddiq. *Witness to Surrender*. Dhaka: University Press, 1997.

Salim, Mohammad. *Bangladesher Muktijuddho o Bharater Rajnaitik Dal* [The Bangladesh Liberation War and Indian Political Parties]. Dhaka: Universities Press, 2004.

Sarkar, Bidyut, ed. *P.N. Haksar: Our Times and the Man*. New Delhi: Allied Publishers, 1989.

Sattar, Abdul. *Pakistan's Foreign Policy 1947–2016: A Concise History*. 4th edn. Karachi: OUP, 2019.

Siddiqi, Brig A.R. *East Pakistan. The Endgame – An Onlooker's Journal 1969–71*. Karachi: OUP, 2004.

———. *General Agha Mohammad Yahya Khan: The Rise and Fall of a Soldier, 1947–1971*. OUP, Karachi, 2020.

Singh, Lt Gen. Depinder. *Field Marshal Sam Manekshaw, M.C.* Dehra Dun: Nataraj Publishers, 2002.

Singh, Kewal. *Partition and Aftermath: Memoirs of an Ambassador*. New Delhi: Vikas, 1991.

Singh, Maj. Gen. Sukhwant. *India's Wars Since Independence, Vol 1: The Liberation of Bangladesh*. New Delhi: Lancer Publishers, 1980.

Singh, Maj. Gen. Lachhman. *Victory in Bangladesh*. Dehra Dun: Nataraj Publishers, 1981.

Sisson, Richard, and Leo E. Rose. *Pakistan, India and the Creation of Bangladesh*. Berkeley: University of California Press, 1990.

Sobhan, Rehman. *Untranquil Recollections: The Years of Fulfillment*. New Delhi: Sage, 2016.

Sood, Maj. Gen. Shubhi. *Leadership: Field Marshal Sam Manekshaw*. Noida: SDS Publishers, 2006.

Subramaniam, Air Vice Marshal Arjun. *India's Wars 1947–71*. Noida: HarperCollins, 2016.

Talukdar, Mohammad H.R., ed. *Memoirs of Huseyn Shaheed Suhrawardy*. Karachi:OUP, 2009.

Thant, U. *View from the UN*. London: David & Charles, 1978.

Umar, Badruddin. *Purba Banglar Bhasa Andolan o Tatkalin Rajniti* [The Language Movement of East Bengal and Contemporary Politics]. Dhaka: Mowla Brothers, 1970.

———. *Samprodayikata* [Communalism]. 2nd edn. Dhaka: Abu Nahid, 1966.

———. *Politics and Society in East Pakistan and Bangladesh*. Dhaka: Mowla Brothers, 1974.

US Department of State. *Foreign Relations of the United States, 1969–1976*, Vols.V, XI, XVII, E-7, E-13 and E-14. Washington, D.C.: US Government Printing Office, 2005.

Van Hollen, Christopher. 'The Tilt Policy Revisited: Nixon–Kissinger Geopolitics and South Asia'. *Asian Survey*, vol. 20, no. 4 (April 1980).

Verma, Maj. Gen. Ashok Kalyan. *Bridge on the River Meghna: The Dash to Dhaka*. New Delhi: K.W. Publishers, 2009.

Wahab, Maj. Gen. A.T.M. Abdul. *Mukti Bahini Wins Victory*. Dhaka: Columbia Prakashani, 2004.

Warner, Geoffrey. 'Nixon, Kissinger and the Breakup of Pakistan, 1971'. *International Affairs* 81, 5 (2005).

Wheeler, Nicholas J. *Saving Strangers: Humanitarian Intervention in International Society*. Oxford: OUP, 2000.

Zaheer, Hasan. *The Separation of East Pakistan: The Rise and Realization of Bengali Muslim Nationalism*. Karachi: OUP, 1994.

Zaman, Arshad-uz. *Privileged Witness: Memoirs of a Diplomat*. Dhaka: University Press, 2000.

Zubok, Vladimir M. *A Failed Empire: The Soviet Union in the Cold War from Stalin to Gorbachev*. Chapel Hill: University of North Carolina Press, 2007.

Zumwalt, Adm. Elmo, Jr. *On Watch: A Memoir*. Quadrangle/The New York Times Book Co., 1976.

Index

A Note on the Author

Chandrashekhar Dasgupta served in the Indian Foreign Service from 1962 to 2000. He was ambassador to China (1993–96) and the European Union (1996–2000), and a member of the Prime Minister's Council on Climate Change. He was elected to serve on the UN Committee on Economic, Social and Cultural Rights for three successive terms from 2007 to 2018.

Dasgupta was awarded the Padma Bhushan in 2008. His publications include *War and Diplomacy in Kashmir, 1947–48* and numerous articles on Indian diplomatic history, climate change and sustainable development.